DISRUPTION

DISRUPTION

Why Things Change

David Potter

OXFORD
UNIVERSITY PRESS

Oxford University Press is a department of the University of Oxford. It furthers the University's objective of excellence in research, scholarship, and education by publishing worldwide. Oxford is a registered trade mark of Oxford University Press in the UK and certain other countries.

Published in the United States of America by Oxford University Press
198 Madison Avenue, New York, NY 10016, United States of America.

Library of Congress Cataloging-in-Publication Data
Names: Potter, D. S. (David Stone), 1957–author.
Title: Disruption : why things change / David Potter.
Description: New York, NY : Oxford University Press, 2021. |
Includes bibliographical references and index.
Identifiers: LCCN 2020036736 (print) | LCCN 2020036737 (ebook) |
ISBN 9780197518823 (hardback) | ISBN 9780197518847 (epub)
Subjects: LCSH: Social change. | Creative destruction. | Human behavior.
Classification: LCC HM831.P686 2021 (print) |
LCC HM831 (ebook) | DDC 303.4—dc23
LC record available at https://lccn.loc.gov/2020036736
LC ebook record available at https://lccn.loc.gov/2020036737

DOI: 10.1093/oso/9780197518823.001.0001

1 3 5 7 9 8 6 4 2

Printed by Sheridan Books, Inc., United States of America

A.A. et W.G.F. in memoriam

CP-S et N.P. amore

CONTENTS

ILLUSTRATIONS

ACKNOWLEDGEMENTS

This book was inspired by my tenure of the Ronald J. Mellor chair in Roman History at UCLA. I would especially like to thank Steve Aaron, who stressed the importance of history as an outward-looking discipline, for creating the environment in which I could conceive of a project which is very different from any other that I have attempted in the past. My colleagues Joan Waugh, Stefania Tutino, Bill Marotti, Teofilo Ruiz, and Nile Green provided further inspiration for the project, as did my immediate, classically inclined colleague, David Phillips. The book was finished in my usual home, the Department of Classical Studies at the University of Michigan, where Sara Ahbel-Rappe and Lisa Nevett listened kindly as I rambled on about what I was doing. It is a particular pleasure to thank Tim Hart, who read through much of the manuscript at an early stage, contributing many helpful comments, as did George Woudhuysen at the University of Nottingham (neither of whom can be blamed for eccentricities that remain); Arianna Zapelloni Pavia read through the whole text at a late stage, saving me from a number of errors. Brittany Pendergraft provided invaluable assistance with the proofs.

Stefan Vranka at Oxford University Press nurtured this project from its earliest stages as the object of dinnertime conversation in Los Angeles through its conclusion, providing excellent editorial advice and seeking immensely helpful input from readers whose attention to detail has made this a much better book.

My wife Ellen has, as always, put up with the burden of the project, stacks of books piling up around the house, and rather a lot of discussion of the unsavory characters who fill the pages that follow. This would not be the book it is without her.

Finally, it seems appropriate in dedicating this book to look ahead and back. As I write, two old friends look over my shoulder from photos taken long ago, men who guided my early steps as an historian and who always stressed the civic importance of historical understanding, George Forrest and Tony Andrewes. Looking to the future and to what will, I hope, be a better, stronger world, the book is also dedicated to two people who bring joy to my life and Ellen's every day: Natalie and Claire.

Introduction

How do things change? Answering this question is a fundamental mission of historical study. It is also a profoundly important question to consider today, as the liberal democracies that set the tone for social and economic development over the past seventy years are facing extraordinary challenges. The convergence of increasing economic disparity and political fragmentation, the presence of alternative economic models offered by superficially successful totalitarian states, and a devastating disease are once again creating conditions in which a disruption like those that are the subject of this book can occur.

Disruptive change always begins on the fringes of society. Throughout time, the "mainstream" has been inherently conservative. Stable societies allow for incremental change but are essentially dedicated to the preservation of existing power structures. In such cases, dominant ideologies justify existing relationships. In the historical studies that follow, we will see how ideologies that develop in reaction to the ones supporting the status quo are necessary to guide profound changes in political and intellectual structures. A study of radical change is also a study of societies in which central institutions have failed and fundamental affiliations are severed.

Not all radical groups are the same, but all the groups that we will be examining take advantage of mistakes that challenged belief in the competence of existing institutions. The coincidence of an alternative ideological system with a period of community distress is the necessary condition for radical change. The agents of change are not the downtrodden and distressed, the disadvantaged or disenfranchised. They are inevitably members of a dominant political class who, when successful, take advantage of existing thought systems to create a new ideology of legitimacy. That said, they would not have succeeded in what they were trying to do if they were incapable of bringing large numbers of people along with them, if they were incapable of speaking a language that people outside their circles could understand, and were not speaking to basic concerns in the broader population.

An important point that will emerge from our studies is that disruptive actions do not always follow paths their original proponents might have predicted. Our studies, therefore, examine structures that can either facilitate or derail change.

A word that I'm deliberately avoiding in discussing "disruptions" is "revolution." One reason for this is that revolutions are very hard to define. In scientific terms, a revolution is simply a completed cycle. In political terms, "revolution" can be used as a synonym for civil war, regime change, or reform movement. Just as easily, it can mean the "substitution of a new system of government" or a "complete change of ideas or methods." Although some of the events I'll be discussing are routinely called revolutions, we'll see that "disruption" is a better term. The French "revolution," for example, substituted an imperial autocrat (Napoleon) for a king, and, when Napoleon was defeated, saw the restoration of the royal family that had been ousted prior to Napoleon's rise to power. What was thoroughly disrupted in the course of all of this was not autocracy as a form of government, but the system that had sustained the autocracy. In France's case this was the alliance between the nobility and the Catholic Church, upon which the monarchy had depended since the Middle Ages. The result of the Bolshevik "revolution," which we'll explore in Chapter 5, for all its rhetoric of social revolution, was the replacement of an incompetent monarch whose authority rested upon increasingly fragile insitutions with a totalitarian dictator. What was disrupted was a traditional way of defining power. That is why the Bolshevik seizure of power differs significantly from the rise of the Communist Party in China, although that too is often referred to as a revolution. But the rise of the Communist Party in China did not involve the overthrow of the ancient imperial political order, which had collapsed decades earlier. Rather, it was the result of the communist victory over the Nationalist Party (Kuomintang) in what was effectively a contest between two ghouls for control of a corpse. As the example of the French or, as we'll also see, Nazi disruptions show, successful parties might not create stable new institutions—but the result of the disruption was that it was impossible to go back to the way things had been.

The successful parties in the disruptions we're looking at in this book are groups who made use of novel ideologies to stabilize their positions. Some of those who failed to create stable new situations did so because they placed ideological correctness ahead of the practicalities of governance. They also lacked, in some cases, the capacity to understand that radicalism unrestrained by realism is inherently self-destructive.

Understanding disruption as a strategy employed for self-advancement on the part of a politically active group means that there is no necessary precondition of socioeconomic dislocation. Students of "revolution" look for explanations in deep structural imbalances, such as the coexistence of incompatible economic systems within a single political entity (e.g., peasant farming and capitalist enterprise). My point is that serious disruption requires the successful exercise of self-interest on the part of the winning side, and that disruption is not the inevitable result of economic change. Economic dislocation can create a problem, but it does not dictate the solution.

Our first two studies will be ones in which the changes were disruptive, successful, and of continuing importance today. These are the emergence of Christianity and Islam as world religions.

The transformation of Christianity from a relatively successful minority cult into a world religion was accidental. The catalyst was a Roman emperor, Constantine, who was trying to solve some problems of his own. He needed to create a narrative to justify his seizure of power at a time when traditional political ideologies had been pretty thoroughly shattered by domestic instability and military failure. He drew upon ideas that had been developed by some of his recent predecessors as a way of creating a myth of legitimacy, chiefly by claiming the favor of a particular divinity.

Constantine chose the Christian God as his protector for quite specific reasons, then worked with a small number of Christians to provide his new religion with an intellectual and institutional framework that could shape the political discourse of his age. It is quite possible that, by the end of his life, Constantine envisaged the possibility that his empire could become a predominantly Christian institution. But the creation of the institutions that made this possible was a process of trial and error. One very important point is that once he had shaped the Christian movement into one that could achieve universal significance, Constantine showed considerable wisdom in leaving the process of conversion to individual consciences.

The emergence of Islam underscores the importance of a number of factors we saw with the rise of Christianity. But there are some important differences. Perhaps the most important was that Constantine made use of ideas that had been in circulation for three centuries after the career of Jesus. There was a long history of interpretation that had already shaped the Christian community before Constantine's intervention. The rise of Islam, on the other hand, was the product of the generation that followed upon those who had known the Prophet themselves.

The circumstances that led to Muhammad's revelation were quite similar to those that lay behind Constantine's adoption of Christianity. Muhammad lived at a time of profound dislocation, in this case caused by an ecological catastrophe followed by the immensely destructive wars waged between the Persian and Roman empires, the two superpowers of his time and place. Muhammad adapted teachings that were well established within the Arabia of his lifetime to unite and inspire his followers to dominate the better part of the Arabian peninsula. At this point, Muhammad died, and the movement was taken up by the companions of the Prophet who took advantage of the self-inflicted wounds suffered by Rome and Persia to sweep existing power structures aside. The rapid collapse of Persia and the withdrawal of Rome made it necessary for the leaders of Muhammad's movement to find a way to turn his revelation into a series of governing principles—a task which, although not without some hiccups, they accomplished. There will appear to be much in common between the decisions made by ʻAbd al-Malik, who stabilized the new Arab empire and shaped Muhammad's message into the ideology of a governing party, and those taken by Constantine. There will also be obvious points of contact between the actions of the Roman emperor Heraclius and the leadership that confronted the Protestant Reformation in our next chapter.

Underlying the disruption caused by the Protestant Reformation was, again, a sense of weakness and unease as the rise of the aggressive Ottoman empire in the Mediterranean and Central Europe was balanced against rumor (and reality) of the discovery of new lands and trade routes. During this same time, the leaders of the two great institutions of the time, the Catholic Church and the Holy Roman Empire, were increasingly detached from the reality of the world in which they were seeking to function. In the case of the Holy Roman Empire, the situation would be further complicated by the fact that, in 1519, its ruler would be the nineteen-year-old Charles V. And there was a new technology, printing, first used by Johannes Gutenberg in 1439. The invention of moveable type made mass communication possible in new ways. Without the printing press, it is scarcely feasible that the statements of an angry clergyman from southern Germany, Martin Luther, could have obtained European significance with such great rapidity, or that many people at all would have learned of the ninety-five theses he posted in 1517. Important support for Luther's thought derived from the work of earlier humanists who had begun the rational recovery of ancient knowledge and questioned the intellectual authority asserted by the Catholic Church in the centuries after the rise of Islam.

Although Luther's views on the Catholic doctrine of Purgatory (that it didn't exist) and the saving power of God's grace were extreme, his movement gave rise to even more extreme revisionist movements which aimed at overthrowing the social order. While Luther resisted the further radicalization of his views, a fact that made it possible for German princes to support him, the explosion of radicalism to extend or suppress a transformative movement is characteristic of major disruptions. The tendency of the political center to collapse toward extremes at either end of the spectrum is one that we will see in other studies, and would inform the reception of the Reformation outside of southern Germany.

When we look at the reformations in the two most successful Protestant states of the sixteenth century, England and the Netherlands, we will see the struggle between centrist and extremist reformers. The central role of the king (Henry VIII) or queen (Elizabeth I) in England meant that the most radical forms of Protestantism were outright rejected by the most effective leaders of the Reform movement. In the Netherlands, William of Orange was able to transform two extremist forms of post-Lutheran Protestantism, which had inspired resistance to the Catholic regime, from potentially destructive forces to the ideological support system for a new system of government that encouraged freedom of conscience as a fundamental feature of the new state. In both Britain and the Netherlands, the Reformation's impact depended upon the ability of dedicated groups of professionals to transform a series of revolutionary statements into principles that could be used to create a unified society.

Although Luther saw himself as a religious reformer, the movement he initiated was profoundly disruptive not only because it insisted that evidence-based thinking replace religious dogma as a path to better understanding, but because it enabled the development of states that upset the European balance of power. The linkage between national identity and conscience that derived from the Reformation, in both Protestant and Catholic lands, encouraged new thinking derived from secular, usually Greco-Roman, political theory in place of the Bible, making it possible to rethink the relationship between government and its subjects. This change laid the foundation for our next great disruptions, the rise of participatory democracy and the demise of royal absolutism.

The idea that a state should have a written constitution based on the idea of "popular sovereignty" is quite a remarkable one. Largely derived from classical models by thinkers of the seventeenth and eighteenth centuries, the idea became foundational in a moment of profound political experimentation at the end of the eighteenth century. The way theory was linked to practice is the subject of our fourth study, or pair of studies. One of the issues we'll be confronting here is why essentially the same sets of ideas worked very well in one case, and failed miserably at almost exactly the same time in another. Our starting point for this study will be 1783, the year the Treaty of Paris ended English rule over thirteen of its North American colonies. The end of centuries of colonial rule was a big disruption; the successful development of a federal government was an unexpected consequence for a movement that began as a protest against government overreach.

The Netherlands had been established by the Union of Utrecht in 1579, but that document was an alliance between independent entities for purposes of self-defense. The constitution of the United States was a response to the failure of the confederation of states that had come into existence in the wake of the war ending English rule over these thirteen former colonies. The constitution that was then adopted was the product of a small group of dedicated individuals who drew upon earlier political theory as well as their own practical experience to shape the charter for a new nation. It was explicitly a revolutionary document, but it was also the product of a series of compromises. The framers of the Constitution were profoundly practical men seeking to fix a system of government that didn't work. Where reality didn't align with theory, theory lost. That is why the Constitution of the United States protected slavery.

The behavior of the framers of the United States Constitution stands in stark contrast to the conduct of the leaders of the movement that, beginning in 1789, initiated an effort to replace the traditional French monarchy with a modern parliamentary government. Although many French leaders were familiar with the ideas that shaped thinking in the United States, and although there were similar structures, including small cadres of committed individuals looking to adapt contemporary political theory to practical purposes, external pressures, and lack of consensus led to the failure of democratic impulses. The result of this failure was the development of, first, a homicidally inclined dictatorship, and then the Napoleonic system.

One important difference between the framers of the US Constitution and the reformist leaders of France was that the former had worked together in running a successful war against the world's most powerful state, while in the latter case, the members of the Committee of Public Safety operated in an atmosphere of ever-increasing mistrust, manipulating hostility to partisan advantage. Another point of contrast lay in their respective understandings of direct democracy. The framers of the Constitution were familiar with democratic voting processes at the local level. They distrusted it, played down its institutional impact, and created a framework within which a political society could grow. French radicals saw democracy as the theoretical opposite of monarchy. They moved rapidly to establish institutions that depended upon responsible voting behaviors despite the fact that most people in France had never voted in an election. That was a disaster. Politics moved rapidly to the extreme, and we see in action—even more clearly in the French experience than in the Reformation—the tendency for radical theory to so transform a debate that centrist positions collapse.

One impact of the great French disruption was the creation of a new way of fighting wars, drawing upon all of a society's resources. The horrors of the conflicts they initiated helped focus the attention of several generations of European leaders on the importance of peace and more limited conquests. Gradually, however, the destructive lessons of the past were forgotten, and there was a widespread failure to appreciate the ruinous potential of the new generations of weapons spawned by the Industrial Revolution. The result of this amnesia and blindness was disaster. There can be no more powerful example of the way bad planning has unexpected consequences than the impact of the errors made by the leaders of Russia, the Austro-Hungarian Empire, and Germany in July and August 1914. All three states descended from entities that had existed for five hundred years, and all three ceased to exist by the First World War's end in 1918.

The horrendous human cost of this war resulting from the industrialization of the previous half-century was accompanied by a belief that science was a rational process. Fascination with progress stemming from the physical sciences led to efforts to understand human society in "scientific terms," giving rise to a pair of particularly powerful theses. One was the idea of an inevitable evolution of mankind from the slave societies of antiquity to a post-capitalist, socialist future. The other, tangentially derived from Charles Darwin's theory of evolution, was the theory of the "survival of the fittest" popularized by Herbert Spencer. By some, Spencer's theory was taken to mean that "weaker" races would disappear before stronger races.

The destruction of the First World War enabled the creation of regimes in the failed states of Germany and Russia that claimed to apply the results of theory to practice. In the rise of Bolshevism and Nazism, we see many of the basic structures we have seen in other periods of disruptive change. These are the collapse of central institutions, accompanied by the twisting of existing theories into governing ideologies. The fact that the ideas of both Lenin and Hitler were widely resonant in the intellectual world of their time made it difficult for outsiders to perceive the particular turn that each had taken. Marx never advocated terror, and social Darwinists, as Spencer's followers came to be known, did not typically advocate racial mass murder. But that did not mean that ideas descended from theirs could not move in this extremely destructive direction. Both Marx and Spencer based their doctrines on notions of struggle, and struggles will have winners as well as losers.

Three points emerge from these studies. One is that ideas around which disruptive movements coalesce are already present in society, though typically imbedded in marginal or fringe elements. The second is that all these thought systems represented a repudiation of the principles that had governed daily life, setting their insights and ideas over and above the existing order and traditional definitions of legitimacy. Finally, in each case, change is driven by a group tightly organized around a charismatic leader, who saw himself as creating a new political order based upon the disruptive thought system identified with an earlier thought leader.

The overall model of change that emerges from our historical studies is not dissimilar to that which informs aggressive contemporary developments in the business community. Innovation tends to come from small companies. These start-ups are absorbed by larger corporations where change has otherwise become an incremental process that simply reinforces a status quo. This pattern is especially clear in the world of technology, where small groups of pioneers drive the ongoing digital revolution and large companies, tied down by the interests of existing customers, cannot justify to themselves the costs of potentially fruitless innovation.

The early twenty-first century is a time when a culture of "disruption" has strengthened radical political movements that aim to alter the existing world order. Major shifts in the political landscape often take their directions from mantras of the business world (e.g., "change is important") to offer increasingly radical alternatives to "the establishment." In recent years, this has been the case with "Tea Party" Republicans and the increasingly potent "democratic socialist" wing of the Democratic Party. In Europe, the normalization of nationalist groups such as *Alternative für Deutschland,* the *Rassemblement national,* or Viktor Orban's Fidesz Party are threatening established political norms. They are dragging more centrist groups away from their base, and eliminating space for compromise while promoting demographic myths based on fantastical images of immigration. And then there is the United Kingdom, where "Brexiteers" have translated traditional English exceptionalism into a destructive form of hyper-nationalism. The ideology of Brexit, like that of Donald Trump's supporters, echoes the doctrines of late nineteenth-century social Darwinists with fantasies very similar to those activating most extreme movements in contemporary Europe. Instead of focusing anger on delusions about migration and fabricating threats of terrorism that "justify" violent police tactics, it might be more reasonable to fasten attention on the impact of monopolistic "surveillance capitalism" that dislocates traditional businesses, and the way a "gig economy" undermines basic protections for workers with a potency no wave of immigrants could possibly achieve. The failure of governments to regulate powerful monopolistic corporations has led to ever greater inequality, the stagnation of living standards for the mass of the population, and has exposed the planet to devastating disease. Frozen in place by dominant financial interests, governments have failed to act in the best interests of their people, undermining faith in public institutions. As a result, extremist fantasies are being allowed to obscure reasoned efforts to promote racial and economic equality, deepening divisions and undermining a social order based on the theory that society should ensure equal justice and opportunity for all its people.

Misery will breed crises The worse the crisis, the harder those in the political center must strive for real solutions. Absent that effort, they will fail. It is not always self-evident (or evident at all) that the response to extremism might be to resort to compromises and the construction of common ground. But that is very often the case. The challenges for liberal democracy are obvious. It remains for us to discover the solutions.

Chapter 1

Constantine and the Christian Church

CHRISTIANITY

The Roman emperor Trajan had a number of subjects who believed a man named Jesus of Nazareth was the son of God. They believed he had risen from the dead and was correct in saying that the world was about to end. They believed he had preached a message of humility before God and rejection of the conventional morality of the time, which held that only rich people were good people. They met once a week, before dawn, to sing a hymn; later in the day they shared a meal. They called themselves Christians. The word derives from the Greek translation of the Hebrew word for messiah, or "savior."

Nowadays we say Trajan was emperor of Rome from the years 98 to 117 of the Common Era. We can only say this because two hundred years after Trajan's death, the emperor of Rome was a man who believed that Jesus was the son of God.

Constantine, for this is the emperor in question, was responsible for the establishment of Christianity as the single, dominant, intellectual force in the Roman Empire. This empire controlled an area that extended from Britain to the borders of Iraq, from the Atlas Mountains in North Africa to the Rhine in Western Europe.

Christianity replaced belief systems that had been in place for thousands of years and were thought to have guaranteed the protection of the Roman Empire by supernatural beings.

How did the followers of Christ change the world so profoundly? How did the belief that the world was protected by many gods give way to the belief that there was only one god. How did old ways of measuring time, based on local traditions throughout the world, give way to the single way many in the West now measure time? How did old ways of thought pass through the crucible of Christianity to shape the way we think about the world today? Even though Roman emperors oversaw the rise of Christianity, our ideas about democracy, the rights of the individual and the rule of law, and our traditions of entertainment and rational thought were all shaped by Greek and Roman thinkers of pre-Christian times. Indeed, the return of many of these ideas, buried in the Middle Ages, will play crucial roles in our third and fourth disruptions.

JESUS AND HIS FOLLOWERS

One of the most important features of Christianity is the simplicity of the basic story. This allows people to bring their own ideas to the faith and shape it into an ideology with meaning to their different communities. Christians often adapted the ideas of others to create their own guidelines for how they should live and understand the ways of the world.

Jesus of Nazareth was himself born into a time of change. The year of his birth may have been the year we now call 2 BCE.[1] That year can be gleaned from the Gospel of Luke because Luke says

1. Our own 1 BCE/CE were established by the sixth-century CE theologian Dionysius Exiguus on the basis of mathematical calculations that have no connection to Gospel narratives.

Jesus was about thirty years old when he was baptized in the fifteenth year of the reign of Tiberius, Rome's second emperor (r. 14–37 CE).

Galilee, where Jesus grew up, became part of the Roman province of Syria, which included not only modern Syria but also portions of southern Turkey, portions of Israel, and all of modern Lebanon in 6 CE. This is one of the years later (and incorrectly) associated with his birth, presumably because the provincial census imposed that year by the Roman governor, Quirinius, was a momentous occasion. The census was imposed because Rome's first emperor, Augustus, had just removed a local king in response to complaints about his brutality. This king was a son of King Herod, who had been on the throne when Augustus established his own position, and been allowed to remain on the throne despite Augustus' disapproval of his homicidal tendencies until his death in 4 BCE. One result of Quirinius' census was a rebellion, as people—especially the poor, upon whom the burden of taxation would fall most heavily—reacted against the intrusive behavior of Roman officials.

In the year Jesus was born, the emperor Augustus was wrestling with the transition of the Roman state from the failed democracy of the Roman Republic—which had created the empire in the first place—to a bureaucratic monarchy. A result of the creation of empire had been that the democratic institutions of Rome had been overwhelmed by the corporate greed which had taken over the governing class. These aristocrats—men like Julius Caesar—ultimately funded a series of devastating civil wars. The theory of government that Augustus introduced was that the "first man," selected through the consensus of the Roman people, would guide the institutions of the state. His power, in turn, would derive from laws passed by the Roman people. This "first man," or *princeps,* would ultimately morph into the figure we know today as the first Roman emperor.

So Jesus grew up in a time of change when the relevance of old beliefs could be called into question. This had been the case within the Jewish community well before he was born, and he now drew upon various traditions to shape his own powerful message about the imminent coming of the world's end and the possibility of resurrection for people who understood his revelation and lived decent lives, treating each other with dignity and respect, no matter who they were. Jesus may have been a bit unusual in this time and place in that he may have known Greek as well as the Aramaic language that most people would have spoken in the countryside where he lived. The Apostle Paul, whose letters provide our most important evidence for Jesus' teachings, says that he was a wealthy person who gave up his wealth as an example to his followers. Jesus also taught that his revelation was not limited to members of the Jewish community, and thus that Jewish scripture had relevance to all people.

Jesus reached some people who were outside the Jewish community directly. In his *Letter to the Romans,* Paul mentions a woman named Junia who was "outstanding amongst the apostles" and "in Christ" before him. In his lifetime she was living in Rome and, if she was "in Christ" before him, she may well have known Jesus personally. The existence of Junia as a leader in the early community reminds us that Paul's belief that women should be silent in church did not apply to everyone. The early Christian community was home to many lively debates, and, indeed, during the first few centuries after Jesus' crucifixion a number of women show up in the community's leadership positions. This is also a sign of the way that Jesus' movement broke down social norms. In ancient Mediterranean societies, women were really not supposed to be leaders in mixed communities of men and women.

In both its message and outreach, Jesus' teaching caused a stir in Palestine. It challenged the traditional Jewish establishment, nor would it have been welcome to a Roman administrator, whose job it was to keep order. It is testimony to Jesus' own conviction and courage that he continued to teach despite the obvious threat of an extremely unpleasant end. Roman administrators favored crucifixion, which caused a lingering death through suffocation, dehydration, and multiple organ failures.

Jesus' crucifixion should have ended his movement. That would certainly have been what Pontius Pilate, the aggressively unpleasant Roman governor of Judea, would have thought. But it did not. Jesus' closest followers said that God, his father, had brought him back from the dead. James, Jesus' thoroughly human brother, managed the resurrection event, during which some 500 people allegedly saw Jesus. The way this happened may have influenced Paul's belief that the body of a resurrected person would not resemble the body of a person while alive.

THE SPREAD OF CHRISTIANITY

Judaism had spread widely around the Mediterranean in the century before Jesus lived. There were well-established communities throughout the areas of what are now western Turkey, Greece, the Balkans, Spain, and Italy. Judaism had found a patron in Julius Caesar, who dealt the Roman Republic its political death blow in the generation before Augustus. Augustus knew enough about Jewish teaching to make a nasty joke about Herod (he said he'd rather be Herod's pig than his son—Herod killed a number of the latter). Tiberius, emperor when Jesus was crucified, had briefly exiled the Jews from Rome after a scandal. They had returned and were well established in Paul's time.

Paul and his contemporaries took advantage of the existing network of Jewish communities around the Mediterranean to spread the word of Jesus' revelations. After considerable debate, in which

Paul was a prime mover, the core community of believers agreed that Jesus' words were really meant for everyone. The connections with Rome that had come into existence pretty rapidly also helped. Rome was the center of the world, the great melting pot and testing ground for new ideas. If a movement was going to have a future, it would have to have a presence in Rome.

The people to whom Paul addressed his *Letter to the Romans* include some interesting names. Not only do we have Junia, who may have known Jesus, but we have a group of people who are said to be "in the house of Narcissus." There are several possibilities here—one is that these people had once served a man named Narcissus who had been one of the favorites of the emperor Claudius (r. 41–54 CE); the other possibility is that this is the Narcissus who served Nero, Claudius' notorious' successor (r. 54–68 CE). Whatever the case, there were some very centrally located Christians at Rome within a decade of Jesus' death.

Christians soon came to Nero's attention. Thanks to his government's incompetent management of a fire that broke out in the summer of 65 CE, a large part of Rome burned to the ground. Nero didn't recite poetry while this was happening (as some people later alleged), but he still took the blame. He tried to shift the responsibility elsewhere, and this is when Christians first came to general notice. Nero accused the Christians who lived in Rome of having started the fire. He subjected those he could catch to hideous punishments, which convinced no one of their guilt and, as the great Roman historian Tacitus, no fan of either Nero or the Christians, tells us, simply attracted attention to the group and increased membership in the movement.

Christians would later say that Nero's victims included Paul and Peter, one of Jesus' original followers. There's no contemporary evidence for this assertion, but the fact that it came up later is a sign of how important Nero's hostility was to the developing sense of group identity. Nero, whose achievements included the assassination of his mother, his adopted brother, and the murder of two wives (one by accident), would soon go down in the annals of imperial history as one of Rome's all-time worst rulers. The fact that he delighted in extravagant expenditure as well as public displays of sexual experimentation made him the symbolic opposite of everything Jesus preached.

Even if Peter and Paul were not actually caught up in Nero's persecution, the last third of the first century was a time when the generation of people who might have known Jesus would have started passing away. The movement was going to have to take on some new direction, especially now that the world showed no immediate sign of ending as promptly as Jesus had predicted.

Even without the end of the world, Jesus' ideas of resurrection and salvation through membership in a countercultural community remained attractive, and the occasional hostility of neighbors strengthened the appeal. The Roman world was often high-risk. Many gladiators (forget the modern Hollywood image of all gladiators as oppressed slaves) were free people, men and women, who were looking for fame and fortune. Other entertainers like professional boxers, wrestlers, and pancratiasts (practitioners of an event that was a lot like today's mixed martial arts) engaged in sports that were very nearly as dangerous as gladiatorial combat. Other people, who voluntarily engaged in hunting wild beasts at public spectacles, both put themselves at huge risk and, like gladiators and theatrical entertainers, were banished to the social margins. At the same time these technically marginalized people could become very wealthy and negotiate their own deals with an imperial government which desperately needed their services to help ensure a contented population. Christians often adopted the language of spectacle in describing their own contests with authority. They called themselves "athletes" in the "contest" to demonstrate the power of their faith.

Risk and fellowship weren't the only appeals of Christianity. Being Christian meant being part of a story that began with Jesus. That was also a prevalent feature of intellectual movements in antiquity, which traced themselves back to founders whose thought they could continue. To be a Stoic was to live a life guided by the principals enunciated by Zeno of Citium at the end of the fourth century BCE; to be an Epicurean was to follow the teachings of Zeno's contemporary, Epicurus. To be a Platonist meant that you felt that Plato offered the persistently valuable rules to guide your life. These philosophical systems offered explanations of how the whole universe came into being, how mortals could understand immortals, and how the world worked; they also passed as science. Being a Christian often meant that a person could engage with the thought of other groups to flesh out Jesus' somewhat rudimentary instruction.

The very simplicity of Jesus' story was an advantage. Jesus' immediate followers were none too clear as to the way his human and divine aspects could be reconciled. Indeed, the accounts that began to be written of his life in the decades after the end of Nero's reign, the four Gospels we have now, contain some pretty significant disagreements on these points. To take one of the most obvious, the Gospels of Matthew, Mark, and Luke all present Jesus' birth as the fulfillment of a prophecy of the Hebrew prophet Isaiah, as mistranslated into Greek, that he will be the son of a "virgin" (the Hebrew merely states a "young woman"). The Gospel of John presents his birth as a result of a process whereby "the Word became flesh" that is borrowed from Platonic theories about the way abstract perfection is translated into earthly reality.

As the second century wore on and turned into the third, more Christians were coming to their faith from among the empire's better-educated people. In this community, new questions arose about how to explain Jesus' revelations, and the ability to draw upon the terms of contemporary philosophy became ever more important. By the beginning of the third century, there may have been as many as a quarter of a million Christians spread across the cities of the empire—there would have been very few in the countryside where something like 80% of the empire's approximately 60 million people lived. People were generally familiar with who they were and, in most cases, willing to accept that they were somewhat eccentric neighbors. There was an active Christian literature in which Christians sought to explain to non-Christians that glimmerings of the truth could be found in their own literatures if they just knew how to look, and that Christians were loyal subjects of the realm.

There were moments, however, when the mood of peaceful coexistence and debate gave way to violence. Sometimes it was the result of prejudice on the part of non-Christians, some of whom regarded Christians as atheists whose refusal to participate in traditional cults angered the gods and caused disasters of various sorts. "If the Tiber floods, if the Nile doesn't, if the heavens stand still, if the earth moves, if there is famine or plague, the cry goes up 'Christians to the lion.'" So said Tertullian, a brilliant rhetorician and possibly practicing lawyer, who was part of the Christian community in Carthage (in modern Tunisia) at the beginning of the third century.

At other times Christians might have provoked pogroms against themselves by openly attacking symbols of traditional cults—it's fair to say that attacking a statue of the god Apollo with a stick and shouting "out, out filthy demon" was about as good a way as one could find of making a date with a lion. Some Christians did this, much to the dismay of their colleagues. But they saw themselves as following in the path of Jesus by giving "witness" to their faith. Such people were known as martyrs in the eastern, Greek-speaking part of the empire, from the Greek word *martys*, which means "witness." In the west they tended to be known as confessors from the Latin *confessio*, which means "to admit." These are both terms deriving from the fact that only Roman magistrates could hand down death sentences, and they did so at trials held in public during which the accused was pressured to confess that he or she deserved the punishment that the magistrate was going to hand down.

Given the strength of the Christian tradition of elevating martyrs to sanctity, it would be easy to imagine that there was something unique about the Roman state's attitude toward Christianity in 200 CE. That would be a false assumption. The Roman state had, at various times, punished people for being Jewish, for worshiping the Egyptian goddess Isis, for being connected with Celtic Druidism, or for promoting immorality through the worship of Dionysus. People were also deeply suspicious of Epicureans, whose denial that the gods took a direct interest in the world was taken by some as being a sign that they were really atheists. Trajan had declared that while he thought people should not be Christians, they shouldn't be hunted down, and governors should not accept anonymous denunciations of people for being Christian. If a Christian appeared in court and refused to offer sacrifice for the emperor's well-being, he or she could be executed because such an action would count as treason.

In 200 CE, the Christian community was successful, known, not always despised, and definitely part of the landscape of the Roman Empire. Christians, aided by their readings of contemporary philosophy, were developing all manner of new ideas about the nature of God, the relationship of Jesus' revelations to Jewish scripture, and the possibility of new revelations. They were beginning to evolve an administrative structure with regional overseers or bishops selected from their congregations.

Given the intellectual ferment of their movement, it is perhaps not surprising that they also began seeking a set of overarching doctrines in which all could believe, and began to limit the books that could be viewed as authoritative revelations in order to create a definable canon. The canon that we now know as the New Testament began to stabilize in the later second century, but disputes about doctrine would continue, and bishops would become ever more interested in defining heresy, even at the cost of declaring that other bishops held heretical ideas. One of the most remarkable books of this period, strictly excluded from the canon, purported to be the recollections of Judas Iscariot, who pointed out that he had done God's will in handing Jesus over to the authorities and that bishops need not be listened to.

The disputes within the Christian community were in many ways a sign of strength, for they reflected the importance people placed on their faith. But they also indicate that at that time, there was not a single Christian message, aside from belief in Jesus' death and resurrection.

CRISIS AND TRANSITION

When Septimius Severus, emperor since 193, died in 211 CE, there would have been few, if any, Christians who thought their faith would replace that of their pagan neighbors as dominant within the Roman world. If a Christian imagined that a fellow Christian would ever be emperor, it's likely that would have been regarded as an exceptionally eccentric point of view. Indeed, nowhere in the surviving Christian literature of this period is the possibility ever mentioned. A hundred years after Severus' death, Constantine would be on the verge of his conversion. What changed and why?

The first thing that changed was Rome's ability to dominate its neighbors. In 225 CE a new regime came to power in Persia (Iran and Iraq), Rome's great imperial neighbor to the east. The previous regime had been reasonably inefficient—"overrated" according to a contemporary—and Roman armies had sacked the capital of

Ctesiphon, an ancient site near modern Baghdad, three times since Trajan's reign (he was the first emperor to do so; Severus had been the most recent). The new regime, which came out of southwestern Iran, was very different. Its leader, Ardashir, believed that he was the agent of the ancient Persian god, Ahura Mazda, who guided him to victory.

The initial Roman response to the new regime had been ineffectual, largely because of problems in the Roman government itself. Severus had left the empire to his two sons, Caracalla and Geta. The two hated each other, and Caracalla had Geta murdered in the arms of their mother on December 25, 211. He celebrated the event by granting Roman citizenship to all the free inhabitants of the empire who did not have it already so they could join him in thanking the gods for his own salvation. This was not so much an act of sensible policy, looking to crown two hundred years of growing unity within the empire, as the act of a narcissistic fool with a short attention span and strong tendency toward fantasy. He was assassinated in 217 by senior subordinates.

Caracalla's assassination was followed by two decades of political rupture in which manipulation of the state religion became ever more important. One example of this tendency was the effort by Caracalla's nephew (installed by a coup which eliminated Caracalla's assassins) to implant a new leading divinity in the Roman pantheon. History knows this young man as Elagabalus, which is actually a Latinized form of the name of his preferred divinity El Gabal (God Mountain), a deity manifested in a great, black meteorite that was the chief god at Emesa (he actually called himself by the family name of Antoninus). Elagabalus took El Gabal with him to Rome, where he appalled people by retaining his native attire in place of the traditional Roman toga and leading dances around his God. He was murdered in January 222 and replaced by his thirteen-year-old cousin, Alexander. El Gabal was sent back to his temple at Emesa. It was in Alexander's reign that the new

Sassanians took power in Persia. The Sassanians crushed Alexander's effort to replace them, and a similar effort by one of his successors—an effort which led to yet another coup, through which a man named Philip became emperor. Like most of Caracalla's successors he was from a provincial family. As both an outsider and a usurper, he needed to find a way to strengthen his claim to the throne, and he too turned to the state religion to do so. He put on a gigantic religious celebration of the 1000th anniversary of Rome's foundation. This was not a success, for he had stripped resources from the provinces and alienated his subordinates. Just one year after celebrating Rome's birthday, Philip fell victim to a man named Decius who led a rebellious army against him from the Balkans.

Drawing inspiration, perhaps, from Caracalla's empire-wide thanksgiving and Philip's recent, well-advertised celebration of Rome's millennial birthday, Decius decided that he needed to make some sort of empire-wide religious gesture. Thus, he ordered all the people of the Roman Empire to sacrifice on behalf of the empire and obtain a certificate to prove they had done so. This caused a good deal of trouble for some Christians, who refused to sacrifice on principle. Others found ways around the edict by doing things such as buying fake certificates from the deeply uninterested local officials who had been charged with administering the imperial order.

In 251, Decius did what no Roman emperor had ever done. He got himself killed in battle by some Transdanubian raiders near Drynovets in Bulgaria. In 253, a new emperor (the third since Decius' death) named Valerian took charge. He was responsible for two further firsts. One was an empire-wide persecution of Christians. The act took many people by surprise, since he had not evinced any hostility toward the Church before his edict in 257. And some Christians, possibly with good reason, saw this as the result of the complicated politics within his own court. For our purposes, however, what Valerian did is important as yet another instance of centrally directed religious policy.

Valerian's second "first" was that he was the first emperor to be captured by enemies of Rome. Taken alive in battle by the Persian king, Sapor, in 260, he died in captivity some years later. The empire then split essentially into three parts. One was a breakaway "Gallic empire," consisting of the provinces in France and Britain. The second consisted of North Africa, Egypt, Italy, and the Balkans, ruled by Valerian's son Gallienus. The third, nominally subordinate to Gallienus, was controlled from the Syrian city of Palmyra and encompassed most of Rome's eastern provinces. The ruler of Palmyra, Odaenathus, had managed to gather an army of Arab tribes and some Roman soldiers to drive Sapor out of Roman territory and eliminate various eastern pretenders to the Roman throne who emerged after Valerian's capture.

In 262 Gallienus reversed Valerian's persecution of the Christian Church and declared that Christianity was a legal religion in the Roman Empire. Odaenathus' wife, Zenobia, seems to have had a soft spot for the bishop of Antioch, a man named Paul, and also showed interest in a new religious movement that had emerged with its prophet, Mani, in Iraq. Mani's revelations combined Zoroastrian Persian and Western traditions of thought (possibly with some admixture of very old Mesopotamian ideas). The reception of his ideas in the West was a sign of the fact that, while not rejecting the worship of the traditional gods, people were becoming interested in new ideas.

The division of the empire ended by 274 when the emperor Aurelian reconquered the western provinces. He had earlier defeated the Palmyrenes, led by Zenobia who had taken power after her husband's assassination. In the course of his victorious campaign, Aurelian had a vision at Emesa, where he won a decisive victory, that El Gabal, whom he now identified as a sun god—Invincible Sun, to be precise—had aided his victory. He now actively advertised the fact that he was the personal favorite of Sol Invictus (Invincible Sun). A junior officer in his army was a man named Constantius (he is about to be very important). Less than a decade after Aurelian's assassination in 275, two other staff members, Diocletian and Maximianus, would find themselves as the rulers of the world.

The events of the decades following Severus' death did not make the further rise of Christianity inevitable, though they do suggest Christians were becoming ever more noticeable on the empire's intellectual landscape. The transformation of the local god El Gabal into the imperially supported, universalizing Invincible Sun; the Persian devotion to Zoroastrian thought; Decius' edict on sacrifices; and the spread of Manichaeism show us that one response to crises was to find new ways to think about human relationships with the divine. There were now important precedents for emperors who might want to advertise novel forms of divine worship as a feature of government.

After a half-century of mayhem, the notion, inherited from Augustus, that an emperor was created through consensus was a thing of the past. Repeated assassinations and defeats dealt the system such a blow that people were starting to think they needed to make some radical changes to make the imperial government functional. The first person to do this effectively was about to take the throne.

DIOCLETIAN AND THE CONVERSION OF CONSTANTINE

In November of 284, the general staff commanding the Roman army in the east met outside of Nicomedia (modern Izmet in Turkey) to select a new emperor. The army had successfully invaded Persia, which had been in political chaos since Sapor's death a decade earlier, and murdered two emperors (father and son). The surviving son/

brother of this pair now controlled the western part of the empire, and a new ruler was needed in the east before the campaign against him could begin. No senior officer, perhaps leery of the short life expectancy of people holding this job, wanted to be emperor. The choice fell upon a mid-level guard officer named Diocles.

Diocles, who immediately changed his name to Diocletian (it sounded classier), proved to be a very different emperor from what anyone could have anticipated. Winning the civil war, he selected a comrade, Maximian, to be, first, his deputy, and later a nearly equal co-emperor. Diocletian advertised the notion that he and Maximian would be the earthly equivalent of the gods Jupiter and Hercules, who defended civilization from all evil.

Maximian would administer the western provinces while Diocletian concentrated his attention on the Balkans and the east. In 293, after some military embarrassment in the west, the two emperors selected two deputies who would see more of the front-line action. Maximian selected his son-in-law, Constantius, for the job; Diocletian selected a man named Galerius, who became his son-in-law.

Constantius had a son by a previous marriage named Constantine, who was about thirteen when Constantius became deputy emperor (a post bearing the title *Caesar*). At the time of his father's appointment to high office, or shortly thereafter, this Constantine was sent to Diocletian's court and then to serve on Galerius' staff.

Constantine was present for the great military triumph of the era, Galerius' crushing defeat of a Persian army. He was also in Nicomedia in 303 when Diocletian suddenly decided to unleash an empire-wide persecution of the Christian Church. Diocletian had earlier tried to purge Christians from the army, and it is quite possible that his decision to launch the new persecution was connected with other policies he was initiating to cleanse "un-Roman" elements from what he saw as his reconstructed and perfected empire. It is also possible that the fact he could see a large Christian church from his palace enhanced his antipathy toward the Christian community.

Constantine would have seen the edict posted, and perhaps stood aside as people he knew were arrested or dismissed for their faith. He may even have known the Professor of Latin at Nicomedia, a Christian from North Africa named Lactantius. Lactantius was not himself arrested, but people he knew certainly were.

Outside of Nicomedia the persecution was carried out with varying degrees of enthusiasm. The chief administrator of Egypt was an eager persecutor, arresting a number of Church leaders and sending them to a mine in Palestine (a form of harsh imprisonment), and seizing a good deal of property. A governor in North Africa appears to have been rather less keen. A document surviving from this period records the actions of the chief magistrate in the city of Cirta who, charged with carrying out the persecution, went to the local bishop, whom he clearly knew, and asked for some books so that he could burn them and tell the governor he had carried out the emperor's order. After a bit of posturing, books were duly delivered. Another bishop suggested that his flock could take advantage of the edict to pass off the works of heretics as scripture so they would be destroyed. This same bishop may also have called the governor's attention to a group of people who were not responsive to his authority so that they would be arrested. When some of their fellow Christians tried to bring them food in the notoriously harsh prison at Carthage, the bishop's men beat them up. In the provinces of western Europe, where Constantius was in charge, the edict was largely ignored. Perhaps aware of its lack of success, Diocletian rescinded his orders in 304.

If Constantine took anything away from Diocletian's persecution edicts (there were ultimately two, issued a couple of months apart), it was that religious persecution was ineffective. It was one thing for an emperor to promote the worship of a god who could be seen as his special protector in the way, for instance, that Aurelian had done with

Invincible Sun, and Diocletian was then doing with Jupiter. It was entirely another thing to tell people that they could not seek salvation as they saw best for themselves.

Constantine was soon to be in a position to make his own decisions. After twenty-one years in power, Diocletian abdicated on May 1, 305. Maximian abdicated at the same time, and Constantius became senior emperor with Galerius as his colleague. The twin abdications were the first in Roman history and were intended to advertise Diocletian's success in creating a new political order.

The problem with Diocletian's thinking was that the staffs of Maximian and Constantius had grown apart from those of himself and Galerius. Maximian's former officials resented Galerius' people, and Constantius' men were not eager to find themselves replaced if and when Constantius, who was in poor health, should die. Galerius was technically Constantius' junior, but he had engineered the appointment of two of his cronies as the new Caesars, which was resented by Constantius' people.

Constantius, recognizing that his health was failing, ordered Galerius to return Constantine, who was still serving at Galerius' court in Sirmium (modern Stara Zagora in Bulgaria). Constantine rejoined his father by the end of 305 and was rapidly adopted by the staff, which put him on the throne on July 28, 306, the day Constantius died. He had been on campaign in Britain at the time, and the building in which he died—the building in which Constantine was proclaimed emperor—is today incorporated into York's cathedral.

Constantine's seizure of power encouraged Maxentius, son of Maximian, to launch a coup d'état at Rome on October 28. Galerius' regional deputy failed to suppress Maxentius' revolt—then, in the summer of 307, Galerius himself failed at the same task. That was a shock. Galerius, conqueror of the Persians, was the greatest soldier of his age.

An uneasy peace reigned for the four years after Galerius' invasion of Italy, until Galerius himself died. Maximian was also dead by this point. He had broken with Maxentius and taken refuge with Constantine, who had previously married his young daughter Fausta to secure their alliance. Maximian then tried to overthrow Constantine, failed, and was invited to hang himself.

Having disposed of Maximian, Constantine had firmly established himself as a renegade. Basing his claim to power on a combination of his father's position and divine favor, he ceased advertising other connections to Diocletian's ideology of collegial power. Emblematic of this shift was his rejection of the physical images of Diocletian's imperial college in which everyone had a beard, to appear clean shaven (see Figure 1.1).

Although he was ideologically at odds with the old system, Constantine was practically enmeshed in the politics of the old order, which took a new turn given the intense hostility between Galerius' surviving deputies: Licinius, whom Galerius had made his co-emperor from 308 onward, and Maximinus, who had been Caesar in the east since 305. Maximinus began to make diplomatic overtures to Maxentius, while Constantine now courted Licinius. When Galerius was laid to rest, the stage was set for a nasty civil war.

At this point, Constantine knew that he would have to invade Italy to deal with Maxentius, his most immediate threat. He also knew that the last three emperors to do so had failed. He was worried. He knew he needed a god who would help guide him to victory. He reflected that Galerius, who had renewed Diocletian's persecution of Christians, had particularly despised their god. The Christian God was identified by some Christians with the sun, and Constantius himself may have recalled how Invincible Sun had helped Aurelian. Constantine's interest in a sun god had been advertised in the wake of Maximian's demise in 310, and now, as he later wrote, he thought deeply about how he could become a better man. At some point in

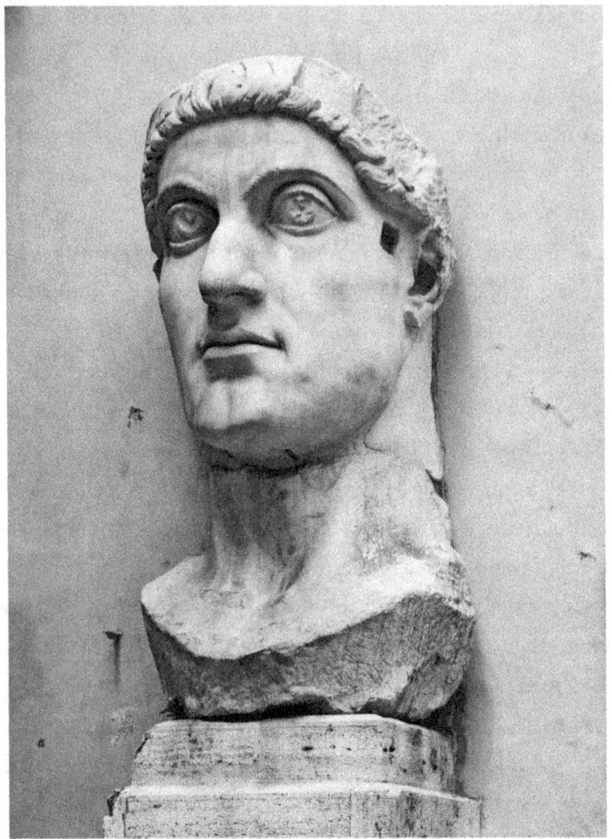

Figure 1.1 Constantine's image eschews connection with the imperial imagery of Diocletian's era, in which all emperors were depicted with beards (something that had been the case, albeit with different styles, since the early second century). Constantine's "new look" was in line with his rejection of the collegial system of government instituted by Diocletian.

the spring of 312, identifying the Christian God with the abstract entity described as Divine Mind (and, it seems, Invincible Sun), Constantine began to worship the Christian God.

People would later make up bizarre stories about what happened, namely that Constantine saw a cross in the sky with the words "in this sign conquer" on it. That never happened, and no one in the western empire even knew it was supposed to have happened for centuries. Those who did not know the story about the cross in the sky made one up that was even more ridiculous. According to this story, Constantine, residing in Rome and persecuting the Christians, was smitten by leprosy and cured by pope Sylvester of Rome, who then baptized Constantine and became titular head of the Church throughout Rome's domains.

That the Christian God was the right god was confirmed, spectacularly, by the stunning success of Constantine's invasion of Italy, culminating in his victory at the Battle of the Milvian Bridge outside of Rome on October 28, 312. His family converted at the same time, and when he married his half-sister Constantia to Licinius at the end of the summer, he seems to have told his co-emperor what had happened. When, in 313, Licinius stormed to victory over his rival in the east, he wrote to all the governors of the eastern provinces instructing them that Christianity was legal and that they should restore property that had been seized from Christian groups during the persecutions of the previous decade. Since Constantine had met with Licinius at Milan, this decree is sometimes, erroneously, referred to as the edict of Milan. It was in fact the letter from Nicomedia.

The letter from Nicomedia underscores just how astonishing Constantine's choice of god was. The letter seeks to restore a community that had been battered by persecution, the bitterness of which can still be felt in the pages of a book that Lactantius wrote as soon as Licinius' victory was complete. It is called *On the Deaths of the Persecutors,* and it celebrates the grisly fates of every emperor who had persecuted the Christians. At the time he wrote, it is not clear that Lactantius knew that Constantine was a Christian. This was something he would learn in the next few years when he journeyed west and was received at Constantine's court.

CREATING IMPERIAL CHRISTIANITY

Constantine now needed to find a way of justifying his own place in the world. The old notion that an emperor was a product of consensus among the people he ruled was long gone, as was Diocletian's effort to instantiate the notion that only an emperor could create another emperor. Constantine's career had done that notion in. Constantine also needed to explain what made his career special; the one point that had survived the turmoil of recent years was that an emperor was guided by divine inspiration.

Constantine arrived at Rome in the company of four bishops: Maternus from Cologne, Reticius from Autun, Marinus from Arles, and Ossius from Cordoba. It was with this very small group that Constantine set about redefining the role of Christianity within the Roman state and, indeed, reshaping Christianity so that it could provide an ideology to assist in the government of empire.

Theology was not a great concern of Constantine's immediate associates. One of the major problems of which they were aware was that of Church discipline, of getting people to actually follow whatever it was their bishops believed they should do. Once this problem was solved it might be possible to create a more wide-ranging theology that would link the story of Jesus with the government of the very empire whose official had put him to death.

In terms of the structures that enable radical change, we may discern at this moment the crucial elements of the process. These included the relatively small number of people who were initially involved in applying a pre-existing set of ideas to a new circumstance, the collapse of previous modes of describing authority, and a malleable ideological system that engaged with dominant modes of thought.

Two points are most obvious in the first decade of Constantine's career as a Christian. The first is the continued advertisement of the divine guidance that had brought the great victory in Rome. On the arch the Roman senate erected for him next to the Colosseum, viewers are told that Constantine was moved to save Rome from the "tyrant" through the inspiration of a divinity and the greatness of his mind. The actual divinity is never mentioned in non-Christian contexts, and Constantine did not deny the possibility that other gods existed. That wasn't necessary. All that mattered was that his god was the best god.

The second process involved defining the imperial government's role in unifying the Church. This was something that got off to a rocky start thanks to the intense hatred that had erupted within the North African Church as the result of Diocletian's persecution. Given the fact that one faction there was charging the leadership of the other faction with collaborating with the imperial authorities, there really wasn't a lot of common ground upon which to build a settlement. Still, when Constantine found out about what was happening (which was already in 312), he summoned the two sides to a church council in Rome. In his view the Church should solve its own problems under imperial supervision and count upon the government to enforce its decisions.

From the perspective of one of the groups involved in the North African dispute, this was a highly disagreeable decision. This group, the Donatists, took its name from the new leader who emerged in 312, Bishop Donatus, and refused to accept the authority of the council held in Rome in 313 and the one at Arles in 315, at which Constantine was present and to which he wrote concerning his own conversion. The documents relating to these events (though not Constantine's letter, which was presumably too hot to handle) were put into wide enough circulation that a bishop named Eusebius, who was in Caesarea on the eastern shore of the Mediterranean, could include them in the version of his *History of the Church*, which he was updating after Licinius' victory in the east. Christians could now know they had a highly sympathetic emperor, unless they were Donatists.

Constantine lost his patience with the Donatists in 317, just about the time that he had to admit that he could not eliminate Licinius as a ruler in the east (their recent civil war had ended in a treaty that slightly advantaged Constantine). He ordered arrests. Then stopped. Presumably Christians at court drew the line at shedding the blood of their fellow Christians. This too was an extremely important point, for it established a limit as to how far the imperial government would go. Christians who were convicted of crimes could still be executed, but being a heretic would not be one of those crimes. People who had been persecuted understood what persecution could not accomplish.

NICAEA

In 324 Constantine eliminated Licinius for good, again advertising the role his God played in assisting him to victory. Possibly on Good Friday of 325 he delivered a very long speech to an assembly of bishops, setting out his understanding of God and the way he saw the deity guiding him. This address possibly took place in Nicomedia, which was serving as Constantine's capital while the new capital he had founded at Byzantium (it was called Constantinople) was under construction. Some aspects of the speech follow the writings of Lactantius quite closely, which again suggests the importance of what appears to have been a small group of advisers in shaping the emperor's faith.

The bishops who listened to Constantine at Good Friday would have been among those who assembled in early June for the first "world-wide" church council, tasked with solving two issues for all Christians. The notion that such a council could take place at all is a result of Constantine's interest in centralizing authority over the

Church in the imperial palace. If the Church was to be effective it needed, like Constantine, to have a single, straightforward message.

There were two issues that the council summoned to meet at Nicaea would have to decide. One was the date of Easter; the other was the relationship between the Father, Son, and Holy Spirit. The issue with Easter was whether it should be celebrated in conjunction with Passover—reasonable enough, since Jesus had been executed at Passover—or whether it should be celebrated on the first Sunday after the first new moon following the vernal equinox. The idea supporting this latter view was that the single most important Christian festival should not depend on the Jewish calendar.

The theological question regarding the relationship between the members of the Trinity was whether Jesus was the same as the Father ("consubstantial") or, having been "created" by the Father, was similar but not exactly the same. The second view stressed the human aspect of Christ and was well grounded in the Gospels, but could allow the claim that Jesus' authority was not the same as the Father's. This view, that the Father and the Son were similar but not identical in nature, was espoused by an Alexandrian priest named Arius, who had a large following. The view that they were identical in nature, or "consubstantial," was favored by a faction backing bishop Alexander of Alexandria.

For Constantine the issue of the relationship between the Father and the Son was not a matter for debate. It was an issue to be legislated. His decision would shape the parameters of belief for the faithful ever after, but the manner through which he devised his "Nicene Creed" was closely aligned with the way that major imperial legislation was drafted. In this process the emperor would consult a panel of experts who would offer him a draft of a proposed regulation. In the case of the Holy Trinity, the expert was a priest from central Turkey named Hermogenes, who was working with a draft proposed by bishop Eusebius of Caesarea. His version was as follows:

> We believe in one God, the Father Almighty, Maker of all things visible and invisible—and in one Lord Jesus Christ, the Son of God, the only begotten of the Father, that is of the substance of the Father; God of God, Light of Light, true God of true God; begotten not made, consubstantial with the Father; by whom all things were made both which are in heaven and on earth; who for the sake of us men, and account of our salvation, descended, became incarnate, was made man, suffered, and rose again on the third day; he ascended into the heavens, and will come to judge the living and the dead. We also believe in the Holy Ghost. But those who say "There was a time when he was not" and "Before his generation he was not," and "he came to be from nothing," or those who pretend that the Son of God is "Of other hypostasis or substance," or "created" or "alterable" or "mutable" the universal and apostolic Church anathematizes.

The creed, which Constantine presented to the council for its approval, betrays, in its final lines, the controversies that gave rise to it. But it also remains the most often quoted and recited product (at least until the last sentence) of the Roman imperial government.

The Nicene Creed was not completely satisfactory to everyone, but most bishops at the time did accept it as a definition of their faith, and even diehard opponents of Bishop Alexander ultimately came around, including Arius himself and Bishop Eusebius of Nicomedia (no relation to bishop Eusebius of Caesarea).

Although briefly removed from his see for supporting Arius, Eusebius of Nicomedia soon exploited his friendship with Constantine's half-sister, the now-widowed spouse of Licinius. Proximity to the court enabled him to join the inner circle. When Athanasius of Alexandria, Alexander's successor, complained about Nicene revisionism and other appalling doctrinal failures, he did so by complaining that the faith was being corrupted by this inner circle. Members of the inner circle, Constantine himself, and later his son Constantius, found Athanasius objectionable not so much for doctrinal reasons as for his thuggish behavior as bishop.

CHRISTIAN AND NON-CHRISTIAN

Athanasius' victims were usually other Christians who were members of groups that did not fully accept his authority. This was typical of the period in which—despite Constantine's creed, somewhat altered by councils under Constantius II (r. 337–361)—Christians were more often concerned with the misdeeds of other Christians than they were with non-Christians. Nonetheless, what Constantine had done was to effectively set the stage for the very gradual ending of traditional belief. His own highly nuanced policies had aimed at preventing strife between what was still the majority of the population of his empire and the minority of Christians, while at the same time encouraging people to become Christian. The tipping point by which most people were Christian came within a few decades of his death and was quite possibly reached because Constantine had done so little to strengthen pagan belief through persecution.

Constantine's own statements about his faith varied in strength according to audience. To outsiders he could be explicit. There exists a letter he wrote to Sapor II, king of Persia, explaining the glory of his God and, among other things, that Valerian's capture was the result of his enmity to God rather than Sapor I's genius. That does not seem to have gone down well in the highly Zoroastrian Persian court. Constantine's further efforts to reach out to Christians in Persian territory were deeply resented. Things seem to have gone better along the northern frontier where Gothic tribes in Central Europe began to accept Christianity, and the same may have been true of tribes north of the Rhine. Constantine also made some efforts to speed up recognition of his faith in the army, which had been slow to catch on prior to the war with Licinius. In the early 320s, a group of soldiers had greeted Constantine with the acclamation, "*Gods* preserve you Constantine Augustus."

Otherwise things were less obvious. When Constantinople opened for business in 330, one of the major monuments (a portion of which survives) was a giant column supporting a statue of Constantine as the sun god in heroic nudity. The city also had two major churches, and its old temples. The point was that old could coexist with new.

Constantine's message of coexistence between old and new ideas was immensely important for the future, in part because the educated, increasingly Christian, governing elite was brought up on classical non-Christian literature. Such Christians united the thinking of the past with the future. St. Augustine of Hippo (354–430 CE) was well trained in classical literature. He said that he wept when he read the scene in Virgil's *Aeneid*, the poem that was the core of an ancient education in Latin, where the hero Aeneas abandoned his new love Queen Dido so he could found Rome. She killed herself. In rewriting the history of Rome in his *City of God*, he also showed a deep command of pagan history (his point was that things had been terrible before the birth of Christ, so people should stop whining about a few contemporary catastrophes). The City of God was going to be better than anything that had happened in the pagan past. We will meet him in later chapters as other aspects of his thought, especially his ideas on sin and God's grace, shaped later Christian traditions.

Another person whose impact we'll be coming across later was Augustine's contemporary Jerome (347–420 CE). He trained as a lawyer and had been immersed in traditional (pagan) Latin texts before taking off to the desert of Palestine, where he produced the Latin version of the Old and New Testaments that would become the versions known in Western Europe throughout the Middle Ages. He also produced a *Chronicle* that united biblical with pagan history. It would be Christians who continued to copy important works of pagan literature, history, and philosophy—the works of authors such as Plato, Aristotle, Livy, Tacitus, and Thucydides that would inspire new ways to think about a state in the seventeenth and eighteenth centuries.

Christian and classical thought may have become more antithetic in the eighteenth century than they were in the fourth century. Indeed, the only serious complaint about this melding of classical (non-Christian) and Christian thought and tradition was raised by Julian, Constantine's nephew who briefly seized power in the early 360s and tried to de-Christianize the government. He died while engaged in an ill-advised, catastrophic invasion of Iraq after eighteen months on the throne. Even pagans deplored an edict in which he stated that only pagans could be teachers of pagan literature.

There would be some moments of greater tension. Constantine himself ordered the closure of several temples where, he was told, ritual prostitution was the order of the day, or housed oracles that were particularly offensive to Christians. At other times he might congratulate people who became Christians. In writing to a place called Orcistus, which was applying for civic status, he said the town had earned the promotion (which had economic benefits) because of its fine amenities. He added that he was pleased to learn that all its inhabitants worshiped his God. One of his officials writing toward the end of Constantine's life to Spello in Italy about the temple it was erecting in honor of the imperial family and the biennial festival it would hold there, reminded people they should not sacrifice, but said they could celebrate the imperial family with the usual entertainments (including gladiators).

Traditional cults at traditional temples required sacrifice in order to make an approach to the gods. It is not clear if Constantine ever banned sacrifice at temples, and the fact that the letter to Spello mentions this particular point suggests he did not. He did, however, tell his officials they shouldn't sacrifice and, when his sons later did ban sacrifice, they claimed they did so on his authority. "Pagans," as non-Christians came to be called, learned to do without it.

There remained plenty of pagans even after the majority of the population had converted. Christians claimed this was particularly true of the countryside. Indeed, the Latin word *paganus*, the root of our word "pagan," just means "country-dweller." But just how many there were by the end of the fourth century remains open to question. Heroic stories of bishops such as Nicholas of Sion in southern Turkey (ultimately our Saint Nicholas) show their subjects chasing pagans well into the sixth century. One of Nicholas' contemporaries even claimed to have converted 50,000 around his home town. This may be a considerable exaggeration. By and large, most people abandoned, at least formally, their old ways, and adapted themselves to the new faith, which was permeable enough to permit local forms of worship that evoked past moments. St. Demetria at Eleusis in Greece, whose worship replaced the cult of Demeter in the same city, is a case in point.

There were also moments of genuine violence, though these were not typically initiated by the central government at any period before the sixth century. One of the worst moments, the slaughter in 391 of a pagan community and the destruction of the great temple of Serapis at Alexandria in Egypt, which held a major library, was the work of the local bishop. So was the appalling murder, in the same city, of the philosopher and mathematician, Hypatia. Stories that pagans supported revolts against Christian emperors tended to be no more than that. The battles involved Christian armies on both sides.

CONSTANTINE'S LEGACY

Constantine died outside of Nicomedia on May 22, 337. He was on his way to visit the Holy Land, where he would bathe in the river

Jordan before going to war with Persia. So the story goes. The one thing that is certain is that he was going to go to war with Persia. One other certain thing is that Bishop Eusebius of Nicomedia baptized him before he died and that he was later entombed at Constantinople in a mausoleum in which it was hoped he would be joined by a complete set of apostolic relics (that never happened).

Constantine passed almost immediately into legend. This is perhaps not surprising, as he kept many of the most important things about himself relatively quiet. There was never a court-authorized story of his conversion. The account he gave to the bishops at Arles was not widely known, and never passed through the organs of imperial propaganda. This meant that people could make things up, as we have seen in the cases of the story of his conversion by pope Sylvester and the tale of the cross in the sky. Working from a different perspective, a pagan historian of the later fourth century claimed Constantine only converted in 326 after a series of unfortunate events at Rome. According to this version, Constantine's wife Fausta told her husband that Crispus, his oldest son by a previous marriage, had tried to rape her. He executed Crispus, then found that Fausta had lied to him. He had her steamed and smothered in a bathhouse. None of this is true. Crispus had started the year 326 in Gaul, where he appears to have engaged in treasonous discussions. He was executed in the early summer. Fausta, who traveled with her husband, was exiled from court at the end of the summer and died a year later. There was more to come.

Visitors to Rome these days might stop at the lovely church of Santa Croce in Gerusalemme, or ascend the Capitoline to see the Church of Santa Maria in Aracoeli. In either place (the latter now retains Helena's remains) there are versions of the story that Helena, Constantine's mother (Figure 1.2), discovered the relics of the cross upon which Jesus was crucified. She didn't. She did go to Jerusalem in 327 and had some role in the establishment of the modern Church of the Holy Sepulcher. Not even Eusebius of Caesarea knew about the discovery of the "true cross," even though he was a neighbor to Jerusalem and, in the early years of Constantius II's reign, was in the process of fabricating a *Life of Constantine* presenting his hero as a die-hard foe of paganism from the moment of his miraculous conversion.

Figure 1.2 Helena's position became increasingly prominent as Constantine's reign progressed; here she is represented with aspects of the goddess Ceres, which is emblematic of the mixed messaging with respect to religion throughout Constantine's reign. She did play a significant role as a patron of the Christian Church.

If Constantine had really behaved the way Eusebius says, we can be certain that Christianity would never have become the religion of the empire. People would have been too angry.

The situation has not improved with the passage of time. Some have wished to believe that Constantine's conversion was a carefully calculated political act, as he aligned himself with a religion that was already threatening to overthrow traditional paganism (false). Others have claimed that he is the founder of modern anti-Semitism (also false), and still others have suggested that he is responsible for eliminating the feminine element of Christianity. (That at least appears in an avowed work of fiction, and female leadership in the Church had been pretty well squelched before the end of the third century.)

PATTERNS OF CHANGE

Fantasy has obscured Constantine's true significance as an agent of change, and the reasons why he was so successful. He became a Christian for very specific reasons of his own. He needed to forge a story with which to claim legitimacy as Rome's emperor. He chose the Christian God as his protector and was then convinced of his God's extraordinary power when he defeated Maxentius.

The reason that Constantine was looking for a new god in the first place was that the established ideology of imperial government had been battered throughout the previous hundred years, a period of internal strife and defeat on the frontiers. He was not the first emperor to look to establish a new ideology; he was the most successful.

Just as the Christian faith had begun and flourished through the efforts of a small number of devout believers, the development of imperial Christianity depended on Constantine's ability to work with a small coterie of Christians to develop a message reconciling imperial power with what had previously been a fundamentally counter-cultural group. Working outward from this group, he then shaped Christianity into an institution with a coherent structure and with a central message that went beyond belief in the resurrection and world's end. He believed that his adherence to the Christian God was good for himself and encouraged others to join him in his faith, for their own benefit and the benefit of society as a whole. He felt rational self-interest to be a far greater inducement to change than force. He understood that to effect true change, he had to allow for people to change themselves.

Constantine's model for change was effective because he understood the limits of the possible and because the Christians with whom he worked were willing to adjust their beliefs to suit new circumstances. A radical movement devoted to imagining the imminent end of the world is not the obvious source of an ideology that could govern an empire. But a religion that allowed for its god to become the great god of battles, the emperor in heaven to guide the emperor on earth, was eminently capable of providing the ideological spine for a new imperial regime. The fact that Christianity was seen as a radical alternative to conventional thought by those who did not understand the teachings of Jesus enabled Constantine to seem radical in the pagan world while seeking a traditional goal: personal supremacy. The result was to create an intellectual movement in his reformed Christianity that would prove appealing to his subjects and shift the intellectual center of Europe.

Chapter 2

The Rise of Islam

THE WORDS OF THE PROPHET

In 610 CE, Muhammad the son of Abdullah, member of the tribe Quraysh and merchant of Mecca, had a vision. He would describe the experience as follows:

> We sent it down on the Night of Glory. What will explain to you what the Night of Glory is? The Night of Glory is better than a thousand months. On that night the angels and the Spirit descend again and again with their Lord's permission on every task. Peace it is until the rising of the dawn.

Muhammad was born in 567 CE. His father died before his birth, his mother when he was six, his grandfather when he was eight. He was subsequently raised by an uncle. It is possible to sense something of his experience as an orphan when later he would say, "do not be harsh with the orphan and do not chide the one who asks for help." At the age of twenty-five he came to the attention of a wealthy widow named Khadija, who hired him to run her caravans north into the territory of the Roman Empire. She later became the first of what would ultimately be fifteen wives.

Muhammad's vision urged him to preach a message of peace in a world riven by deadly strife. The God whose messenger came to him was the God of Abraham, and the God who had inspired Jesus of Nazareth. The God whose messenger came to Muhammad wished him to unite people who had previously benefited from God's revelation, to help them to better understand that revelation, and to transform unbelievers into believers, guaranteeing them salvation when the end of the world arrived.

Muhammad, like Jesus of Nazareth, must have been an extraordinarily charismatic individual. To this day we can feel the power of his revelations through the Koran, the book in which we now know are recorded visions he reported to his followers. One of the extraordinary developments of modern scholarship has been the discovery of two manuscripts, containing portions of the Koran, which date to Muhammad's lifetime or the years shortly after his death. The existence of these manuscripts disproves what was once the widespread consensus among Western scholars that the Koran was assembled more than fifty years after his death. One of these manuscripts resides in the Mingana Collection at the University of Birmingham. It was written by 645 CE and contains two Suras (chapters) from the Koran. The date of this manuscript therefore appears to confirm the tradition that Muhammad's immediate successor, Abu Bakr (632–634 CE), ordered the creation of an authoritative text of the Prophet's visions. The other manuscript, from Yemen, represents a version of the Koran that precedes the edition prepared on Abu Bakr's instruction, based upon records made by people who wrote down statements recited by the Prophet himself. The significance of these discoveries is that they prove that the Koran really is the best guide to Muhammad's thought. It is not a later reconstruction of his views.

A further development is the publication of a Chronicle describing the last wars between Rome and Persia, as well as the early Arab conquests. It dates from the middle of the seventh century. It is written in Syriac, the principle language spoken by people living in Syria, western Turkey, and Iraq during the period of the conquest, and, indeed, for centuries before these events. The perspective is that of Iraq's Christian community. These people were not enthusiastic supporters of the Persians who ruled them directly, or of the Roman government across the border. The seventh-century date of the Chronicle, known as the Chronicle of 660 from the last events it describes, means we can more readily test the extensive later narratives of the events after Muhammad's death, which have hitherto provided the bulk of our information, against a contemporary source.

What the Koran tells us is that Muhammad advocated the reconciliation of people whose faith descended from God's revelation to Abraham. It tells us that he preached a powerful message of moral probity, that he delivered a potent vision of heaven as the future home of the faithful, of hell for enemies of the true faith who refused to be reconciled to Muhammad's truth, and of the world's end. What he did not do is predict the sudden takeover of the Roman and Persian empires, the extension of the community of his followers, within a century, to lands running from Spain to India, or even the necessity of waging war for his revelation. When Muhammad used the word *jihad*, which now is understood to mean "holy war," he used it to mean "ethical striving."

The rise of the new Arab state means that we must also pause for a moment to contemplate the phenomenon which is often referred to, since Montesquieu's book *On the Greatness and Decline of the Romans* and Edward Gibbon's masterful *Decline and Fall of the Roman Empire,* both composed in the eighteenth century, as the "Fall of the Roman Empire." The result of the Arab conquests in the seventh century was that the Roman Empire declined but did not fall. It ceased to be a Mediterranean entity and would henceforth be limited to portions of what is now Turkey, modern Greece, and, occasionally, Bulgaria. We conventionally refer to this reduced entity as the Byzantine state, a name derived from the ancient name of the city that had become Constantinople. The rulers at Constantinople, who called themselves "Roman," would have been surprised by this terminology.

Stressing the decline of Rome has the unfortunate tendency to obscure the fact that the fates of Rome and Persia were linked. The two empires controlled the major agricultural regions of Egypt on the one side and Iraq on the other, and were surrounded by a ring of tribal societies whose welfare depended upon access to the products controlled by these empires. The true impact of the Arab conquest was to bring this system to an end, replacing it with an extensive new political system based on states sharing a common religious identity that stretched from central Asia, ultimately to southern Spain. This powerful Islamic world was flanked by tribal societies in Asia or relatively weak polities whose most important common feature was their adherence to some form of Christianity in Europe.

Because the concept of the "Fall of Rome" doesn't reflect the complexity of the situation, many scholars have now substituted the term "Late Antiquity" to encompass the period from roughly the reign of Constantine until the period in which the new world order stabilized in the seventh to eighth centuries CE. This has the advantage of stressing change as the dominant aspect of this period, of allowing for ascent as well as descent, and for the agents of change being neither Roman nor Persian.

The spread of Muhammad's message into the world of Late Antiquity stemmed in part from the exceptional talent of Muhammad's followers, and the exceptional incompetence of the leadership of both the Roman and Persian empires. The failure of the governing class in both the Roman and Persian empires arose from the heady combination of economic failure, natural disaster, bigotry, and boneheaded refusal to recognize new realities imposed by changed economic circumstances. Traditional government incapacitated itself prior to confronting the threat that emerged from tribes united by Muhammad's vision.

The failure of traditional government is insufficient in and of itself to explain the success of the new order, or even the existence of what would become the new order. It took nearly fifty years after the disruption of the old world order in the 630s for a new regime to emerge that was able to unite the areas that had suddenly fallen under Arab control around a coherent vision for the future. The success of the Arab conquest stemmed not only from the failures of Persian and Roman governments but also from the ability of ʿAbd al-Malik, a successor to the leaders who won the initial victories, to bureaucratize Muhammad's teachings. In so doing, ʿAbd al-Malik provided the ethical basis of a new government.

ECONOMIC DISLOCATION

A natural disaster initiated the terminal spiral of the Roman and Persian empires. In the summer of 541 the bubonic plague arrived in the Mediterranean and spread rapidly throughout Europe, the Middle East, and North Africa. The bacterium came from Central Africa; the first outbreak was at Alexandria in Egypt, where trade from the south and east was funneled into the broader economy.

The effect on Alexandria was catastrophic. Then, in the spring of 542, ships from the city carried the infected rodents to Syria, Asia Minor, and Constantinople, where the pestilence ran its course for four months. Contemporaries interpreted the outbreak as both the vengeance of God and as a play date for demons. A historian of the period wrote that many people saw apparitions in human form which struck them; another says that some demons appeared in the form of monks. Doctors knew not what to do; they had never seen the disease, and those who recovered did so for no obvious cause.

The death toll was horrendous; five or ten thousand people perished in a single day. The total number of deaths at Constantinople may have reached 300,000, while in one town on the Egyptian border all but eight people were found dead. People were seen to totter and fall in the streets; merchants or customers might be suddenly overcome in the midst of a transaction; a house was filled with nothing but the dead, twenty bodies in all; infants wailed as their mothers died. At Constantinople the authorities filled the tombs around the city, digging up all the places where they could lay the dead and finally filling the towers in the defensive walls. A plague victim recalled how he was afflicted with the swellings, and how later the disease took his wife, many of his children, and relatives, servants, and tenants. For some, he said, the first symptoms were in the head, making the eyes bloodshot and the face swollen; the symptoms then descended to the throat. For others there was a violent stomach disorder, while for those whose lymph nodes swelled up there was a violent fever, then death, if it would come, by the third day.

The plague devastated the economy—signs of expansion in various areas came to an end in the middle of the sixth century. An immediate effect of the plague was also to short-circuit an effort on the part of the Roman government in Constantinople to rebuild effective control in the western Mediterranean. In the previous century a collection of Germanic successor states had arisen in territory once controlled by Rome in North Africa, Spain, France, and Britain. Rome had regained control of North Africa in the 530s and had ousted the Germanic regime in Italy a few years later, but it had not yet built a stable regime of its own to replace the one it had unseated. That would now not happen. When the empress Theodora, in many ways the brains behind the government, died of cancer in 548, the imperial regime would blunder from failure to failure for the rest of the reign of her husband, Justinian, who didn't die until 565. Most significantly, Rome lost effective control over the central Balkans where a new, Bulgarian, state was developing. Justinian's successor Justin was of very limited ability, losing control of most of Italy and faring badly in a war with Persia before his abdication in 578. His two successors, Tiberius and Maurice, stabilized the situation, but what was really needed was peace, and peace required strength that Rome no longer had.

It is in the Balkans that the economic transition away from the Roman imperial economy first becomes obvious. Politically, the plague-weakened, over-committed empire progressively lost control in the half century after Theodora's death. The most serious problems were connected with the arrival of a new group of Turkic peoples, the Avars, from the Ukraine into the region north of the Danube. In 567 the Avars assisted one Germanic tribe, the Lombards, in destroying their long-term enemies, the Gepids (the safety of the Roman frontier had depended upon the Roman ability to play these two groups off against each other). The Lombards, however, recognizing that they were likely to be the next target for Avar expansion, headed south into Italy to continue the by now seemingly endless struggle for control of the peninsula. There was worse to come. Even before the Avars arrived, Slavic tribes had been moving into the area north of the mouth of the Danube. Once the Avars established themselves, the Slavs tended to join them to raid Roman territory. On their own the Slavs, who were rather badly organized, were not a great threat. Linked with the Avars, they constituted a force that required powerful Roman armies to control, and those armies were soon stretched too thin. In 582 the Avars launched a series of devastating raids that culminated in the capture of Sirmium, the long-time bastion of Roman rule on the upper Danube.

As chaos encompassed the frontier, local land owners, feeling betrayed by an imperial regime that could not keep hostile neighbors under control, began to look to their own protection. And they started eating differently, preferring legumes and millet to winter-sown grains. They had nothing now to exchange with other parts of the empire, which in turn lost markets to which they could previously have shipped surplus. Cities in the imperial core of western Turkey showed signs of decline even as the plague-ravaged economies of Syria and Egypt stabilized. Stabilizing does not, however, mean fully recovering. Urban decline had the collateral effect of lowering the empire's tax receipts, and that had the further effect of weakening the military.

The Roman Empire's problems were not just economic. There was also a serious split over the proper way to understand the relationship between the members of the Holy Trinity. In 451 a council was summoned at Chalcedon (across the Bosporus from Constantinople) to produce a new creed, stating that Christ had two natures, human and divine, that became one after "he was made man." This statement was anathema to many bishops in Syria and Egypt, who believed that Jesus had but one, divine, nature. The split between the two sides worsened with the passage of time, dividing communities throughout the eastern provinces against themselves, and some of Persia's numerous Christians against those within the empire. The faith which Constantine had used to explain his great success and justify his new order now became a divisive force.

As the seventh century dawned, and Muhammad began to bring Khadija's caravans north into Palestine, the empire was suffering progressive economic failure and profound ideological division. Muhammad's message of religious unity may have been influenced in part by what he experienced of the divisions within the Roman community. His observations in the Koran that God had no human son look like a reformulation of Chalcedonian theology. He also understood that the intense hostility generated by the controversies over Christ's nature profoundly weakened Roman society.

Rome's weakness was not translating into Persian strength. This simple fact raises questions about much later accounts which imply that the Persian kings were fabulously wealthy. This suspicion cannot be tested, as in the case of the Roman Empire, through examination of contemporary documents and a well-articulated archaeological record. What we can do, however, is look at the institutions of the Persian state and at the way the Persians behaved.

One reason to be suspicious of statements that the Persians were wealthy is that the Persian Empire, occupied less—and less productive—territory in modern Iran and Iraq than the Roman Empire did in North Africa and the Near East. Another factor that makes it unlikely that Persia was incredibly rich is the fact that when we can recover actual details of their revenue system, we find that it was based on exactly the same sort of taxes that were characteristic of the Roman Empire; that is to say, a head tax collected from adults, a property tax, and taxes on trade. So, either Persians were much more productive than Romans, or the vast sums of money the Persian kings are said to have raised are a fantasy of later traditions.

There are two considerations that favor the fantasy idea. One is that Persian land and head taxes were paid to an agency that turned the money directly over to the army, suggesting that the Persian kingdom had little discretionary money for infrastructure and other projects. Another issue appears to have been the fact that Persia's rulers continued a tradition of Near Eastern kingship that stretched for millennia in maintaining a vast royal treasury, probably filled up with gifts from foreign embassies and plunder from successful wars rather than taxes. This was a royal heirloom from which kings, even in extreme distress, were loath to withdraw money. So, even though he might have the resources to alleviate the hardship that increased taxation in time of war caused his subjects, a Persian king was acculturated not to do this.

Lack of liquidity and a tendency to hoard existing resources meant that Persian kings had great difficulty securing their northern borders from Turkic peoples of central Asia. Their repeated efforts to get the Romans to finance the defense of this frontier (only occasionally successful) are indicative of financial problems at the empire's core. Their failure to reach agreements with these tribes would ultimately play into Roman hands.

Another sign that the Persians were having trouble is that they spent a good deal of time in the sixth and seventh centuries trying to extend their reach into southern Arabia. Yemen, as a result, came gradually under their control in the later sixth century, provoking occasional responses from the king of Ethiopia, a Christian and ally of Rome. One of his most notable interventions was in the very year of Muhammad's birth. That was the year an elephant was seen at Mecca, the result of one of these interventions.

The Persian regime was not only poor, it was also divided against itself. The Syriac Chronicle of 660 is written from the perspective of the Christian community. Its members are conscious of living in a mythic land of great antiquity, and of the history in which a Westerner, Alexander the Great, had destroyed an earlier Persian regime. These Christians, divided into two sects which were both considered heretical by the government in Constantinople, fought with each other, had no love for their Persian government, and loathed their neighbors. They believed that Jews—Iraq had a large Jewish population—would crucify their children and that their Manichaean neighbors would eat them. They also loathed the small, highly stratified, and politically potent Zoroastrian community, the group most closely aligned with the interests of the monarchy. It is emblematic of this relationship that the Chronicler of 660 believed Kusru (r. 591–628) pretended to love the Christians because of the emperor Maurice, but in truth he hated them. The feeling was mutual.

THE GREAT WAR

The Roman emperor, Maurice, who ascended the throne in 582 was successful in checking the power of the Avars and had won notable successes against the Persians, installing a client—Kusru, whom he adopted—on the throne in 588. In 602, his run of success ended. The Balkan army, commanded by a general named Phocas, mutinied and marched on Constantinople. On November 25, 602, Phocas occupied the imperial palace. Maurice and his children were executed two days later, or so it would seem. Shortly after the massacre, a man named Theodosius, claiming to be the son of Maurice, appeared in Ctesiphon asking that Kusru, who owed the family a debt stemming from his installation and adoption, restore him to the throne.

Whether this Theodosius really was the son of Maurice we cannot know. We do know that his appeal started a war between the Roman and Persian empires. From 603 to 610, the war went slowly but surely against the Romans—so much so that in the autumn of 610, the governor of Africa launched a fleet under the command of his son, Heraclius, to overthrow Phocas. On October 5, Phocas was dead, and Heraclius was emperor. For the next fourteen years, things went from bad to worse, beginning in 611 when Kusru captured Antioch, still Syria's chief city, and began to establish a permanent administrative system. In 614, the Persians destroyed Jerusalem as an example to cities that might think of resistance rather than surrender, and in 619 they occupied Alexandria. Most cities in fact had simply paid ransom to the Persians—one reason for the brutal treatment of Jerusalem was that, having surrendered, it had rebelled, killing its Persian garrison. In the absence of effective imperial defense, the people of the east saw no reason to risk their necks for the regime.

The stage was set for the destruction of the empire. Kusru allied himself with the Avars and began a series of immensely destructive invasions of Asia Minor, culminating in a siege of Constantinople (assisted by the Avars) in 626. Heraclius, however, was not in the city. He had taken the bulk of his army into Armenia, and even as the siege of Constantinople fell apart, he advanced, at the head of an army that included a very large number of Turkish auxiliaries, into Persian territory. On December 12, 627, Heraclius destroyed the Sassanian army in a battle at Nineveh, near Mosul in northern Iraq. Negotiations to end the war dragged on for a while, with the result that Persian armies did not finally evacuate Roman territory until 629. This was in part because of the chaos that engulfed the Persian court.

Kusru was deposed in the immediate aftermath of the battle at Nineveh, tried, and killed. This happened by the end of February 628. The agents of his deposition were a senior general and one of his younger sons, Kavad. Kavad lived for eight months, during which time he murdered the majority of his male relatives while also presiding over his father's execution. When Kavad died of the plague, he was replaced by his young son Ardashir, who was in turn murdered by the Persian general who had recently negotiated the restoration of Roman territory to Heraclius. This general was murdered after a reign of forty days and replaced by Kavad's widow, who finalized the peace treaty and then died, being replaced by Yazdgerd, a grandson of Kusru and the one nephew Kavad hadn't managed to kill. Yazdgerd was eight years old when he was placed on the throne.

The economic stress caused by the war, and the inherent weakness of the regional economy as a whole, is revealed by the circumstances of Kusru's removal from power in the months after Heraclius' victory. At his trial, the king was accused of the murder of his predecessor (true), the ill-treatment of his sons, the brutality of his lengthy prison terms, lack of affection toward his harem, treacherous behavior toward Maurice, and:

> [Fifth] What you have inflicted on your subjects generally in levying the land tax and in treating them with harshness and

> violence. [Sixth,] Your amassing a great amount of wealth, which you exacted from the people with great brutality so that you drove them to consider your rule hateful and thereby brought them into affliction and deprivation. [Seventh] Your stationing the troops for long periods along the frontiers with the Byzantines and on other frontiers, thereby separating them from their families.

There is no obvious reason to believe that taxation was not in fact a serious issue, for Kusru's successor promptly repealed some of the taxes that Kusru had imposed. And the charge that Kusru hoarded his wealth means no more than that Kusru was a traditionally inclined Persian king. Speaking in his own defense, Kusru says that only a fool does not realize that a king maintains his authority through wealth and armies, but that was not much of a defense. The fact financial issues are at the heart of complaints about Kusru suggests that, although having taken possession of Syria, Osrhoene, and Egypt, he was unable to extract sufficient surplus from these lands to fund war and avoid alienating his subjects. In Roman lands it is apparent that he retained the Roman tax system and many of the collectors who had been in their posts at the time of the conquest. Persia was essentially ruined by the war.

The situation was not much better for the Romans. The progressive degeneration of western Turkey's urban fabric, which had suffered severely from Persian invasions, could not be immediately reversed, nor could money be conjured from nowhere in the recently reconquered areas from Syria to Egypt. It did not help that Heraclius saw himself as very much the hero in his own story. An extant narrative of the victory outside Nineveh tells us:

> And when he had found a plain suitable for fighting, he addressed his troops and drew them up in battle order. Upon

> arriving there, Razates also drew up his army in three dense formations and advanced on the emperor. Battle was given on Saturday, 12 December. The emperor sallied forward in front of everyone and met the commander of the Persians, and, by God's might and the help of The Mother of God, threw him down; and those who sallied forth with him were routed. The emperor met another Persian in combat and cast him down also. Yet a third assailed him and struck him with a spear, wounding his hip; but the emperor slew him too. And when the trumpets had sounded, the two sides attacked each other, and as a violent battle was being waged, the emperor's tawny horse, called Dorkon, was wounded in the thigh by some infantryman, who struck it with a spear. It also received several blows of the sword on the face, but, wearing as it did a helmet made of sinew, it was not hurt, nor were the blows effective.

A less dramatic version simply says that he "descended on the northern territories, destroying, ruining and capturing all the northern lands." The damage he did to the densely populated hinterland of the Persian capital would not be repaired before the end of the Sassanian dynasty.

Heraclius seems to have believed his own press releases, and did little to ease the reintegration of the eastern provinces into the empire. While he advertized his recovery of the "True Cross," the object Helena had allegedly discovered centuries earlier, from the Persians with a massive celebration, he also installed a Chalcedonian hierarchy in regions whose people were largely anti-Chalcedonian. This was most unwelcome. People had grown used to living without the stress of an administration that treated them as heretics. The leaders of these areas would soon see no reason to sacrifice themselves for a regime that had proved more ineffective than effective in recent decades, and which they had tacitly opposed through years of collaboration with the Persians. Heraclius' aggressive stance against the anti-Chalcedonian population just added insult to annoyance. It did not help that he had entered an incestuous marriage to his niece a few years earlier.

In addition to alienating his newly reclaimed subjects, Heraclius appears to have broken with the allies upon whom he depended for his victory against Persia: the Turkish tribes who occupied the area between the Caspian Sea and Iran's northern borders. Given their long-term enmity with Persia, it did not require a diplomatic miracle to acquire their services. But they would be notably absent from the campaigns that would result in the creation of the new Arabic state after Muhammad's death in 632. They would long resist the invaders from the south, but not in alliance with Rome. Why? Perhaps Heraclius did not pay them what they thought they were owed.

MUHAMMAD AND MECCA

Mecca was a commercial and religious center centuries before the arrival of the Quraysh, Muhammad's people. The city's prominence, attested as early as the second century CE, was due to a combination of factors. One was its location on the eastern edge of the Hijaz, the region of what is now western Saudi Arabia bounded in the north by the Gulf of Aqaba and in the south by Yemen. Mecca sits in a valley that is fourty-three miles east of the Red Sea, at a point where there is a pass through the Hijaz mountains, giving access to the north. For some period before Muhammad's birth it was the center for the cult of a god named Hubal, worshiped in the central temple or Ka'ba. Also prominent among Mecca's cults were those of three female divinities: Al-Lat, al-'Uzza, and Manat, who, Muhammad would say in speaking to those who rejected his revelation, "are nothing but names you have invented yourselves, you and your forefathers. God has set no authority for them." At the time he said this, it was an eccentric point of view.

Mecca's location made it a hub for one of the caravan routes leading north into Roman territory. Muhammad himself mentions the winter and summer journeys of the Quraysh in which he must have participated. They would have traded in leather goods from their own district, and in spices that came from Yemen with the people to their north—probably more of the former than the latter in Muhammad's time, as there was less money for luxury goods in the post-plague poverty of the northern lands. Lack of profit might also be a reason why the emperor, or Nagus, of Ethiopia, gave up on trying to dominate Yemen and the Hijaz before the end of the sixth century, and why the subsequent Persian takeover of Yemen yielded them no appreciable gain. That said, Mecca was still a center for trade and the exchange of ideas. In addition to the worshippers of Mecca's ancestral divinities, Muhammad would have met members of the substantial Jewish community in southern Arabia, Christians, and a few Zoroastrians in the Persian-occupied zones.

Prior to the reign of Maurice, contact between southern Arabia and the great empires to the north was mediated by two coalitions: the Roman-supported Jafnids, based at Jabala in southern Syria, and the Nasrids, based at al-Hira near the Persian border. Of these two groups the Jafnids had the greatest contact with the Hijaz. Even before the outbreak of the great war in 602, the Roman relationship with the Jafnids had collapsed. This was Maurice's doing, and the result was that Rome lost its traditional point of contact with the political groups in the peninsula's south and center. Kusru had wrecked Persia's association with the Nasrids, claiming they were insufficiently obedient. He then tried to claim control over Arabia. That was impractical, and Persia was now no better off than Rome.

It was against a background of war and dislocation that Muhammad began to have his visions. His point, initially, appears to have been that proper understanding of the one God was necessary for salvation, and this God was the God revealed to Abraham, and Jesus too was his prophet. In a city which profited from the pilgrims who came to view its holy sites, this message was not uniformly welcome. "If they call you a liar" he said, "many messengers before you were called liars: it is to God that all things will be referred." "Those who disbelieve will have severe torments; those who believe and do good deeds will have forgiveness and a rich reward." Those who worship idols are deluded, he said, asking what part of the earth those false gods had created. "When will this promise be fulfilled?" asked his critics. Muhammad's revelation was nothing more than poetry he had made up.

As Muhammad's group of followers expanded, relations worsened with the authorities at Mecca. Muhammad urged his followers not to respond with violence, for "the servants of the Lord of Mercy are those who walk humbly on the earth, and who, when the foolish address them, reply 'Peace'." Muhammad's message of unity between his followers, Christians, and Jews became more complicated after the Sassanid army captured Jerusalem, slaughtering many of the inhabitants, allegedly with the assistance of the area's Jewish population. Still, Muhammad would say, even well after the fall of Jerusalem, that "the believers, the Jews, the Christians and the Sabians—all who believe in God and the Last Day and do good—will have their rewards in their Lord." The Sabians mentioned here are another group of monotheists. Belief in the one God, for Muhammad, should be a unifying force, and he warned the Jewish community to be moderate in success, saying that they had in the past been punished for arrogance. Christians were told to stop fighting each other: "If God had so willed, their successors would not have fought each other after they had been brought clear signs. But they disagreed: some believed and some disbelieved."

The power of Muhammad's message and his increasing success in building his community of supporters—as well as the death, both in 619 CE, of Khadijah and his uncle Abu Talib, who had insulated him to some degree—led to a thorough break with the authorities governing Mecca in 622. He was mad, so people said. He lied about God.

As the situation in Mecca deteriorated, Muhammad reached out to the authorities at the city of Yathrib, later known as Medina (the name comes from the Arabic *madinat al-nabi*, "the city of the Prophet"). In June of 622 he departed Mecca for Medina with his followers, by night.

It is at the time of the establishment of Muhammad's community at Medina that we get the clearest documentary evidence for the way Muhammad envisioned the relationship between his followers and those around them. This document, known as the Constitution, or community document (*umma*) of Medina, sets out the obligations the immigrants from Mecca, the *muslim* (believers) who follow the *islam* (teaching) of the Koran, have to each other and to "those who follow them and attach themselves to them and struggle alongside them." Full members of the community, those who believed Muhammad's message replaced earlier revelation, were expected to live morally upstanding lives, to pray regularly (before dawn, during the day, at sunset, and at night), fast during the year's ninth month, and provide alms to support the poor. The associated groups include "allies" from among the Quraysh, who must have come with the believers from Mecca, as well as a number of pagan tribes in the area of Medina and one tribe that is Christian. Included in the broader community are a number of Jewish groups affiliated with the otherwise pagan tribes.

Muhammad's immediate followers, the believers, swear to exact vengeance for members of their community who are killed and to aid the poor among them in matters connected with ransom or the payment of the blood money due in the event of a killing. Believers will act against those who seek to divide their community; they will not kill each other; they will honor the obligations members of the community undertake to outsiders; and they will not make separate treaties. It appears that they agree to raid in an orderly fashion and only with Muhammad's permission, to treat Jews fairly, and that the center of Medina will be a sacred area. This sacred area, "the place of prostrations" or *masjid,* was the first mosque (the English word derives from *masjid*). Disagreements both among the believers and between the believers and their allies will be resolved by Muhammad, who is the messenger of God. In the Koran, Muhammad says "those who believed and emigrated and struggled for God's cause with their possessions and persons, and those who gave refuge and help, are all allies of one another."

The Constitution of Medina suggests Muhammad was a well-known figure by the time he and his followers arrived in their new home, and that he was trusted as a person to deal fairly with people. Crucially, the Constitution reveals Muhammad's comfort in leading a group that included people with differing degrees of belief in his message. And it shows that the community was shaped by the persistent violence surrounding it. The authorities of Mecca are identified as obvious enemies, but the emphasis in the document on raiding reflects a generally combative environment. Muhammad's community seeks to unite people of different beliefs. It was plainly a powerful message even before Muhammad proved himself as a strategist as well as a prophet.

It would be eight years before Muhammad triumphed over the Quraysh at Mecca. There are numerous indications in the Koran that neither Muhammad's army nor that of his Meccan rivals was especially well disciplined. Muhammad appears to have found it necessary to point out that it behooves people to do what they are told if their commander is the messenger of God. In a Sura reflecting an early conflict, he says, "Believers, when you meet the disbelievers in battle, never turn your backs on them: if anyone does so on such a day—unless maneuvering to fight or to join a fighting group—he incurs the wrath of God, and Hell will be his home, a wretched destination." On another occasion, after he was nearly killed, Muhammad said that, "he is only a messenger before whom many messengers have been and gone." He also found it necessary to forgive those who had run away: "you fled without looking back while the Messenger was calling out to you from behind, and God rewarded you with sorrow for sorrow. [He has now forgiven you] so that you will not grieve for what you missed or what happened to you." Moments like these were, however, less frequent than moments of victory as Muhammad's movement grew in strength.

After six years at Medina, Muhammad announced that he would make a pilgrimage back to Mecca. The return was put off while Muhammad negotiated with the Quraysh. In the end, the two sides agreed to the Treaty of Hudaybiya, according to which Muhammad would be allowed to make a pilgrimage to Mecca in ten years' time. Two years later, Muhammad claimed the Quraysh had violated the agreement and announced that he would come immediately to Mecca. His power was also now irresistible, and so the return in 630 was without violence. Muhammad's peaceful entry into Mecca marked the end of the struggle, and his former rivals among the Quraysh—able soldiers such as 'Amr ibn al-'As and Khalid ibn al-Walid—now joined him. "God has truly fulfilled His messenger's vision: 'God willing, you will most certainly enter the Sacred Mosque in safety, shaven headed or with cropped hair, without fear'—God knew what you did not—and he has granted you a nearer triumph."

Now Muhammad becomes ever clearer that his new revelation corrects errors and replaces the old. Jewish and Christian teachers are now people who have promoted ignorance of divine truth:

> They take their rabbis and their monks as lords beside God, as well as the Messiah, the son of Mary. But they were commanded to serve only one God: there is no God but Him; he is far above whatever they set up as his partners! They try to extinguish God's light with their mouths, but God insists on bringing His light to its fullness, even if the disbelievers hate it. It is He who has sent his Messenger with guidance and the religion of truth . . .

Monks and rabbis are now people who take the property of others, monasticism is something "they" invented. Such a statement does not mean that Christians and Jews were no longer welcome. What it meant was that their teachers were leading them astray. Given that Muhammad had earlier expressed horror at the outrages committed in the name of Judaism by a chieftain named Dhu Nuwas, memorable even at a century's distance, and that he plainly objected to what he considered Christian misunderstanding of the nature of God's relationship to Jesus, such statements represent a development rather than a departure from his other teachings.

Muhammad's more strident tone was accompanied by the dispatch of armies to bring more of Arabia under the sway of the believers. Just as he was strengthening his condemnation of what he saw to be "false teachers" for Christians and Jews, so too he was changing his position on the acceptability of continued pagan practice among allies to the community. He decreed an end to treaties between the believers and these people, warning them that:

> On the day of the Great Pilgrimage [there will be] a proclamation from God and his Messenger to all people: 'God and his Messenger are released from [treaty] obligations to the idolaters. It will be better for you [idolaters] if you repent; know that you cannot escape God if you turn away.

These pagans are given four months to repent, after which it will be open season for the believers to kill them. If, however, they did repent, pray to God, and pay tax, they would be forgiven. At no point, even now, does Muhammad appear to envision a world in which there will only be believers. He is concerned that the believers will live moral lives—that had always been a theme of his revelations—but he does not lay down a specific code of conduct they must follow. The believers will be received in "the Garden that those mindful of God have been promised: flowing streams and perpetual food and shade. This is the reward that awaits those who are mindful of God; the disbelievers' reward is the Fire." As had been true of Jesus' earliest followers, Muhammad's had been taught that the Day of Judgment was imminent. Added to this was a doctrine that self-sacrifice for the faith would be especially rewarded.

Muhammad's effort to subdue the Bedouins took his forces into areas once controlled by the Jafnid and Nasrid federations, shadows of their former selves in the postwar period. How would Persia and Rome react? Muhammad's early ties with Palestine had left him with a distinctly pro-Roman bias. Even as Syria was being overrun by the Persians, he had said, "The Romans have been defeated in [their] nearest land. They will reverse their defeat in a few years' time." It is possible that Muhammad made this observation as Heraclius was beginning his counteroffensive against the Persians. This was in 626. Did he see Heraclius' struggle as somehow parallel to his own? Could the good feeling continue? There were signs that they would not. There had already been conflict before Muhammad died in 632.

Through his period of success, Muhammad remained accessible to his followers. He did wish they would not yell outside his private chambers. But he had led from the front and been visible to his followers. There is no sign that changed in the last years of his life. He was still trying to find new believers up to the very end.

CONQUEST

Abu Bakr was one of Muhammad's earliest supporters and the father of 'A'isha, the one of his fifteen wives whom Muhammad had loved best. He was rapidly accepted as the community's new leader, probably taking the title *amir al-mu'minim,* "commander of the faithful," a title reflecting the somewhat fraught military situation that arose as news of Muhammad's death spread. The title also indicates that Abu Bakr did not lay claim to Muhammad's religious authority. Muhammad had been the messenger, the *rasul,* of God.

Muhammad's political community had been based upon treaties through which groups submitted to his authority and agreed to pay tax. When he died, many groups tore up their treaties. Abu Bakr therefore appointed four commanders, *amirs,* who took off in various directions to bring tribes that had rethought submission to Muhammad, or, in some cases, found another prophet, back into line.

The situation along the Roman frontier was complicated. It appears that shortly after Muhammad's entry into Mecca, Khalid ibn al-Walid entered southern Jordan with a raiding force and was heavily defeated. In the immediate aftermath of this victory, the Romans cut off the subsidies they were paying tribes along the Arabian border. We are told of an imperial official who met with the local rulers of the Arabs, telling them that, since the emperor could barely pay his own men, he could certainly not pay them. These tribes promptly went over to the believers, and people would notice members of the invading army who were actually Christians. Heraclius seems not to have understood the severity of the situation and proceeded to further alienate his subjects by ordering the forced conversion of the empire's Jewish population.

Instead of persecuting the Jews, Heraclius might have been better advised to think about his army's nepotistic command structure. In 634 an Arab army destroyed the garrison of Arabia, commanded by Heraclius' brother. It then captured the weakly defended city of Damascus. As worrying as the destruction of the Roman garrison should have been, the subsequent response of the city of Bostra, capital of the province of Arabia, was even more so. The city council made a deal with the Arabs, offering payment in return for peace. Such arrangements had been frequent in the war with Persia, and they represented a continuing lack of confidence in the imperial regime. They also freed Arab armies, which were ill-equipped for siege warfare, to maneuver freely in the countryside, which played to their strengths.

It was said, in the Arabic tradition, that the last news Abu Bakr received before his death was of the victory in Syria. He was succeeded by another of Muhammad's close companions, 'Umar. The definition of leadership in this generation therefore began with a requirement for close association with the Prophet. Added to that was an insistence upon living a moral life. 'Umar's succession marked the opening of a new, more aggressive, phase of conquest.

The existence of a new organization in Arabia remained unclear to outsiders. Immediate reactions to the emergence of Arab armies recorded in Western sources suggests a great deal of ignorance. The patriarch of Jerusalem, for example, complained of ". . . the Saracens who, on account of our sins, have now risen up against us unexpectedly and ravage all with cruel and feral design, with impious and godless audacity." The description of the invaders as "Saracens," a traditional term for nomadic inhabitants of the Arabian peninsula, suggests he did not understand the religious movement lying behind the raiders. A near contemporary of his, who wrote a dialogue between a Jew and a Christian, does a little better, in that he mentions a prophet who is inspiring the Arab invaders—but not much better, given that he doesn't know that the prophet had died before the invasion. Such comments are significant because they reveal the deep and continuing level of ignorance, among well-educated contemporaries in the

Roman Empire, about the people who are coming out of the desert. It is perhaps then not so surprising that Heraclius doesn't seem to have appreciated the depth of the problem he was facing when he sabotaged the defense of his own frontier by ending payments to allied tribes.

The final blow, as far as Roman Syria was concerned, fell in 636. The commander of the army for the previous year had been a man named Baanes. He had served under Heraclius with some distinction in the Persian campaign and now tried to prevent an invasion across the Golan Heights in the area of the Yarmouk Valley. The confused accounts of this event suggest a struggle that lasted several days, ending in a total defeat of Roman forces. As early as the Syriac Chronicle of 660, the battle is mentioned as a total disaster for the Romans, who are alleged to have lost 100,000 men (a number which should be read simply as meaning "lots of people"). The Arab commander at this point was Khalid ibn al-Walid, who would soon be shifting his attention to Iraq while 'Umar moved his capital to Damascus. Then, in 638, 'Umar got on his camel and rode to Jerusalem, which surrendered without a fight.

The surrender of Jerusalem was a repeat of events that had become pronounced as early as 635, when 'Umar began to peel cities away from Roman control. As had been the case in the Persian war, people saw no reason to back a loser. Perhaps the most stunning illustration of what this meant in practical terms appears on a papyrus surviving from the period of the Arab conquest of Roman Egypt that would begin after the capture of Jerusalem. It contains a letter from the local official named Athanasius to his superior in which he says:

> The letter carrying *moagaritai* having come asking for boats, give them the boats where they want in your district so that in the future they do not come to me if they wish to get on the boats.

The term *moargites* is a Greek rendition of *muhâjirûn*, a term indicating "militarily active members of the community of believers," or, it seems, more simply, Arab soldiers serving in the armies of the *amirs*. The use of the technical term suggests that the Romans were beginning to learn more about the invaders. That didn't seem to be making them any more ready to deal with them.

In light of the evidence quoted above, and extensive evidence in other contemporary sources, for deep divisions within Egyptian society caused by ongoing divisions between Christian communities, it is scarcely surprising that the Arab invasion, led by 'Amr ibn al-'As, culminated in a negotiated settlement. This was in 642, and the Roman Empire now consisted only of portions of modern of Turkey and Greece, as well as some territory in Italy and North Africa. The situation for the Persians was even worse.

The expansion of Muhammad's movement into Yemen dislodged a Sassanian client state, and the believers had been in conflict with the Sassanians for years before Muhammad's death. But the Persians had few resources with which to respond. Moreover, King Yazgerd was still a child. He depended upon his leading general, Rustam, to lead the resistance to the Arabs. After a victory on the south-eastern edge of Mesopotamia in 634, Rustam found himself in serious trouble. Later traditions, both Arabic and Persian, suggest that he was aware that his army was no match for Arab forces.

Rustam was right to be worried. Khalid ibn al-Walid brought an army from Syria to join with troops under the command of Sa'd ibn Abi Waqqas, one of Muhammad's early followers. Together they crushed the Persian army at Quadisiyya in 638. Rustam was killed. Elite units of the Persian army promptly changed sides and served thereafter under Arab command. The young Yazgerd was left to defend his capital, Ctesiphon. That effort failed, and the Persian government withdrew into Iran, where it was finally crushed in 640. Our Chronicler of 660 can point to a Christian official who welcomed the Arabs and won the respect of their leaders. A bishop of Nineveh would write that "The Arabs to whom at this time God has given control over the world . . . are . . . no enemy to Christianity, but they are even praisers of our faith, honorers of our Lord's priests and holy one, and supporters of churches and monasteries."

The Persian Empire now ceased to exist. A political order that had existed for more than 700 years was ended in a decade of fighting. Or not. It would be better to see the Arab victories of the 630s as an appendix to the ruinous war of the previous thirty years. That war destroyed the economic power and moral authority of both states. Errors such as those Heraclius made in managing his victory compounded the problem, but those errors reflected the fact that he had no plan to restore his empire, to build a consensus for a new way forward. Yazgerd and the members of his court didn't have a plan, either.

In none of these cases were the armies involved very big. What is striking, however, especially in the case of descriptions of battles pitting Arabian armies against the Romans, is that Roman armies seem to have been prone to rapid collapse, while the Arab armies are presented as being extremely well motivated. Certainly, the forces commanded by Khalid ibn al-Walid covered an enormous amount of ground and showed up ready to fight. The Sassanians too do not seem to have been motivated by devotion to the imperial regime. Leadership was either divisive, the Roman case, or discredited, the Persian case. Arab armies, commanded by men who knew the Prophet, were filled with people who may have shared the belief that the last days were at hand, and hoped for the rewards that would come to them because they struggled for the message of truth.

The question facing 'Umar and his compatriots was whether they could do a better job than the people they were replacing. They had taken on the old administrative apparatus of the Roman and Sassanian regimes. Documents, in addition to the one already quoted, reveal that the transfer of officials from one regime to the next was quite seamless, but, as the failure of Rome and Persia had just shown, an administrative system does not necessarily yield a successful state. Tax collectors, ancient or modern, are not the world's most popular people. Taxpayers need to feel they are getting something they can believe in.

THE RISE OF ISLAM

States that expand very rapidly are often very unstable. Alexander the Great, for instance, conquered an earlier Persian empire in eleven years between 334 and 323 BCE. After his death, his generals spent more than forty years fighting to grab bits of that empire for themselves. So too, Genghis Khan. The Mongol leader created a massive empire stretching from China to the Ukraine in the twenty-one years between his achievement of sole rule over his people in 1206 and his death in 1227. That empire fractured almost immediately thereafter. 'Umar would not have time for serious state building after the conquest of Egypt completed his demolition of Roman power. He was mortally wounded by an assassin in 644. His successor 'Uthman, another close associate of the Prophet, lost the support of luminaries such as Khalid ibn al-Walid and 'A'isha, Muhammad's widow, and botched a naval expedition aimed at capturing Constantinople before his assassination by military mutineers at Medina in 656. When 'Ali ibn Ali Talib, nephew and son-in-law of Muhammad, tried to seize power for himself, Mu'awiya, one of 'Uthman's relatives, allied with 'Amr ibn al-'As to prevent him from securing the position of *amir al-mu'minim*. With 'Amr's support, Mu'awiya ousted 'Ali, who withdrew to Iraq, claiming, as his supporters, the Shia, do to this day, that he was Muhammad's rightful successor and that Mu'awiya was a usurper. He was assassinated in 661.

The central issue in the civil war that ended with 'Ali's death was the qualification for leadership. Piety, it was generally agreed, was still crucial. But what else? 'Ali claimed that relationship to the Prophet mattered, as did early support for Muhammad (Mu'awiya had joined late). Others claimed that effectiveness in service to the community mattered. That was certainly Mu'awiya's view, but he had not managed to articulate a more robust ideology of government before his own death in 680. The result was yet another civil war. It was to be twelve more years before Mu'awiya's nephew, 'Abd al-Malik, suppressed his sundry rivals.

Now, fifty years after Muhammad's death, 'Abd al-Malik would use the Koran to create a governing ideology. The generation of Muhammad's immediate followers had passed away, the world hadn't ended, and if the cycle of destructive internal conflict was to end, it was necessary to create a belief system around which a government could be assembled. Earlier actions which looked to separate the community of believers from the newly conquered included 'Umar's foundation of new garrison cities such as Fustat (now Cairo) in Egypt and Kufa on the border of Iraq as administrative centers, their primary public buildings being a mosque and a palace for the regional governor. The new regime decided to take over more directly. 'Abd al-Malik was explicit about the ideas that were central to the community.

One of the earliest and most powerful statements of 'Abd al-Malik's new ideology was the great mosque he built at Jerusalem, the Dome of the Rock (Figure 2.1). Using the architectural pattern typical of Christian buildings devoted to martyrs, its octagonal pattern indicates that it was seen as a commemorative building. Just as martyrs had triumphed over the forces of evil through their sacrifice, the Dome of the Rock represented the triumph of the believers. The inscriptions on the walls of the mosque make it clear that Muhammad's message was distinct from any that had gone before. Specifically, Christian beliefs in

Figure 2.1 Built on the plan of a Christian martyr shrine, the Dome of the Rock. The plan may have been chosen to symbolize paradise and the Judgment Day. The inscriptions inside the building stress the indivisibility of God and expressly reject Christian Trinitarian doctrine.

the Trinity are deprecated. "In the name of God, the Compassionate, the Merciful: there is no deity except God alone; he has no partner. Muhammad is the messenger of God." "The Messiah Jesus son of Mary was only the messenger of God and his word, which he cast unto Mary, and a spirit from him." Included with statements such as those in the previous sentences, which might be taken as interpretations of Muhammad's message, are quotations from the Koran, which is presented as the authoritative revelation for the community of believers. In addition to spelling out the difference between Muhammad's revelation and Christian belief, 'Abd al-Malik introduced legislation which enjoined specific lifestyle choices. One of these was an order for the slaughter of all pigs in Syria and Iraq. Also, he regularized, as the title for the leader of the community of believers, the title *Khalifa*, which means "deputy." The community's leader would henceforth be seen as God's deputy. The Khalifa issued new coinage, removing the images inherited from earlier Roman and Sassanian coinage, which, on the Roman end, had featured the image of the *amir* on the obverse (front) and a depiction of the globe mounted on a pole on the reverse (back) (Figure 2.2). Sassanian versions had a portrait of the *amir* on the obverse and images on the reverse that were evocative of the fire altars standard on Sassanian coins. The new coinage did away with images in favor of inscriptions quoting verses from the Koran and the "double *shahada*" (statement of faith), "There is no God but God" and "Muhammad is the messenger of God." In tandem with the clear statements on public documents, the more extensive use of the Arabic script to express the government's message was an effort to delimitate the boundaries of the community of believers. One novelty appears to have been the creation of a prayer service on Friday, which included a sermon delivered from a pulpit by a prayer leader. The number of prayers to be said each day was set at five, and a new body of written material elucidating the revelations of the Prophet, *hadiths*, which would guide community practice, began to emerge. So too did a professional priesthood to interpret the tradition and develop elaborate rules for the community of believers. Local bureaucracies which had been using their native languages since the arrival of Arab armies now began using Arabic.

Christians, in describing their conquerors, still used the traditional word *Saracen*, if writing in Greek or Latin, or, if writing in Syriac, usually *tayyaye*, also a traditional term for an Arab nomad—or, as is the case with a very early account in Syriac, they would speak of "the Arabs of Muhammad" without any explicit religious sense, or, as we've seen in other cases, with an understanding that Muhammad was no longer alive when the major raids began. Other terms that appear are *Hagarene*, a term that stressed the belief that Arab peoples were descended from Hagar, the slave wife of Abraham, and *Ishmaelite*, referring to Hagar's son, who was the ancestor of the Arab peoples. Tombs of both were said to have been near the Mecca's Ka'ba (this is not in

Figure 2.2 Depicted on the obverse is the *Khalifa,* with the inscription that reads, "The Servant of God, 'Abd al-Malik, Commander of the Faithful." The reverse of the coin is inscribed with an image of a pole symbolizing the caliph's role as the center of the community, and is inscribed with the *shahada* (confession of faith), "There is no God but Allah, and Muhammad is the messenger of Allah."

the Koran), and Hagarism was seen as a distinctive sect whose worshippers prayed while facing east to the Ka'ba. The Chronicler of 660, for instance, introduced his account of the conquest of Persia by writing, "Then God brought against them the sons of Ishmael who were [as many] as the sands on the seashore." A roughly contemporary text, purporting to be prophetic, predicts the ruin of the Roman empires at Ishmaelite hands, while as late as 684, an eighth-century gloss on a seventh-century letter by an eastern bishop differentiated between the "pagans" and "the Hagarenes who now rule." In 700 there is finally evidence for Christians equating Muslim dates (their era begins with Muhammad's withdrawal to Medina in 622) with Christian reckonings. The admission that there was a new way of reckoning time was a clear indication that a new understanding was taking hold.

FROM MUHAMMAD TO 'ABD AL-MALIK

Muhammad attracted followers through the power of his personality and the conviction of his preaching. His followers trusted him to be fair, and they believed in him sufficiently so that they would abandon their homes to follow him into exile. Having been his associate was a requirement for leadership in the community after his death, as was living an upright life. Moral rectitude was a quality Muhammad's contemporaries associated with him. Muhammad saw himself as providing spiritual guidance in a complicated and violent world, a path to salvation for those who would believe, a true message to replace those which had been corrupted. He developed a system of governance for his followers, but it does not appear that he saw the Constitution of Medina as a foundational document for a great empire. His followers did not understand it that way, either. For all the power of Muhammad's personality and conviction, he did not preach the destruction of the empires of his era. He appears to have deplored the Persians and seen the Roman Empire as an entity that would endure. He did not see either as self-immolating. But they were.

Neither Persia nor Rome could afford endless war in the wake of the vast disruption caused by the plague of the sixth century. The emperor Maurice appears to have understood the gravity of Rome's situation when he could no longer guarantee the security of the Balkan frontier. He did the best he could to prevent the outbreak of further conflict between the Roman and Persian states when he adopted Kusru. The failure of neither state was certain in 600. Both were weak; neither the regime in Constantinople nor that in Ctesiphon commanded much in the way of the love and affection of their subjects. But this had happened before. The Roman Empire of the third century was heading toward dissolution before Diocletian and then Constantine provided stability and a sense of purpose. The Roman Republic, centuries earlier, had collapsed into chaos, but the Roman state recovered under the leadership of Augustus and his heirs, and indeed, the failure of the Arsacid regime which ruled Persia for centuries before the Sassanian takeover was not a major change of direction. The failure of central authority does not inevitably result in social collapse or radical reorganization. It was the specific choices made by Kusru and Heraclius, at the time they made them, that fatally weakened both regimes. Counterfactual argument is by its very nature ahistorical, but it is worth considering what might not have happened if Heraclius had spent some of what was left of his money rebuilding alliances along his Arabian frontier. Things might have been very different. Indeed, the fact that the Roman Empire recovered, to some degree, and was able to reshape itself, while the followers of Muhammad descended into civil war, shows that all should not have been lost and underscores the importance of contingency in history. The rise of Islam was a function of Heraclius' failure.

The collective failure of the Roman and Persian empires opened the door for the Arab conquest. But the conquest was not itself a guarantee that a successful Arab state would emerge in the aftermath. Muhammad's followers fell to fighting each other. The memory of the Prophet was insufficient to stabilize a system of succession or shape a new system of government. His immediate successors governed in a variety of languages, with whatever systems they had inherited from the Romans and Persians. The ideological messaging was sufficiently unclear that Christians seem not to have realized just who their conquerors were. Other conquest states had failed, and even Muʿawiya, victor in the first civil war, had not found a way to build a better world. It was ʿAbd al-Malik who was able to reshape Muhammad's revelation into the centerpiece of a governing ideology, to bring out the originality of his teachings and shape them into an ideological system that could command the loyalty of his followers. His actions are in many ways similar to those of Constantine, in that he was working with a small group of dedicated followers to shape the new regime—not just soldiers and administrators, but, to judge from the coherence of the message, intellectuals, who were drawing out the essence of Muhammad's teaching to create the practices which would set the new Arab governing class apart. Having established a new center, 'Abd al-Malik and his supporters spread their new system outwards from their political core.

Crises of state may have similar taxonomies: central authorities collapse, and confidence in prior institutions is shattered. The causes may be substantially political, as in the case of third-century CE Rome, or may combine economic with political factors, as happened in the seventh century. But a disruption on the scale of the creation of the Islamic state required human intervention.

Chapter 3

The Protestant Reformation

CHURCH AND STATE

If Constantine had risen from the dead in 1500 AD he would have been shocked by what he found. His city, Constantinople, was ruled by a non-Roman! It had fallen to the army of the twenty-one-year-old Sultan Mehmed II on May 29, 1453. The defense had been led by the emperor Constantine XI, Palaeologus, who had died in the final assault. He was the last ruler in the direct line of Roman emperors that began with Augustus in 31 BCE.

Mehmed was the ruler of a state created by the descendants of nomads who had settled in Turkey after escaping Genghis Khan, a mightier emperor than any Roman, in Central Asia. These escapees invented a history for themselves and came to be known as the Ottoman Turks. The defenders of Constantinople, meanwhile, had received minimal help from other Christians, and their empire had been horribly compromised by a piratical expedition which had sacked the place at the behest of the ruler of Venice (a city that had not even existed in Constantine's time) in 1204. The Venetians and other European states were now having to deal with the consequences of their actions, as Turkish fleets ranged the Mediterranean and Turkish armies were advancing into Central Europe.

Constantine would also discover that his hopes of a unified Christian Church had ended in 1054, when a ferocious dispute had divided the Church ruled from Rome by its bishop (now styling himself the pope) from the church that operated out of Constantinople. The Constantinopolitan, or Orthodox Church (which recognized Constantine and Helena as saints) was now subordinate to Muslim authority in all the areas ruled by the sultans, and, outside the sultans' realm, was most important in a region Constantine would never have heard of: Russia. In Russia, the Orthodox Church was the central institution in a kingdom ruled by a person who called himself the tsar (*caesar*).

The pope's church regulated the lives of people living in the Christian kingdoms of Europe, the most important of which were Spain, England, France, and a German polity known as the Holy Roman Empire. Each kingdom had two administrative systems: one based on the political system, the other based on the religious. The political structure of a kingdom was determined by the way land was devolved from what was theoretically the original territory of the king—or land that had come under his governance (that is to say, pretty much everything not owned by the Church)—to his most important subjects. These great lords could, in turn, grant some of their lands to lesser followers. At the bottom of the heap were the peasants, whose work on the land supported whatever lord held them in his direct control. This distribution of land in return for service was the essence of the feudal system of government throughout Europe. For its part, the Church divided the territory of a kingdom into districts ruled by bishops, whose appointments were negotiated with varying degrees of animosity between the pope and local kings. Once appointed, a bishop directly administered lands owned by the Church, and supervised the pastoral care of the king's subjects in land held by the king's secular retainers.

In addition to their roles as landholders, bishops were charged with oversight of the religious personnel who resided in their districts, acting either as priests to the parishes in which each district was divided, or as occupants of institutions wholly owned by the Church, such as monasteries or convents. Given that they tended to obtain a significantly higher level of education than the average person, ecclesiastical personnel often served as administrators for kings and other important people. They also served as instructors in the universities that were beginning to appear across Europe.

In addition to their effective control of the institutions of intellectual life, bishops administered their own legal system, with their own courts in which to try cases connected with Church affairs. The notion that there could be courts for Christian matters was something Constantine would have recognized. The independence from secular control that was now exerted by these courts was something that he could not have imagined. To take one notable example, which will have an impact on the story we're looking at: on July 6, 1415, a Church Council assembled at Constance in what is now Germany determined that the theologian Jan Hus "does not desire to return to the bosom of holy mother the church, and is unwilling to abjure the heresies and errors which he has publicly defended and preached." The Council ordered that he be burned at the stake, even though he had been granted a safe passage to address the Council by no less a figure than Sigismund, then "king of the Romans" (official heir apparent to the throne of the Holy Roman Empire), who was trying to assert his control over Hus's Bohemian homeland (now Czechoslovakia). The result was a massive revolt by Hus's supporters. They defeated Sigismund in a series of campaigns over the next several years, making Bohemia largely independent and inadvertently preventing any effective response to Ottoman encroachments on Hungary. In other matters, often inheritance issues where property was being left to the Church, these courts likewise asserted their authority, thereby depriving secular entities of what they were coming to see as potential sources of revenue. Throughout Europe there was a division between the "canon" law that applied in the courts of bishops, and the secular laws of each region.

It will be in a monastery supporting a minor university in the German city of Wittenberg that the story of our next great change will take shape, in a setting where the academic and judicial aspects of the Church were commingled. Wittenberg was a city in the Duchy of Saxony, a part of the Holy Roman Empire, and the proximate cause of this change was a disagreement about the amount of control the Catholic Church should exercise in non-spiritual matters. The spark that would light this controversy would be a highly technical dispute about the way Christians should imagine personal salvation and the operation of divine will. The initial driving force would be a single man, Martin Luther. Luther's personal crusade to correct what he regarded as erroneous Church doctrine drew upon new ways of arranging knowledge that challenged traditional thought patterns, and on a new technology, printing, which made it possible for him to reach large audiences with a speed and impact hitherto unknown in human experience. Luther's stand proved exceptionally useful to local princes who were looking to restrict imperial power, and provided the model for other radical changes, first in England, then in the Netherlands, which profoundly altered the political landscape of Europe and set in motion the development of modern nation states.

Although theology provided the vocabulary framing the debates of this period (a reflection of the fact that theology was closely aligned with ideas of political legitimacy), the most important changes came to be in the power and effectiveness of increasingly centralized states. While the conflict that we will be looking at would become known as the Protestant Reformation, the resulting disruption of the long-standing alliance between the Catholic Church and secular authority enabled the development of new political institutions that would profoundly change Europe and the rest of the globe.

THE HOLY ROMAN EMPIRE

In 1756 the French philosopher Voltaire observed that "the creature that called itself and still calls itself the Holy Roman Empire is in no way holy, nor Roman, nor an empire." That was true when Voltaire wrote, and had been true for a very long time. But it was also somewhat unfair. The empire which, in Voltaire's time, went by the name of the Holy Roman Empire did not aspire to be the sort of empire that Constantine would have recognized—the product of conquest and war, with centrally appointed ministers reporting up a bureaucratic chain of command.

The empire Voltaire described had initially been created through agreement between the Frankish king, Charlemagne, and pope Leo III, in 800. Leo had refused to accept the authority of the empress Irene, who, after deposing her son and taking power for herself three years before, now ruled at Constantinople. After a number of vicissitudes, the empire as it existed in 1500 had descended from a meeting (called a Diet) of lords, which, in 1356, issued a charter known as the Golden Bull. The point of the Golden Bull was to establish the terms under which a college of seven electors, three of them bishops, would elect a new emperor.

The terms of the Golden Bull make it clear that imperial authority depended upon the agreement of the important members of the imperial aristocracy, whose own authority was negotiated with leaders in the territories they controlled. It would have been at this point that the spirit of Constantine, if it had come visiting, would have given up in disgust. The fact that the emperor was elected, much as it would have appalled Constantine, will, however, be extremely important for understanding how the Reformation began.

The biggest problem the Holy Roman Empire faced was not lack of holiness or Romanness, but rather the lack of a coherent bureaucratic government. As the core of Charlemagne's empire passed to the kings of France, the German lands to the north remained under the control of emperors who largely split their time between Germany and Italy, negotiating and renegotiating their power with the papacy as well as their sundry vassals.

In 1440, with the election of the first member of what would become the longest serving dynastic group—the Habsburgs—to hold the throne as emperor, there began to be serious efforts to make the system work better. Frederick, the second Habsburg emperor, settled the formal relationship between the papacy and the empire through the Concordat of Vienna in 1448. The two parties agreed that the emperor could influence the selection of senior clerics in his territory, while the pope would retain the right to collect taxes from Church lands and determine matters of theological importance. The corollary of this arrangement was that local princes began to assert greater control over Church hierarchies in their own bailiwicks.

The settlement with the Church by no means solved all of Frederick's problems. In 1457, Frederick, whose central European base was in Austria, tried to stabilize direct control over Hungary and Bohemia, still a stronghold for followers of Jan Hus. His claim was rejected. When he tried to assert control by force of arms, he was defeated and essentially withdrew, leaving power to his son Maximilian, whose election as "king of the Romans" in 1486 marked him out as the heir apparent.

Maximilian, a better diplomat than his father, earned considerable goodwill by acting as a buffer between his father and the numerous princes who were opposed to him. He exploited the goodwill he'd earned by summoning an imperial Diet at the city of Worms in 1495.

Maximilian used this occasion to declare a universal peace and establish a new imperial court to handle disputes between his vassals, and a new system of regional administration. Additionally, Maximilian introduced more centralized systems of taxation. Ideally this would supplement or replace the existing system of taxation through which vassals were assessed contributions for imperial defense. The problem with this system was that it meant people had to own up to what they actually had, while the old system allowed them to state their own worth, and use that to provide levies of troops, or contributions of cash to the imperial treasury in lieu of soldiers.

A more efficient tax system was increasingly crucial, because war was getting a great deal more expensive. The Turks had taken Constantinople, in part, because they had a large artillery train that allowed them to batter the city walls into rubble. Artillery required professionals who could handle the basic math necessary to construct and fire the guns. Also, as Turkish armies ran into traditional feudal armies, the result was routinely catastrophic from a European perspective (it is fair to say that the early Ottoman interests in securing the Middle East spared the empire an invasion it might not have been able to resist). War had to professionalize, and it did so through the development of increasingly powerful bands of professional military contractors who were now largely used against each other as the emperor sought to enforce his control, usually against French opposition, in northern Italy. The emperor Maximilian spent huge sums of money on wars in Italy that began in 1494 and lasted throughout his reign.

The princes of Germany were just as aware of these facts as was the emperor. They rapidly shed his preferred system of taxation for the older contribution system. If they were to remain factors in the brave new world of military contracting, they needed to husband their resources.

The fact the powerful needed money created problems for the poor. Throughout southern Germany, peasants were finding that access to what had previously been common land was being restricted; that they were prevented from gathering firewood; that new services were demanded; and that new regulations were being imposed upon them. The bitterness engendered by these circumstances was reaching a boiling point when the Church discovered that it needed even more money for its own purposes in the decades after 1500, and sought to suck that money out of Germany for use in its Italian heartland.

As we approach the fatal year 1517, the year Martin Luther would post the ninety-five theses that sparked the Reformation, there are three characteristics of the Holy Roman Empire to bear in mind: (A) power had to be negotiated between the emperor and his subjects; (B) princes had a say in the religious organization of their own territories; and (C) money was in short supply for everyone.

THE UNIVERSAL CHURCH

The Church Martin Luther would challenge asserted its power through its control of two ways of reckoning time. One way was cyclical, featuring a calendar based on annual festivals celebrating the life and ministry of Christ. The other was linear, based on sacraments that defined a person's relationship with God at various points during their life.

The theory of these sacraments, as enunciated by Thomas Aquinas in the thirteenth century, was that they were established by Divine Law as a reminder of the passion of Christ, an indication of the grace resulting from Christ's passion, and a forecast of salvation. There were seven, of which "the first five ones are ordained for spiritual perfection of each and every one in himself, the last two for the government and increase of the Church." Baptism, the first sacrament, was the gateway to spiritual life. Confirmation, the second sacrament, represented "spiritual growth." The Eucharist, the third, provided nourishment for the soul; penance, the fourth, cured the "disease of the soul" contracted through sin; while the fifth, extreme unction, purified the soul for entry into heaven. The remaining sacraments were ordination, which provided for the continuing governance of the Church, and marriage, through which the Church was increased.

Each sacrament had two parts, matter and form. The matter was the substance or action that was used to perform the sacrament—water, for instance, for baptism, or bread and wine for the Eucharist—while the form was the formula used for the performance of the sacrament. The form of the sacrament could be captured in objects that had been made holy and could provide succor if they were approached with suitable reverence. These included holy water, which could be used to bless a house or a field; the palms used in processions on Palm Sunday, commemorating Jesus' final arrival in Jerusalem; or even the bells of a church. One's relationship with God could be improved through devotion to exceptional people or things. Saints were special people whose souls had been admitted immediately to heaven. It was generally believed that saints could expedite appeals for divine intervention if they were shown appropriate reverence. So too could contact with objects from the Christian past. Among the most popular items were fragments of the cross on which Jesus had been crucified. These had been spreading across Europe ever since the fourth century, when the story arose that Helena herself had been shown its location in a dream. Objects once touched by Jesus were joined by such things as body parts from departed saints as objects of everyday veneration. So popular was the trade that there developed a doctrine to the effect that these objects could perpetually regenerate as bits and pieces were divided among the faithful. All churches had some relics, and major collections could expand to number thousands of items.

The average Christian was in constant peril of falling short of the spiritual state needed to gain admission to heaven, and it was only by strict observation of the sacraments that he or she could be saved. Christians were expected to learn about God by listening to Mass (the term comes from the ceremony's concluding words, *ite missa est* "the <service> is dismissed"). The average person stood throughout the Mass on the far side of a screen which separated the congregation from the priests who were performing the rituals. The Mass would be spoken in Latin, and the word of God was available only through Jerome's fourth-century CE Latin translations of the Old and New Testaments. Once a year—by 1400—each person would confess his or her sins, publicly, so as to be allowed partial participation in the distribution of the body and blood of Christ that was the core of the Eucharist. The ordinary person would only be given the bread, miraculously transformed into Christ's body, but not the wine, which was his blood. People could learn more about what Jesus stood for by attending the various theatrical performances that the Church sponsored throughout the year, usually in association with major feasts. People were also reminded of the importance of keeping the faith by the necessity of observing dietary restrictions imposed by the Church's calendar (e.g., fasting during Lent, the forty days before the commemoration of Christ's resurrection at Easter). Good Christians were people who did what their priests told them to do, and contributed 10% of their family's income (the "tithe") each year to support their parish priest.

In addition to its spiritual message, the Church had more physical methods of driving home the importance of conformity. Of particular importance were the courts. The leaders of the Church routinely asserted independence from secular control, denied that they could be bound by arrangements made by temporal authorities, and claimed the right to impose horrific penalties on persons who defied their authority. They were quite often successful in getting temporal authorities to participate in the persecution of their enemies.

One thing Church authorities could hold over the heads of temporal officials who did not hasten to hew to their moral guidance was a dire vision of painful eternity. The distinctly judicial aspect of Church doctrines dealing with divine punishment was enhanced over the centuries by the discovery of a place called Purgatory. This was where pretty much everyone who died without having permanently offended the Lord was going to end up. The idea of Purgatory, not one Constantine would have encountered, developed slowly in the course of the centuries after the death of Augustine of Hippo in 430. Augustine had been disturbed by the notion that the souls of the departed could go only to heaven or to hell, that there was no way to accommodate those who were good though not saintly, or bad but not truly evil. In his great work, *The City of God*, he had posited a period of time during which the imperfect could be purged of their sins while awaiting final judgment. These souls resided in the same space that the ghosts (whom one might see in a dream) occupied, and, he said, it was helpful for the future of those souls if people would remember them in their prayers. From these beginnings emerged an increasingly complex division of the time that a soul would spend between death and the final judgment, with the result that by 1400 the Catholic Church had created a European Union of penitential prayer.

The reality of Purgatory was revealed to people by the ghosts of their relatives returning to tell them how they were suffering. The sense of the looming presence of penalty was suggested by various discussions of where one could go to find the actual entrance. In Irish imagination, for instance, the entrance to Purgatory was at a monastery at Lough Derg. For Dante Alighieri, the Mountain of Purgatory stood among the Atlas Mountains of North Africa.

It is to Dante that we owe what is perhaps the most abiding vision of the medieval afterlife. On his way to explore the seven circles of hell, with the poet Vergil as his guide, Dante had learned that people like Vergil, or infants who had no opportunity for baptism, existed in Limbo, in longing for heaven, for all eternity. As he ascended the Mountain of Purgatory he was told that, after death, the soul forms a new body, and then "just as a flame will follow its hearth whenever it is moved, the new form follows the spirit." This shade forms the senses that enable it to feel the torments of hell or pains of Purgatory. Those sinners who repented before the very end were permitted to make the ascent of Purgatory, but it was a long, miserable trip, and some had to wait at the foot of the mountain for many years before they could even begin. Eloquent as Dante's vision of the future was, there were others that were available, often even more dire. This was especially true in the art and literature of northern Europe. A German book, the *Compendium of Theological Truth,* offers a vision of Purgatory as the mouth of a dragon, containing naked people, one of whom is lifted out of the crowd by an angel. Next to it is a vision of hell, also in the mouth of a dragon, with devils tormenting the damned. A fourteenth-century book, once the property of Philip IV, king of France, depicts the damned in what appears to be the mouth of a cat; other visionaries imagined devils poking the people in hell, and flaming cauldrons full of souls.

How could friends and family not wish to lessen the suffering? How best to do this? In January 1343, pope Clement VI provided the answer. Mary, the mother of Jesus, and all the saints had created a massive treasury of merits, which was committed to the care of the popes "to be dispensed for the good of the faithful, both from proper and reasonable causes," for the complete or partial remission of sins which were set for purgatorial punishment.

Clement did not invent the idea that the remission of sin was available to those who performed special services for the Church.

Promise of remission of sin, or an indulgence, had first begun to be issued for Crusaders in the eleventh century, but the doctrine of a treasury of merits meant that anyone who was willing to pay could apply. You could acquire prospective redemption for yourself, and, for a further contribution, you could help out a deceased relative or friend by arranging for Masses to be said on their behalf—something you could also arrange for yourself. In addition to purchasing an indulgence and/or Masses, you might even create a charitable or educational institution that would contribute prayers on your behalf (Oxford's All Souls College is a classic instance of such a foundation).

The result of the purgatorial economy was to funnel ever more money away from the state and into the coffers of the Church, especially in northern Europe, where it appears that the mercantile aspect of the system of indulgences was especially appealing. It was so mercantile, in fact, that after 1476, pope Sixtus IV finally expanded the trade and allowed people to purchase indulgences for the relief of souls in Purgatory if they did so within ten years of their loved one's decease. The widespread distribution of indulgences was greatly facilitated by the development of a new northern European technology, printing with moveable type. Early publishers found their bottom lines were significantly enhanced when they could take on jobs that required minimal effort on their part, which was certainly the case when it came to mass producing certificates of salvation. Records attest an order for 200,000 printed indulgences at Monserrat in Spain. In 1452, when a mass order for indulgences was sent to hand-copying shops in Mainz, only 2,000 could be produced.

PUBLISHERS AND SCHOLARS

Johannes Gutenberg trained as a goldsmith in southern Germany in the first half of the fifteenth century. At some point in the later 1440s he came up with the idea that letters could be mass produced in lead and then arranged in a form that could be attached to a press. After a few practice runs on shorter works, including a popular school book and some pamphlets, he set his hand to a gigantic project: the Bible. The work, which ran to 1,282 pages, took two years to finish, and the first print run was only 180 copies. Even though all copies were sold by the beginning of 1454, the income could not cover Gutenberg's costs. He had borrowed the money he needed to complete the project, and he lost his printing shop pretty much as soon as the job was done. His partners, Johann Fust and Peter Schöffer, continued the business and rapidly proved that it was possible to make money by printing books.

Fust and Schöffer may not have been the most ethical of men, but they realized they had at their disposal a unique technology with which to transform the book culture of their time, hitherto built on individual copies made by scribes. Mixing larger and smaller projects (they printed many indulgences), Fust and Schöffer rapidly expanded their marketing reach, setting up a printing shop in northern Europe's intellectual capital, Paris, in the early 1460s; business soon boomed. By the time of his death in 1466, Fust had the net worth of a member of the nobility.

Well before his death, Fust was starting to have competition, a process accelerated by the sack of his original base, Mainz, by one of the two men who claimed the position of the city's archbishop in 1462. As trained printers moved away, new printing houses sprang up in places like Cologne and Strasburg, new design features such as a title page and table of contents were added, and printers learned how to include illustrations. Just as important was a change in what was being printed: books in German. These included translations of the Bible, histories, medical books, and books on law and philosophy. Prestige projects continued to be editions of classical texts and religious works, often designed to resemble handwritten books, but these were now joined by works for daily use such as almanacs and newsletters. Print was democratizing learning, and the availability of low-cost works in the native language was building new audiences. The technology had spread to Belgium and the Netherlands by the early 1470s, and in 1473 William Caxton published the first print book in the British Isles. The Oxford University Press published its first book in 1478. Book fairs, especially at Nuremberg and Frankfurt, created a European market for the printed word.

The spread of print books soon gave rise to a new phenomenon as the fifteenth century turned into the sixteenth: the public intellectual. For the better part of the previous century, a small group of dedicated scholars, calling themselves humanists, had been recovering classical texts and, using their new-found knowledge of the past, had started to shape intellectual discourse. The most influential of these figures in the early fifteenth century were Poggio Bracciolini and Lorenzo Valla. Poggio took it upon himself to "rescue" copies of classical texts buried in monasteries of southern Germany and France, having new copies made, and asserted that the study of human letters was a new area of learning. Valla, whose accomplishments included a Latin translation of Thucydides' *History of the Peloponnesian War*, took a different view. He believed humanistic studies should be used to correct errors in the Christian tradition. One example was a stunning demonstration that a document known as the *Donation of Constantine*, which recorded Constantine's proclamation of the pope as the leader of the Church, was an eighth-century fake.

Despite their disagreements and ecclesiastical connections, Poggio and Valla showed that intellectual life need not be totally dependent upon the Church, and with the new-found taste in books that could act as guides to life, new opportunities were opening up for a fresh generation of intellectuals. Chief among these men was

Desiderius Erasmus, who, by the first decade of the sixteenth century, was unquestionably Europe's most famous intellectual.

Erasmus, widely read in classical literature and possessing a good knowledge of Greek, burst upon the intellectual world of the sixteenth century with a collection of wise sayings, *The Adages*, published by Aldus, a path-breaking publisher in Venice. Aldus departed from the earlier habit of trying to make print books look as much like manuscripts as possible by creating small volumes in a typeface he had devised (we now call this typeface *italics*). His was an astute realization that a new technology could be used to create novel forms of communication.

After the publication of the *Adages*, Erasmus, who was from Rotterdam, suddenly found himself welcomed in Italian high society, even at the Vatican, where the current pope, Julius, saw himself as a patron of the arts. It was Julius who commissioned the frescoes of Raphael that still adorn the Vatican, and paid Michelangelo to paint the Sistine Chapel in the vicinity of the vast new cathedral of St. Paul he was beginning to erect. A warrior as well, Julius sought to enforce papal control in central Italy and was noted for riding a white elephant in Roman processions.

Erasmus found Julius excessive and his projects extreme. He contemplated a return to a more spiritual form of Christianity. An astute satirist, Erasmus departed Rome for Britain—he was a close friend of Thomas More, a rising star on the edges of the English Court—with plenty to think about. It was on this journey that his satirical side came to the fore, as he conceived what would become one of his most famous works, *In Praise of Folly*, which appeared in 1511. While poking fun at pretension of all sorts, he had particularly sharp observations on the subject of ignorant monks, grasping bishops, and extravagant popes, who really ought to live lives without the ostentation now so evident in Julius' Rome. A striking work, *In Praise of Folly* articulated what many already thought about a Church whose representatives seemed to have lost their way. Without the medium of print, Erasmus' book would have had minimal impact. With the new technology, however, it commanded a European audience. People wondered what else he might do. Erasmus answered with books setting out new programs for humanistic education, editions of classical texts, and a major project editing the works of a man he much admired. This was Jerome, the author of the Vulgate Bible. Studying Jerome, Erasmus was smitten with the ambition to go one better. His Greek, enhanced by years of study, enabled him to recognize errors in the Vulgate. Erasmus announced that he would produce a new edition of the Greek text with a new translation.

The official doctrine of the Catholic Church was that the Vulgate was perfect, and in some places—most notably England—the suggestion ordinary people should read a Bible in their own language was regarded as acute heresy. In the brave new world of print, however, it was possible to question old certainties and to mock authority. The first decade of the sixteenth century was a time when change was in the air, when old institutions were quivering in the face of new challenges—but also a time when there was no obvious alternative to the status quo. That is when pope Leo X decided that he needed more money for his ambitious reconstruction of the Vatican. He decided to get the money by selling more indulgences in Germany. At the same time the aging Holy Roman emperor, Maximilian, made it clear that his son, Charles, already king of Spain, would also succeed him as emperor, a move that Leo X opposed. So did Francis, king of France, for they saw the election could make Charles the most powerful European ruler since the end of the actual Roman Empire. What say would imperial electors have in the process? Would Germany remain a cash cow for Mediterranean powers and nothing more, and, if so, what would be done about the Turks? An entirely unexpected answer was about to emerge from the obscure German city of Wittenberg.

MARTIN LUTHER

Martin Luther was a difficult man. He had a bad temper and was exceptionally confident in his own convictions. He was also possessed of unusual energy and courage.

Born on November 11, 1483, at Eisleben in Germany, Martin Luther grew up in Mansfield, where his father, Hans, had taken an entrepreneurial interest in the local mining industry as a smelter and mining supervisor. Hans hoped Martin would follow him into the metal trade, and had been successful enough to provide his son with the advantage of a college education. Perhaps more importantly, he provided his son with an example of successful risk taking in a developing industry, as mining then was.

Hans Luther's hope that Martin would follow him into the business world was severely disappointed after his son's arrival at the University in Erfurt. The younger Luther soon abandoned the study of law. After, so he said, his miraculous preservation from a lightning strike as he was walking home in July 1505, he came to a new understanding of God's mercy and decided to join an order of Augustinian monks, in whose company he wrestled constantly with his conscience. His family was initially appalled.

Luther entered a monastery in Erfurt and advanced rapidly in his studies—there was no question about either his diligence or his intellectual ability—and, by 1508, was ready to be appointed to a senior academic position in the town. In 1511, he moved to the new university that had been founded at Wittenberg, which was, coincidentally, the preferred residence of Frederick, duke of Saxony and one of the seven imperial electors. A rising academic star was just the sort of person Frederick wanted for his university, and it is likely the two men established contact in the period after Luther's arrival. It may even have been the one and only trip Luther ever took to Rome, in 1512, that gave the two men something to talk about—including, perhaps, the very negative opinion Luther had formed of the moral and intellectual quality of the Church's leadership.

Luther's relationship with Frederick was to prove extremely important. Without the duke's patronage and protection, Luther would never have survived, and the Protestant Reformation would have flamed out before it had a chance to get started properly.

At first glance, Duke Frederick was not an obvious supporter for Luther. After all, he was a devout Catholic who had made a large investment in salvation through the creation of a collection of relics, including bits of the whip used to flog Jesus and of the cross upon which he was crucified. But first glances can be deceiving. Georg Spalatin, Frederick's librarian, was one of Luther's patrons, as was his colleague John Staupitz, head of the Augustinian monastic order to which Luther belonged. Staupitz himself would preach sermons against the excesses of people selling indulgences in 1516 and subsequently have them circulated in print form. Frederick himself was plainly concerned about imperial overreach, and may have had more than a few doubts of his own about the holiness of the Holy Father in Rome. He was not the only person to be worried. For decades, German princes had treated meetings of the imperial council as a place to complain about the Church, and emperors had listened. Maximilian, for instance, had recently refused permission for cardinal Peraudi, a master of the indulgence trade, to remove to Rome the bulk of the money he had collected a decade earlier. Rome's response to growing resistance to the expansion of the indulgence industry reveals a stunning lack of comprehension: it was to declare that the announcement of a new indulgence voided the benefits of previous indulgences.

The problem facing enemies of indulgences was that they had no theological alternative. People could complain about corruption, but complaining about corruption in the Church was, by this time, a virtual sport. Even Erasmus had written about his shock at the impieties he had heard from leaders of the Church when he was in Rome and Dante had placed some popes in hell. Luther's great contribution would be to provide an alternative to Purgatory based on his superior knowledge of scripture.

While he was preparing to assume the degree of Doctor of Theology (a degree he received in 1517), Luther concentrated on the letters of Paul and Augustinian theology. He was especially interested in Paul's *Letter to the Romans*—not, as we were in the first chapter of this book, because it can tell us so much about the earliest Christian community, but because of Paul's statement that the Gospel, by which he meant the teaching of Jesus, was the power of God, and that God's truth was revealed from faith to the true believer. If salvation came directly from God, then why did one need to worry about Purgatory? A person of faith was either saved or not. Augustine had addressed this same question in his *Confessions,* where he said the grace of God gave him the strength to change his life for the better. The importance of God's grace was an issue to which he would return later in his career in denouncing what he says was the outrageous heresy enunciated by the British priest Pelagius, who claimed that Augustine's position would prevent people from doing everything they could to avoid sin. For Augustine, it was the duty of the righteous person to submit to the will of God and not think it possible to move God through mortal endeavor.

If God's will determined whether or not a person was saved, what need was there for the sophisticated penitential theology that lay at the heart of the fifteenth-century Church? If the Church was not necessary for salvation, what was the need for its elaborate bureaucracy? If, thanks to Valla, it was well known that the authority the pope claimed over all churches in the West was based upon a fraud, on what grounds could the pope exert control over regional churches? These questions would all come to the fore on October 31, 1517, when Martin Luther nailed ninety-five propositions, or theses, to the door of the cathedral church in Wittenberg. These theses, composed in Latin, were concerned with the sale of indulgences.

Indulgences could not save a soul. Luther observed that "it is certain that when money clinks in the money chest, greed and avarice can be increased; but when the Church intercedes, the result is in the hands of God alone"; and, "those who believe that they can be certain of their salvation because they have indulgence letters will be eternally damned, together with their teachers"; that "to consider papal indulgences so great that they could absolve a man even if he had done the impossible and had violated the mother of God is madness"; and, "we say on the contrary that papal indulgences cannot remove the very least of venial sins as far as guilt is concerned."

It was not, however, only indulgences that came into Luther's line of fire. There was also the question of the authority of the pope to grant them. Luther (Figure 3.1) wrote that "the pope neither wishes nor can remit any punishment except that which he imposed by his or canonical authority"; "therefore the pope, when he uses the words 'plenary remission of all penalties,' does not actually mean 'all penalties,' but only those imposed by himself"; "thus those indulgence preachers are in error who say that a man is absolved from every penalty and saved by papal indulgences."

Luther's radical alternative to indulgences was the idea that Christians should seek salvation by following the teachings of Jesus.

The immediate inspiration for the posting of the ninety-five theses was a spectacular indulgence issued by pope Leo X through Albrecht, bishop of Mainz, which was then being distributed in Saxony by a man named Johann Tetzel. The opening of Albrecht's "summary instruction" on the topic makes it plain how direct was

Figure 3.1 Martin Luther, by Lucas Cranach, an artist whom Luther knew well, dating to 1529. Luther is shown here with what were then the distinctive black vestments of the reform movement.

the connection between this action and Luther's thinking when he posted his theses, for Albrecht announced:

> We do herewith proclaim that our most holy Lord Leo X, by divine providence present Pontiff, has given and bestowed to all Christian believers of either sex who lend their helpful hand for

> the reconstruction of the cathedral church of St. Peter, the prince of the Apostles, in Rome, complete indulgence as well as other graces and freedom, which the Christian believer may obtain . . .

When Albrecht's representative arrived in a town to sell the indulgence, the papal bull was brought to the church with a solemn procession of civic and church officials, with flags and candles, with bells tolling and organs playing. Tetzel would then assure people that "even if someone slept with Christ's dear mother, the pope had power in heaven and on earth to forgive as long as money was put into the indulgence coffer," and that God would have to forgive if the pope had forgiven.

The sale of this indulgence was especially fraught, as it was actually the revival of a sale that had begun several years earlier. The reason for the revival was Albrecht's investment of very large amounts of money, borrowed from the German banking family of Fugger, in obtaining his office, which carried with it the role of an imperial elector. A new election to the imperial throne was in view, as Maximilian was aging and also borrowing heavily from the Fuggers to ensure Charles' succession as emperor.

The doctrinal issue cannot readily be separated from the political. Duke Frederick had already taken a stand when he refused to allow Albrecht's representatives to preach his indulgence within his territories. Frederick knew Luther, knew his friends, and would receive a print copy of the ninety-five theses within days of their publication. He could have made sure that Luther was fired, had he wanted to, but plainly he did not. To some extent Luther was speaking for the court as well as for himself. Frederick clearly felt that a political pot needed to be stirred, and that the context of the forthcoming election made it possible to assert regional concerns against the broader interests of the pope and the emperor. In addition, the Turks were again on the move in central Europe. It was not a good time to be shipping resources elsewhere.

THE LUTHERAN REFORMATION

Luther's instant celebrity may have strengthened Frederick in his resolve. Luther obtained this status through his ability to exploit the printing press.

On the same day he posted his ninety-five theses, Luther sent a copy to the university press in Wittenberg. Other presses in Nuremberg, Leipzig, and Basel produced their own editions. The press at Nuremberg even produced an edition in German. Then Tetzel published a response to Luther. Luther responded, in German, with his *Sermon on Grace and Indulgence,* which was an instant publishing phenomenon. Tetzel's further response to Luther was generally ignored. What Luther had created with the *Sermon on Grace and Indulgence* was a court of public opinion.

Unaware that the world was being transformed by the new technology, the Catholic Church resorted to medieval means to silence its new nemesis. In the late summer of 1519, pope Leo declared Luther a heretic, and his representative in Germany, cardinal Cajetan, summoned Luther to make a formal submission at Augsburg, having promised him safe passage. Cajetan, who had once written a negative appraisal of indulgences himself, demanded that Luther recant his views. Luther asked why. Cajetan was furious. Luther returned to Wittenberg, and Cajetan demanded his surrender. Frederick refused.

Luther kept on writing. Between 1518 and 1519, he produced forty-five works which appeared in 291 editions. As these numbers suggest, Luther had a natural understanding of the realities of the contemporary publishing industry. Short was good. So was simple. Interest in Luther meant there was an immediate audience for anything he turned out, and, given that the profits on short books outweighed the costs, there was ever more cash on hand to print more new books. The success of the shorter works, in turn, created an audience for longer books, three of which Luther produced in 1520 (along with twenty-five shorter ones). Those three big books—*To the Christian Nobility of the German Nation, The Babylonian Captivity of the Church,* and *The Freedom of the Christian Man*—go beyond his earlier criticisms of indulgences and lay out a new theology, announcing that religion needed to be freed from the corrupt clergy and that all baptized persons could be priests by virtue of their baptism and their faith.

In the address *To the Christian Nobility,* Luther seeks to overthrow the three walls which he says the Church has constructed around itself to prevent reform. The first was to claim that spiritual power is superior to temporal; the second was that only the pope could interpret scripture; the third was that Christian belief was regulated through Church councils. None of these "walls" has the support of scripture. Any Christian man could be a priest in his own right, for "between spiritual and temporal persons, the only real difference is one of office and function, and not of estate." There is no scriptural evidence to support the notion that the pope alone can interpret scripture, and likewise there is no evidence in scripture to support the notion that only a pope could call a council. What a person learns from the Apostle Paul is that "every town should elect a pious learned citizen from the congregation and charge him with the office of minister." The crucial point was that religion should be united with the state, under secular control. He had opened the work by calling upon the "young leader of noble blood," the incoming emperor Charles V, to start restoring the purity of Christ's teaching. Charles, whose relationship with Leo was deeply troubled, was advised by Erasmus to avoid immediate condemnation of Luther, and by another adviser that Luther might be a useful tool to use against the pope.

The sacraments are the subject of *The Babylonian Captivity.* Luther claims there is scriptural support for only three of them—the Eucharist, baptism, and penance—and that it was Jesus who absolved a truly penitent person. *The Freedom of the Christian Man* addresses the issue of salvation: this is not something that comes about through "good works," but rather through faith. In Luther's words, "anyone may clearly see how a Christian man is free from all things; so that he needs no works in order to be justified and saved, but receives these gifts in abundance from faith alone." Even as these works were pouring off the printing presses, the pope issued a bull excommunicating Luther if he did not recant. When he received a copy, Luther staged a public incineration of the document at Wittenberg.

So long as Frederick protected Luther, there was really nothing the pope could do about him, and there was nothing that the emperor could do, either. Charles V (Figure 3.2) was scheduled to succeed his father at the imperial congress, or Diet, at Worms in 1521, and could not afford to offend his electors. With the Turks advancing into Hungary and a war with France in prospect, the last thing he needed was a civil war in Germany. It also did not help that he was plainly uncomfortable in a German environment. The attitude that led to his being quoted as saying that he spoke "Latin to God, Italian to women, and German to my horse" may already have been in evidence.

Charles seems to have been unaware of the extent of Luther's celebrity and to have been overly impressed with thoughts of his own significance when he summoned the monk to appear at the Diet of Worms. Instead of overawing Luther with his imperial magnificence and forcing him to recant, Charles created an event that overshadowed his own election as emperor.

When he arrived at Worms, Luther was greeted as a hero by crowds in the streets. Miscalculation then followed upon miscalculation when Charles provided him a stage upon which to stand at 6 pm on the afternoon of April 18. Asked if he acknowledged authorship of the books circulating under his name, Luther spoke at length, explaining his thought and the purposes of his writings. He concluded by saying:

Figure 3.2 Charles V, painted by Barent van Orley in 1519, shows the ruler in the year that he was elected Holy Roman emperor. Charles' youth and inexperience were important factors in the beginning of the Protestant Reformation.

Since your Imperial Majesty and Lordships demand a simple answer I will do so without horns and teeth as follows: Unless I am convinced by the testimony of Scripture or by evident reason (for I trust neither in popes or in councils alone, since it is obvious that they have often erred and contradicted themselves). I am convinced by the Scriptures which I have mentioned and

> my conscience is captive to the Word of God. Therefore, I cannot and will not recant, since it is difficult, unprofitable and dangerous indeed to do anything against one's conscience. God help me. Amen.

It was later recorded that before "God help me" he said, "here I stand. I can do no other." The scene is remarkable enough without the addition (which does echo other statements Luther made). A man, standing alone, asserted the primacy of his conscience against the majesty of the emperor and his assembled nobility.

It is said that the German audience hoisted Luther on their shoulders and carried him from the room in triumph after Charles had departed in dudgeon. As cries of "burn him" from Charles' Spanish officials were drowned out by the Germans, Luther made a gesture evocative of a victorious knight at a joust. Charles declared him an outlaw the next day. Frederick whisked Luther away to Wartburg Castle, where he remained in seclusion for the next nine months (often discussing the troubled state of his digestive system with anyone who cared to listen or receive a letter from him). By 1522, Charles was back in Italy fighting the king of France, while his brother took charge of what was proving to be an ineffective defense of Central Europe against the Turks. Luther was free, safe and sound, to return to Wittenberg from Wartburg.

While Luther provided an ideological rallying point for Frederick and his immediate allies, his defiance of Charles inspired others to join in. Since returning from Wartburg, Luther developed a valuable circle of friends, most significantly his younger academic colleague, Philip Melanchthon, who would help spread his developing doctrines while also trying to repress people who were seeking to take Luther's ideas to extremes (an extreme was essentially anything Luther hadn't thought of first). This was especially the case with people who sought to link religious change to social reforms. Luther's steadfast opposition to a major peasant revolt in 1525 solidified his position as the establishment's anti-establishment figure, while opening some space to his left which others could fill.

The most important of alternative reformers were Ulrich Zwingli, who launched a reformation at Zurich in 1521, and then, after his death, a young French lawyer named John (Jean) Calvin in Geneva. Beyond Zwingli and Calvin there were even more radical preachers who saw themselves as prophets for true faith. The most significant of these prophets were those who believed that baptism should only be for adults. The practitioners of these beliefs, known collectively as Anabaptists, took their name from the belief that only adult baptism could wash away sins (the term literally means "re-baptizers"). They were soon in particular disrepute after one of the founders of the movement, Thomas Müntzer, led a massive peasants' revolt in southern Germany in 1525, and even more so after 1532, when an Anabaptist group declared that the city of Munster was an earthly paradise grounded in free love and communal property. The repression of this group was especially brutal, and helped solidify a tendency to regard the mere assertion that a person had Anabaptist tendencies as grounds for immediate incineration. This situation will become significant to us when we come to consider events in England and the Netherlands after 1530.

The growth of more extreme anti-Catholic movements after the Diet of Worms accords with a pattern of development we've seen before, for instance with the Christian Church in Constantine's time. There were many Christians making extreme demands—the end of pagan cults, for instance, or the suppression of "wrong thinking" within the Christian community. Constantine had not planned to intervene on the subject of the nature of God when he converted, yet he did. Christians like Eusebius, who wrote Constantine's biography, would have liked to see him take a more proactive stand against continuing pagan practice. But Constantine stopped well short of this, and the imperial government would usually follow Constantine's lead in resisting demands for the violent suppression of traditional cults. Lack of imperial support did not, however, mean that the more extremist wing of the Christian Church disappeared, and that would also be true of the extremist movements of Luther's period, some of which would soon be integrated into political movements outside of Germany.

Returning to Luther, any coherent response to his stand at Worms on the part of either the empire or the Church collapsed in the face of other pressing concerns. In 1526, the Turks occupied Hungary; in 1527, Charles' war in Italy took a remarkable turn when pope Clement decided to ally himself with the king of France. Short of money, as he often was, Charles pointed his unpaid mercenary army (including a substantial number of Lutheran-leaning soldiers from Germany) toward Rome. Charles' army sacked Rome, murdering some 8,000 people, and delivered the pope into his custody. Two years later, a Turkish army advanced on Vienna.

PROTESTANT GERMANY

The military situation in Italy and Central Europe played into the hands of German princes who wanted greater freedom from imperial control. Luther provided these rulers with a useful ideological antidote to divinely supported imperial authority. In 1526, there was a meeting of the imperial assembly at Speyer, with Charles in Italy and his brother Ferdinand facing the Turkish invasion of Hungary. There it was agreed that princes, including Frederick's son and successor, John of Saxony, as well as the rulers of Brandenburg (ancestors of the later kings of Prussia), Hesse, Anhalt, and Brunswick, in addition to a number of independent imperial cities, could decide whether or not they would continue to follow the religious ordinances of the

Catholic Church. The result was the de-Catholicization of much of Germany from Saxony to the Danish border as well as of the two Scandinavian kingdoms of Denmark and Sweden. Catholic institutions were abolished and Church property was confiscated to serve local governments, while Luther worked to provide coherent instruction for the new priests who were appointed throughout the area. In this he was assisted by a small group of colleagues who had gathered around him in Wittenberg. Luther's movement shifted from protest against the status quo to the construction of new institutions to serve the princes who found him useful.

In March 1529, as Turkish armies were preparing to attack Vienna, a second Diet was summoned at Speyer. Ferdinand denounced the actions of the princes who had adopted religious reforms after 1526, and denied their rulers and other local governments the right to determine the religious direction of their realms. The reforming princes and cities replied in a document in which they "protest and testify openly before God, our soul's creator, preserver, redeemer and savior (who, as we mentioned before, alone searches and knows all hearts, and therefore will judge justly) likewise before all men and creatures, that we for our subjects and on behalf of all, each and every one, consider null and void the entire transaction and intended decree." It is from this document that the concept of a unified "Protestant" movement arose.

With a Turkish army showing up in front of Vienna in September, Ferdinand had his hands tied. A year later, although the Turkish army had been driven back, Ferdinand was in no position to impose his will on the German princes. At the Diet that was summoned at Augsburg, the assembled princes adopted a joint statement of faith which had been composed by Luther's closest friend and associate, Philip Melanchthon. Melanchthon's document, which became known as the *Augsburg Confession*, laid out the beliefs of the reformed Church, chiefly that mortals are wholly reliant upon Jesus for reconciliation with God (which is to say, salvation cannot be purchased); that Jesus' body and blood are truly present in the bread and wine at the Eucharist (a major issue separating followers of Luther from others who were rejecting Catholic teaching); and that there can be only two sacraments, baptism and the Eucharist. They stated that in celebrating the Eucharist, both the bread and wine should be offered to the congregation, that priests should be able to marry, and, crucially, that the only power granted to priests was the power to administer the sacraments and preach. Any civil or military authority a priest might wield would have to be granted to them by civil authorities. They had no divine right to such powers.

Having agreed on the principle of a unifying faith, the princes who had agreed to the *Confession* met at the small town of Schmalkalden in central Germany to establish a formal league. At the same time, an alternative Protestant movement was growing stronger in the Swiss cantons. The first leader of this movement, Zwingli, had differed from Luther primarily in his understanding of the Eucharist, stating that the doctrine of transubstantiation, the belief that the bread and wine offered at the Eucharist actually became the body and blood of Christ, was nonsense. Luther had retained the Catholic understanding of transubstantiation, and neither man, both of whom were exceptionally stubborn, would yield an inch on that point. Zwingli also differed from Luther, who wrote numerous hymns as a way of spreading his message, in believing that instrumental music and traditional plainchant should be eliminated from church services.

Zwingli made the German-speaking cantons of Switzerland, which were generally hostile to the imperial Habsburgs, something of a safe haven for alternative thought (though not too alternative). So it was that John Calvin moved from Paris to Basel in 1530 to escape the bestial persecution that had been launched against Protestants in

France by King Francis I. In 1535, having acquired a reputation as a theologian, Calvin moved to Strasbourg, where he preached until 1540, at which point he moved to Geneva to set up his own version of the kingdom of heaven on earth. For all that their views on many matters appeared to overlap, Calvin never met Luther in person, and Luther was on record as disapproving of Calvin's Zwinglian views on the Eucharist. Other significant aspects of Calvin's developed theology would be hostility to any kind of image in a church, a strong belief that the Church should be able to police the morals of its members, and a thoroughly articulated doctrine of predestination. It was a basic tenet of Luther's theology that a person gained God's grace through faith, and that those capable of doing so were destined for this happy fate. Calvin took this idea in a new direction by developing a theory suggested in the work of Martin Bucer, one of Luther's friends. He now argued that the grace of God predestined salvation to only a fortunate elect. In Calvin's view, God knew ahead of time that some people would be more devout than others, and thus some people would be saved while others would not. Just as God had chosen the people of Israel for his own, he chose—or "elected"— those members of his Church who were destined for salvation.

For all that he never had the overt political support that Luther obtained from the leaders of the Schmalkalden league, Calvin's version of Protestantism would prove even more potent than that of Luther. Calvinism would exert the strongest influence over the dominant theology in the two most powerful states that would burst upon the stage of world affairs in the second half of the sixteenth century. These would be England, which had essentially exited the European scene when its domestic political crises degenerated into the Wars of the Roses between 1455 and 1487, and the Netherlands, which emerged from the northern provinces of the Habsburg possessions at the mouth of the Rhine.

THE ENGLISH REFORMATION

King Henry VIII of England had a lot of problems (Figure 3.3). His father, Henry VII, had won the throne in battle against King Richard III on Bosworth Field on August 14, 1485. Henry VII had, at best,

Figure 3.3 This portrait of Henry VIII was originally part of a mural painted by Hans Holbein, Henry's official painter. The mural also depicted Henry's father Henry VII, his mother Elizabeth of York, and Jane Seymour, Henry's third wife and the mother of his son Edward, and illustrates Henry's concern to assert the legitimacy of his regime for the present and future.

a tangential claim to the throne and was desperate to strengthen his family's claim by building a stable dynasty and securing good marriages for his sons. He succeeded in so far as his elder son Arthur was concerned when he secured for him the hand of Catherine of Aragon, daughter of King Ferdinand of Spain and aunt of Charles V. Arthur died within a year of the wedding, but Catherine had remained in England, a virtual prisoner of Henry VII, who was unwilling to return the portion of her dowry he had received and trying to collect the rest from her father.

When it became clear that a proposed marriage between Henry VII and Catherine was not going to work, it was agreed that she would marry Henry VIII as soon as her marriage to Arthur could be annulled. The grounds were non-consummation (a convenient fiction). Catherine married Henry VIII shortly after he assumed his father's throne in 1509.

Henry and Catherine had a robust relationship as the king sought the heir who would provide dynastic stability. They were, however, not well matched. Catherine had a series of miscarriages and lost one son in infancy before giving birth to a daughter, Mary, in 1515. That was not good enough. Henry felt he needed a male heir. He also needed money. Henry VIII liked grand spectacles and felt he should be able to play a role on the world stage. To do so, he needed a lot of cash, particularly given that he (like everyone else) equated importance with army size. To improve his finances, he employed the exceptionally able son of a butcher from Ipswich, Thomas Wolsey.

Wolsey owed his position in large part to the fact that Henry VII, who had made him royal chaplain, distrusted the traditional aristocracy. As soon as he took the throne, Henry VIII appointed Wolsey to the royal, or privy, council, and rapidly turned over much of the day-to-day management of the kingdom to the man who was now his most trusted servant, elevating him to the rank of lord chancellor in 1515. Once a priest, Wolsey also advanced in

Church circles, becoming bishop of York in 1514 and a cardinal in 1515.

One of Wolsey's first acts as lord chancellor was to manage the scandal that had broken out when a man named Richard Hunne died in Church custody. Hunne had been engaged in a series of legal battles with the Church over payments the Church claimed as its due, arguing that the Church's courts were infringing upon English sovereignty. Henry VIII ordered an inquiry into Hunne's death, and now, for the first time, heard an argument that priests could be tried in civil rather than Church courts for civil infractions. Wolsey, who, despite his exalted position in the Church, understood that he owed his entire advancement to the king and was therefore unwilling to infringe on his royal authority, permitted the inquiry to go forward in a royal rather than Church court. For his part, Henry stated that "the kings of England in time past have never had any superior but God alone." The court found for Hunne's relatives, and Wolsey was left to patch things up with the pope, which he did. But the seed was planted in Henry's brain that he need not succumb to papal authority.

Even if he could assert independence of papal authority, Henry was still keen for papal recognition. In 1521 he published a book (probably ghost-written by Erasmus' good friend, Thomas More) attacking the heresies of Martin Luther. Luther responded with a book on the stupidity of Henry.

At about the same time Henry was producing his attack on Luther, that a young man named Thomas Cromwell entered Wolsey's service. After an adventurous youth, Cromwell, who was, like Wolsey, the son of a commoner, had entered the clothing business, making something of a fortune in trade with Northern Europe. In so doing, he had become familiar with Luther's teachings and appears to have become a genuine, if secret, convert to the reform movement. Cromwell moved up in Wolsey's service throughout the 1520s, taking charge of building projects near and dear to his employer's heart, such as the magnificent tomb he was designing for himself, and the colleges he had founded, one at Oxford (now Christ Church), and the other (which had no future beyond Wolsey's day) in Ipswich. For financing these and other projects, Wolsey made use of money he extracted from minor monasteries and convents he closed, usually using rampant immorality within their walls as an excuse. Work for Wolsey gave Cromwell a detailed knowledge of the contents of monasteries, large and small. It also brought him into passing contact with a man named William Tyndale, who, before the 1520s were done, would be living in exile while translating the Bible into English. In translating the Bible, Tyndale was engaging in an act that was regarded as the apogee of heresy in the England of his day. We may still appreciate what he accomplished, however, as his translation formed the basis for the translation later commissioned by England's King James I.

In the later 1520s Wolsey's position at court came under threat from the king's penis in a scandal that came to be known as the king's "great matter." Early in the decade, Henry had an affair with a woman named Mary Boleyn, a lady in waiting to Catherine and a former lover of the king of France. In 1526, Henry became enamored of Mary's younger sister, Anne. Anne, who may have learned something from her sister's experience, refused to sleep with the king unless they were married. Henry, who had fathered a son by another of his mistresses, was now convinced that his relationship with Catherine would never produce the male heir he believed would be crucial to the political stability of his realm. The reason, he claimed, was that his union with Catherine was unholy, since she had, in fact, consummated her prior marriage to Arthur. Henry wanted the pope to grant an annulment for his marriage so he would be free to marry Anne Boleyn. He charged Wolsey with getting him one.

1527 was not a good year in which to seek the annulment of a marriage to the aunt of Charles V, for Charles now held the pope a virtual captive in the wake of Rome's sack. Wolsey finally thought he'd found a way to have the annulment granted through a hearing before the visiting papal legate cardinal Campeggio in May of 1529. Campeggio betrayed him, refusing to grant the annulment, and invited Catherine to appeal to Rome. Wolsey's subsequent fall from royal grace was swift. Cromwell deeply resented what he saw as the Church's betrayal of the master he genuinely liked. This resentment now mingled with his reformist inclinations when he emerged from Wolsey's shadow to a meteoric rise, first as a potent parliamentary figure and minor courtier, then to a dominant position in government while Henry contemplated making the thorough break with Rome, which was finalized in 1533.

As he looked around him, Henry had now before his eyes the successful separation of the Schmalkalden states from the Catholic Church. He even thought of repairing his relations with Luther, from whom he asked advice on his prospective divorce in 1531. Luther responded by telling Henry that divorce was immoral, and he should consider the Old Testament practice of bigamy! There would be no further communication between the two men.

That Luther's response did not stop the English Reformation in its tracks underscores the importance of tight-knit organization in securing radical change. A couple of years before Wolsey's downfall, probably in 1528, Cromwell had made the acquaintance of a young scholar from Cambridge named Thomas Cranmer. Cranmer and Cromwell would enable Henry's divorce, separate England from Catholicism, and lay the foundation for a modern state. The quality the two men shared was simple pragmatism: neither was an overt ideologue, but both were outsiders to the aristocratic world of medieval government, which they were effectively dismantling to make space for people like themselves.

Cranmer and Cromwell were extremely competent people, willing to mix and match continental ideas with English traditions.

Together, they built a bureaucratic alliance capable of withstanding the vagaries of Henry's temperament. Cromwell (Figure 3.4) owed his increasing prominence at court to his willingness to support the king in his search for an answer to his "great matter," despite his personal dislike of the Boleyn family. Cranmer, hitherto a rather obscure

Figure 3.4 Thomas Cromwell's portrait was painted by Hans Holbein toward the beginning of his period of ascendency in 1532 or 1534. The placement of the portrait low in the frame may be a subtle reminder that Cromwell was a man of humble birth; Cromwell's simple clothing, by the standards of the day, and the presence of a devotional book on the table may suggest his Protestant sympathies.

cleric, was an established client of the Boleyn family—which is why, when the sitting archbishop of Canterbury died in 1532, the Boleyns made sure that he got the job. Cranmer understood why he was appointed, and so managed the matter of Henry's divorce with dispatch. Thomas More, who meanwhile had risen to the position of lord chancellor, protested. His term in office had been notable for the brutal pursuit of heretics and the publication of a book defending Purgatory, whose torments he described with what can strike the modern reader as excessive zeal. Cromwell saw to it that More lost his head.

The separation from Rome was mainly the result of an effective coup d'état by the uneasy alliance between Cromwell and the Boleyn family, and only partly informed by any ideology, given that the king did not share his new wife's enthusiasm for reform. Henry's declaration of himself as the head of the English Church at this point was dependent upon the notion that the king was subordinate only to God in religious matters. This was the view that had emerged in the matter of William Hunne some fifteen years before.

It was only after Henry's marriage to Anne in 1533 that Cromwell could operationalize the royal takeover of Church properties. His assault on these properties, which had precedent in the Baltic and Schmalkalden appropriations of Church property, was thorough, efficient, and supplemented by an increasing ideological support from Cranmer, who tempered Cromwell's assault on monasteries by maintaining the essential superstructure of the Church when he retained the regional control of bishops (anathema to more hardcore reformers). Throughout 1535, while Cromwell's agents collected evidence of deep corruption in northern English monasteries (nuns seeking abortions, priests fornicating, etc.), Cranmer was devising a new order of service and arranging for the publication of a Bible in English. The version that would finally be printed in 1539 was largely the work of the exile William Tyndale.

In 1536, after facilitating Anne Boleyn's decapitation for adultery, Cromwell forced an act through Parliament for the dissolution of monasteries, while Cranmer published ten articles of faith to govern the new Church of England. These articles tracked the Augsburg *Confession* rather closely in eliminating all but two of the Catholic sacraments, which is all the more striking in that Henry, who feared for his soul, was often averse to scrapping Catholic teaching and died thinking that he was still a Catholic. But the king's attention was engaged elsewhere. He was trying to father an heir to the throne with his new wife, Jane Seymour.

The centerpiece of Cranmer's reform, a necessary accompaniment of Cromwell's attack on the monasteries, was the abolition of Purgatory. A collateral aspect of Purgatory's demise would be the destruction of images, a feature of the Swiss reform movement that had been picked up by Tyndale. Indeed, Cranmer asserted that as a result of his work, "Purgatory, pilgrimages, praying to saints, images, holy bread, holy water, merits, works, ceremony, and such other be not restored to their late accustomed abuses." So, while Henry continued many old practices in his personal life, Cranmer and Cromwell proceeded to end those same practices for others. There would soon be push-back from the provinces.

People brought up to believe that their relatives would suffer horrible tortures (the English vision of Purgatory tended to be more violent than Dante's) found it difficult to believe they had been living with a lie for generations. The movement of officials outward from the palace, appropriating local landmarks and often destroying familiar works of art as idolatrous, caused intense distress in many quarters, especially in the more conservative areas of northern England. In the fall of 1536, a major protest movement, the Pilgrimage of Grace, broke out in Lincolnshire and Yorkshire. While it initially appeared to threaten Henry's regime, the movement soon collapsed, largely as a result of its own disorganization. The pace of reform quickened in the next year as the first edition of the English Bible appeared, blessed by the king, who now had his long-sought male heir, Edward. But he no longer had a wife, as Jane Seymour died within weeks of Edward's birth. That led to complications that might have derailed the reform movement. Cromwell engaged in some ill-advised matchmaking, seeking to strengthen relations between England and the Schmalkalden league by arranging for the king to marry a German princess, Anne of Cleves. The marriage was a disaster. Anne did not live up to her handsome portrait, and barely spoke English. Henry was appalled, Cromwell was exposed, and conservative elements leapt at the opportunity to dispose of a man they hated and, hopefully, reverse the course of reform.

In 1540, Henry's marriage with Anne was annulled, and Thomas Cromwell, charged with treason, was executed on July 28—the same day Henry married Catherine Howard, a relative of Anne Boleyn. In the previous year, he had started walking back some of Cranmer's reforms, and with the conservative Stephen Gardiner now installed as bishop of London, people too closely identified with reform were being executed at the same alarming rate as devout Catholics. Catherine Howard's rapid demise, she was executed for adultery, shifted the balance of power back to Cranmer and his fellow reformers, especially when Henry married Catherine Parr, who was favorable to the cause of reform.

When Henry died on January 28, 1547, his realm did not resemble the one he had inherited. Royal finances had, to some degree, been improved by the professionalization of a secular administrative class that was the legacy of Cromwell's career. Cromwell, as ambitious as he was able, had seen that the cause of reform was critical to his own. His advancement had involved the displacement of traditional administrators drawn from the clergy or traditional aristocracy. Despite the political advantage he obtained from his actions, it would be wrong to assume that Cromwell did not believe in the Reformation. He took genuine risks in promoting the cause and it's supporters. Of equal importance was Cranmer, who created an English Church that could absorb the new wisdom from abroad. Henry himself, worried for much of his reign about potential threats from within the aristocracy, was willing to promote new men as a protection to himself. Administrators from outside the traditional aristocracy had been significant under Henry VII, so Henry VIII's displacement of traditional aristocrats was not an especially novel practice, but the direction his reign ultimately took was the result of a cabal of able men who used Lutheran, and later Zwinglian/Calvinist, ideas to shape a new nation on their own behalf. Political outsiders were attracted to Reformation theology as a useful complement to their program of upsetting the status quo.

THE BIRTH OF THE NETHERLANDS

In the sixteenth century, the city of Antwerp, now in Belgium, was a major center for the trade in books and in cloth. It was also—as were all the lands that now form Belgium, Holland, and Luxembourg—a part of Charles V's empire. Once the possession of the dukes of Burgundy, these lands had passed into the Holy Roman Empire after the death of the last duke, Charles the Bold, in 1477. Mary, the daughter of Charles, was the wife of Maximilian and Charles V's mother.

The former lands of Charles the Bold had been divided into seventeen provinces, of which seven were north of the Rhine. Dutch was the primary language spoken in these areas, which were unlike the rest of Europe in that feudal forms of governance had never really taken hold there. The main language of the ten provinces south of the Rhine was Flemish, and the major cities within each province maintained "ancient privileges" conferred upon them by the dukes of the past, as here too, feudal traditions, never strong, had largely evaporated over time. The result was that people in these provinces had greater traditions of self-government than was the case in most of Europe. Among the most important aspects of civic government were that cities had the power to determine who was a citizen, the autonomy of their courts, and the right to elect their own administrators. Another major difference from most of the rest of the Europe is that these provinces had elective assemblies known as states. In the middle of the fifteenth century, the dukes of Burgundy had begun to summon an assembly of all the states, known as the States General.

Charles V had been in Antwerp while he prepared to take up his position as emperor and clearly was somewhat uncomfortable with the independence of the people he found there. Indeed, his decision to order the mass incineration of Luther's works, widely read in Antwerp, may have been as much a statement about the people of Antwerp as it was a statement about Luther, toward whom his behavior would be more restrained.

Luther was not the only nonconformist who found a Belgian publisher. On the far side of the North Sea, Thomas More was incandescent when he contemplated the inflow of what he regarded as dangerously heretical works from Antwerp. The area itself was soon home to the likes of Tyndale and Simon Fish, whose violently anti-establishment *The Supplication of Beggars* drew forth from More his *Supplication of Souls,* the work in which he laid out a grisly vision of the torments imposed on the souls in Purgatory.

Despite Charles V's hostility, publishers in Antwerp continued to print Luther's writings. The fact hundreds of copies of Luther's various works were burned between 1520 and 1522 simply shows how popular they were. There were various reasons for this popularity. One was the humanist movement, which had shaped Erasmus and spawned greater levels of literacy than was typical elsewhere in Europe; another was the generally greater sophistication of the region's well-developed urban society. Yet another was the introduction of early forms of capitalism connected to the area's thriving cloth trade, brewing, and bulk trading, as well as its publishing industry. Economic change was loosening the vertical bonds that had (in theory) kept people in thorough submission to their overlords. Within this setting, persecution of pro-Lutheran publishers around Antwerp simply drove them a bit further north to cities like Leiden and Amsterdam. At the same time, persecution of individuals rounded up by the Inquisition, which Charles had dispatched to the region, simply fanned the flames of discontent, even as more literal fires ended the lives of the small number of persons who actually fell into the hands of the inquisitors.

Initially, the steadfast loyalty of the area's administrators to Charles V prevented any reformation along the lines of what was occurring in Germany or Switzerland. Lutheran sympathizers learned to keep their views to themselves. The lack of a publicly organized reform movement opened the door to the sorts of extremists (chiefly Anabaptists) who were shunned or persecuted in Protestant lands. By the 1530s, there was a distinct division between crypto-reformists of a Lutheran stamp and activist Anabaptists, whose rejection of the validity of infant baptism was generally a feature of a wholesale rejection of societal norms, which included willingness to experience a hideous death for their beliefs. One hundred thirty-nine of the one hundred sixty-one persons executed for heresy at Antwerp between 1522 and 1565 were Anabaptists, as were fifty of the fifty-five individuals executed at Ghent.

Not every Anabaptist wanted to die a painful death, and as the 1530s ended, the further one was from Antwerp the more likely it was that an Anabaptist could survive and behave in less overtly antisocial ways than had the reformers of Munster. Two men in particular stand out, Menno Simons and Dirk Phillips, whose more pacific form of Anabaptism was spread through publications in Dutch. When Calvinist preachers began to arrive in the area in the 1540s, they found that much of the population had turned from the Catholic Church, and most people were finding ways of concealing their true thoughts from the authorities. The literature that accompanied their arrival stressed subordination to the will of God, the notion that martyrdom was a supreme act of faith, and that the authority of princes was ordained by God. People were not yet ready to explore the implications of Calvin's statement, in his *Institutes of the Christian Religion,* that minor officials in ancient states, such as the tribunes in Rome, had been appointed to limit the power of kings, and that there might be a similar power inherent to assemblies of the three orders of society (the three orders being the clergy, nobility and commons). That view, which challenged the notion that royal power was sanctified by God, would ultimately become Calvin's most important intellectual legacy.

The late 1540s and early 1550s witnessed a newly aggressive effort to counter the reform movement. The Catholic Church worked to reform itself at the Council of Trent between 1545 and 1561, and promoted a new, intellectual response through the Society of Jesus (better known as the Jesuit order), founded at Paris in 1541 by the Spanish priest, Ignatius Loyola. On the battlefield, Charles V won a smashing victory over the forces of the Schmalkalden league at Mühlberg in 1547, and in 1553, Henry VIII's older daughter Mary (Figure 3.5), a devout Roman Catholic, succeeded her brother Edward VI (a firm reformer) as ruler of England.

The lesson Charles and his soon-to-be successors—Ferdinand in the Holy Roman Empire and Philip in Spain—should have taken away from the battle of Mühlberg was that there was no going back. Charles found he could not exploit his victory, and finally conceded the point a year later at yet another Council of Augsburg, agreeing that Protestant princes could continue to rule their lands until the Council of Trent finished its work.

Charles' moderation at Augsburg was not matched by conduct in England or the Netherlands. Mary adopted a hard ideological line when she took the English throne and tried to undo Cranmer's reforms, which had put down deep roots in the six years of her brother's reign. Cranmer was but one of numerous victims of her efforts to

Figure 3.5 Mary Tudor. Painted in 1554 by Anthonis Mor, who was assigned to the task by Charles V. This painting was done while negotiations were in progress for Mary's marriage to Philip V of Spain.

restore the old Catholic ways. Rather than die at the stake, many intellectuals fled to Switzerland and elsewhere, the Netherlands included. The years of repression, associated with the queen's marriage to Philip II, had the effect of linking religious reform with national identity, so that when Mary died in November of 1558, renewed reform returned with her half-sister Elizabeth (Figure 3.6). Indeed, Elizabeth's

Figure 3.6 The "Coronation Portrait" of Elizabeth I, by an unknown artist, makes a point about the legitimacy of her claim to the throne. Elizabeth's claim could have been questioned both by those who did not accept the legitimacy of Henry's marriage to Anne Boleyn, and by others because Henry annulled his marriage to Anne after her execution. The robe, decorated in Tudor roses, was previously worn by Elizabeth's sister Mary, whose legitimacy could also have been questioned because Henry had annulled his marriage to her mother Catherine. The point is that both sisters had equal and legitimate claims to the throne despite what happened to their mothers.

own religious views, always malleable according to circumstance, were less staunchly in favor of reform than those of the advisers who pushed the reestablishment of the national, but notably not Calvinist, Church in the immediate aftermath of her succession. The key figures of this era were members of the newer nobility. They tended to be as hostile to what they perceived as socially disruptive doctrines from Geneva—such as democratic election of Church leaders, radical changes in the liturgy, and the notion that society's leaders had to act responsibly in their dealings with their social inferiors—as they were to Catholicism. That would change, but not until the issues dividing Protestant from Catholic had reached new levels of violence on the continent.

In 1549, Charles had taken a major step toward the centralization of imperial authority in the former Burgundian lands, by issuing the "Pragmatic Sanction," which united the government of all seventeen provinces while stating that each region would retain its ancient privileges. Just how that was supposed to work was never made clear, and the hamfisted actions of Philip II, who succeeded as ruler of the area when the exhausted Charles abdicated in 1556, created immediate tension.

Philip had been excluded from any claim to the English throne by the terms of his marriage to Queen Mary, and was tied up with a war against France as his wife lay dying. Now, operating from bases in Belgium, he won a major victory over the French. Unfortunately, he had not learned the lessons that had gradually dawned on his father, who had died a few months before Mary, namely that battlefield victory rarely led to political success and that all power had to be negotiated.

In the long run, pretty much the only thing Philip gained from his treaty with France was an end to the expense of fighting a war. The cost of the war had put a severe strain on his relations with the local nobility (especially those based north of the Rhine) who had been called upon to pay for it. Philip was somewhat suspicious of this group, as he sensed that they were unenthusiastic about Catholicism. So it was that when he returned to Spain, he divided the government of the region between his half-sister Margaret (the result of an illicit affair between his father and a palace servant many years before), who ruled over the ten southern provinces, and William of Orange, a local notable, who was granted the seven northern provinces. William, whose father was duke of Nassau, a territory in the heart of the modern Netherlands, had obtained princely status when his uncle, prince of the region of Orange in southern France, had died in 1544.

William, known also as William the Silent because of his ability to conceal his true thoughts from those with whom he dealt, was cautiously supportive of the Calvinist tendencies among the people in the regions under his charge. This was despite the fact that he had been given a strongly Catholic upbringing as one of the terms of his inheritance of the state of Orange. Prior to his appointment in 1559, he had also been among Philip's favorites.

The tensions between Margaret's Catholic administration and the sentiments of William's subjects, as well as those of other nobles, led to rifts within the governing group in the years after Philip's departure. Simply put, the inquisition into the religious beliefs of the people of the seventeen provinces by Mary's court seemed an outrageous violation of the principle that the states would retain their ancient privileges. Detesting Antoine Perrenot de Granville, Margaret's chief minister and manager of the Inquisition, William became increasingly outspoken in his opposition to the active repression of reformers, which he blamed on de Granville.

At the same time that William was attacking de Granville, a new theme begins to emerge in contemporary literature. In 1557, for instance, Peter Dathenus published a book entitled *Christian Account of a Dispute Held within Oudenaarde* in which he argued, following Calvin, that while good Christians should be subordinate even to tyrannical authority, lower secular magistrates had a duty to resist tyrants. Five years later, a group of Protestant ministers gathered at Antwerp and stated that it was permissible to break co-religionists out of jail. A year earlier Guy de Bray, a minister at Antwerp, while arguing that all people should obey their princes, boldly claimed that princes should avoid persecuting people for their faith. A contemporary, Pieter de Zuttere, went somewhat further in stating that government should limit itself entirely to secular affairs. These views accorded well with those of civic magistrates who were concerned about what they saw as wholesale violations of their ancient privileges.

The writings of de Bray and de Zuttere articulated the issues lying behind the bold statement that William of Orange made at a meeting of German princes in 1564, that monarchs should not rule over the souls of their subjects (a point that was likely just as shocking for Protestants as it would have been for Catholics). He then joined a protest against religious repression launched by notables of his region in 1565, in which protestors maintained their loyalty to Philip while objecting to the conduct of his officials. There was worse to come.

In 1566–1567, widespread rioting broke out in Antwerp and rapidly spread throughout the region, as mobs began destroying religious images in churches. There were occasional efforts on the part of the imperial authorities to suggest that the mass action was carried out with such assurance that it appeared the rioters had been appointed to their task by members of local governments. On the other side, as in the *Remonstrance* written by de Bray shortly before his execution, it was plainly stated that when the demands of conscience clashed with temporal authority, the good Christian should follow conscience. The critical point which distinguishes de Bray's statement from Luther's at Worms is that Luther was explicitly speaking for himself, while the author of the *Remonstrance* was speaking for a society as a whole. Johannes Michaellam, writing a *Declaration of the Church or Community of God,* went even further. He stated that government officials who infringed on the freedom of those for whose protection they were appointed were "traitors," and lower magistrates were appointed by God to silence evil kings. This was a very long way from the doctrine that martyrdom was good for someone.

The gradual coordination between theological and political thinking on the subject of tyranny and political legitimacy was given a rapid shove by the arrival of the duke of Alva, the Spanish general whom an enraged Philip had charged with reestablishing Catholic authority and eradicating reformers. He immediately ratcheted up the level of violence. One of the first things the duke did was to set up a local inquisition, which he called the Council of Troubles. Among the many who were executed in the next few months were several leading nobles. A powerful response and cry for aid, composed by Marnix van St. Aldegonde, asserted that a prince had no right to take any action with respect to his country without the assent of the governed. According to van St. Aldegonde, the regional councils, or states, were the true source of legitimate power, and so, a ruler needed to govern "after a prescribed form of laws and the ordinances of the states." According to this emerging line of reasoning, no longer was Philip II the victim of evil ministers. Rather, he, himself, was now the source from which evil flowed.

William of Orange was now summoned to appear before the Council of Troubles. With him went a man named Jacob van Wesembeke, who enunciated with clarity the view that legitimate government rested upon community liberties and privileges and the authority of the states. Assisted by van Wesembeke, William set his own pen to paper, producing a series of pamphlets blaming the current troubles on the brutality of Granville and asserting that:

> You well know that by the king's own proper consent you are free and released from the oath and obedience you owe him, if he or others in his name infringe on the promises and conditions on which you have accepted and received him, until finally every right has been restored.

William and his supporters continued to write, even when his attempt to expel Alva by force of arms failed miserably. As a result, he was confined to bases in Germany until, in 1572, the seven northern provinces named him their governor or Sta(a)tsholder. The crucial point here is that political theorists had moved away from delegitimizing their rivals to conferring legitimacy on a leader whom they chose.

The interplay between the prince and regional governments continued for the next few years, with the lead tending to come from regional governments—something that would presumably not have been imaginable were it not for the congruence that had been achieved between Calvinism and political practice. In 1576, William led the northern provinces in an ultimately unsuccessful effort to assert control over the south. This "Pacification of Ghent" had been sparked by a major mutiny, which had destroyed Antwerp and temporarily incapacitated the Spanish regime in the region. Following the failure of William's intervention, magistrates in the seven provinces of Holland took matters into their own hands, declaring their union. This treaty, the Union of Utrecht, would be the first formal constitutional document in European history. It declared that:

> So those from the Duchy of Gelderland and county of Zutphen, and those from the counties and regions of Holland, Zeeland, Utrecht, and the Ommelanden between river Eems and Sea of Lauwers have thought it advisable to ally and to unite more closely and particularly, not with the intention of withdrawing from the General Union set up at the Pacification at Ghent, but rather to strengthen it and to protect themselves against all the difficulties that their enemey's practices, attacks or outrages might bring upon them, and finally, to make clear how in such cases the provinces must behave, and can defend themselves against hostilities, as well as to avoid any further separation of the provinces and their particular members.

They further stated that the United Provinces would work together in the future, have a common currency, a common army, and:

> Concerning the matter of religion: Holland and Zeeland . . . may introduce . . . such regulations as they consider proper for the peace and welfare of the provinces, towns, and their particular members and for the preservation of all people, either secular or clerical, their properties and rights, provided that in accordance with the Pacification of Ghent each individual enjoys freedom of religion and no one is persecuted or questioned about his religion.

The Union of Utrecht as a pact for mutual defense stopped short of declaring independence from Spain. That would come two years later, when the Dutch states, on July 21, 1581, decided to "unanimously and deliberately" declare that Philip had forfeited "all hereditary right to the sovereignty of these countries," and, on the advice of William, invited the French duke of Anjou to take charge. The French alliance failed miserably, and the states came back to William (Figure 3.7). By the time William fell victim to an assassin's bullet in 1584, making him the first world leader to be murdered by a gunman, a new nation was emerging and developing the capacity to stand on its own.

At first glance, William's story looks different from those of earlier Protestant movements, but Luther might have been pleased to draw a line from his assertion of individual conscience to the statement that human communities should be based on moral principles. The sixty years from the Diet of Worms to the Dutch declaration of independence changed the intellectual direction of Europe and made it possible to imagine the creation of territorial states based upon the rights of citizenship rather than dependency on lordships, on the free exchange of ideas rather than the threat of Purgatory.

At first sight, the Dutch achievement might seem different from the German and English Reformations. In fact, the similarities are

Figure 3.7 William of Orange as painted by Adriaen Thomaz Key in 1579, when he was at the height of his power. It is notable that William is depicted in civilian clothing rather than armor.

greater than the differences. First and foremost was the ideological failure of Philip's regime; without that, there would have been no revolt. Second, the realities of modern warfare meant that a king had to work with his subjects so they could see a benefit from supporting the costs imposed upon them. This, Philip appears to have been constitutionally incapable of doing. Third, for all that John Calvin ran a theocratic state in Geneva, there was nothing in his teaching that especially enabled the creation of a new political entity. A belief in predestination, that images should be destroyed, that services should be conducted in the indigenous language, that priests should be able to marry, and that the substances of the Eucharist were not transubstantiated, in and of themselves were insufficient doctrines upon which to build a state. It was William's additional belief, one that Calvin would have rejected out of hand, that a state should be built upon freedom of conscience that made the big difference. This, combined with his ability to support armies in the field and his capacity for working with local governments, made him successful. Without the religious reform movement, William would have remained a Habsburg functionary. Without William, the religious reform movement in the Netherlands would have continued to offer little more to its members than a fast track to incineration.

THE REFORMATION'S IMPACT

The Reformation of the sixteenth century disrupted the centuries-old alliance between secular and religious authority that defined Europe's social, political, and intellectual order, making possible the emergence of societies that admitted a diversity of religious opinion and intellectual experiment. The effect of the Reformation was to extend the notion of a state from a society bound by shared practice, to a society bound by both practice and belief.

By creating space for new styles of thought, the Reformation opened the door not just to discussions of abstruse concepts, but also to new ways of studying the natural world, further undermining religious authority by making it clear that there were natural laws that could be understood without reference to the authority of religious texts. Even though the two greatest scientists of the sixteenth and seventeenth centuries—Copernicus and Galileo—were Catholic, their discoveries were far more welcome and influential in Protestant lands than they were to Catholics.

Accurate observation of the natural world encouraged new thinking in a wide range of areas, which included the exploration of different ways in which societies could be organized. Demonstrable fact would replace dogma as the driving force in the generation of new knowledge that could then be a force for further change. It is not accidental that the century after the Reformation would see the transformation of the world's balance of power in favor of states on Europe's Atlantic fringe, areas that had been of minimal significance in previous millennia.

The course of the Reformation is similar to the disruptions we have already explored, first and foremost because it arose from a loss of faith in existing institutions, which stemmed from political, economic, and intellectual challenges. There can be little doubt that Luther would have failed in taking his stand against indulgences if he could not have counted on support from Frederick of Saxony. Nor is it imaginable that Cranmer and Cromwell could have built a new Church that was a hybrid of reformist thinking and traditional episcopal governance if Henry had not been desperate for a solution to his marital problems. But Henry's break with Rome was made possible by the fact that Luther had shown how papal authority could be challenged. William of Orange's achievement was perhaps most astonishing of all, because he built on the passions of persecuted extremists to construct a new state independent of what appeared to be the greatest power Europe had seen since the end of the Roman state in the fifth century CE. The common factor here is the government of Charles V.

Charles V as Holy Roman emperor is a figure who is in many ways evocative of the Roman emperor Heraclius. Heraclius failed to recognize the weakness of his own empire in the wake of the Persian war, and then proceeded to alienate many of the subjects who returned to his sway after years of Persian rule. If he had realized that he needed to negotiate his authority rather than impose it, the door to the Arab conquest might not have opened. Charles' open contempt for his German subjects and his evident weakness in the face of the challenge of the Ottoman state invited revolt. Like Muhammad, Luther emerged from the context of a religious reform movement so as to play a crucial role in uniting opposition to the status quo. Also, like Muhammad, he did not shape the state that emerged as a result of his preaching—that was left to others who took his ideas in directions that he quite often did not approve of. His poor relationship with Henry VIII is a case in point.

Like Heraclius, Charles V was actually a decent general. But, also like Heraclius, he was unable to recognize, until too late, that victory on the battlefield is insufficient, in and of itself, to ensure a political result. Heraclius and Charles were not the only people to have this problem. The bloody course of European history in the ninety years after Charles' abdication led to even greater changes. The principles of royal absolutism were now undermined by thinkers who, released from the bonds imposed by Biblical thought, would study the classical texts that had survived the Middles Ages to be recovered by the humanists of the previous century, and made widely available through print.

The ability to control media, the key to Luther's initial success, will remain a critical aspect of disruptions to come. The dissemination of ideas beyond the reach of government censorship will be a crucial factor in the development of new ways to analyze a society and new concepts about the nature of authority. None of this would have been possible, at least not possible in the form it would take, were it not for the Reformation. The Reformation demonstrated once and for all that efforts to repress modernity with the tools of medievalism, appeals to mystical authority, and ghastly penalties, were doomed to failure.

Chapter 4

Popular Sovereignty

PEACE

On the 3rd of September, 1783, peace commissioners acting on behalf of an entity styling itself the United States of America finalized a treaty with representatives of "the most Serene and Potent Prince George III, by the Grace of God, King of Great Britain, France and Ireland." They agreed "to forget all past misunderstandings and differences that had unhappily interrupted the good correspondence and friendship" they wished to restore. In the first article of this treaty, the British king relinquished "all claims to the government, property and territorial rights" of the United States, now recognized as free, sovereign, and independent.

Representatives of the United States had been asserting that independence since July 4, 1776. They were only now obtaining British recognition of their claim because of a striking victory won by the army of the Unites States, aided mightily by a French army and fleet, that culminated in the surrender of a British army at Yorktown in Virginia on October 19, 1781. The claims the Americans made, based upon theories of the implicit sovereignty of a people and the rights of humans to be free of tyrannical authority, derived ultimately from the theories of John Calvin, through the work of various thinkers who had articulated novel theories of government during the previous century. Four years after the conclusion of the Treaty of Paris, the Americans would bring forth a new constitution based on these theories. At the same moment, the French would be on the edge of a titanic upheaval of their own. The national bankruptcy resulting from the war with Britain on America's behalf had undermined the authority of their king.

Both the Americans and the French asserted the rights of the individual, popular sovereignty, the protection of property rights, and freedom of conscience. One movement yielded a constitution that remains, albeit with significant changes, in effect today. The other gave way rapidly to mass murder, aggressive war, and a new form of imperial monarchy. The central question of this chapter is how two movements whose ideologies were shaped by similar intellectual inheritances could yield such radically different results.

A coincidental result of the French experiment was that King George III would stop claiming to be king of France. That would be in 1800, seven years after the decapitation of Louis XVI, who was France's actual king in 1783.

CIVIL SOCIETIES: BODIN AND HOBBES

The emergence of political theory in the English-speaking world is largely due to the impact of Thomas Cromwell's great grandnephew. His name was Oliver, and he beheaded a king in 1649. The great theorist of his era was Thomas Hobbes, who was joined, at the end of his life, by John Locke. In France, the intellectual path is a bit more convoluted, beginning with Jean Bodin, whose thinking was unleashed by brutal wars between Protestants and Catholics that tore sixteenth-century France apart, and then to the subtle theorizing a century later of the Baron de Montesquieu and Jean-Jacques Rousseau.

Jean Bodin was born into a middle-class family at Angers. After a youthful attachment to the Carmelites, a monastic order devoted to improving the lot of the poor, he was released from his vows and acquired a substantial humanist education through university study in Paris. This secular education is exceptionally important for what follows, because it separated Bodin's approach to social theory from traditions based on Calvin's reading of Christian scripture. Instead, Bodin's approach was based on his reading of classical literature.

Bodin was an astute reader of ancient texts, and his *Six Books on the Republic*, written at the height of his career in 1576, transformed him into a public intellectual of note. He was also a man of principle, and, while he could have thrived in public service, he placed principle ahead of profit when he was chosen as a deputy for France's "third estate," or commoners (the clergy comprised the "first estate" and the nobility the "second estate"). In this role, he opposed a proposal for taxation that had come down from King Henry III, who said he would use the money to impose religious unity. Bodin saw this as a threat to public order and succeeded in convincing his colleagues to reject the king's request. High royal office was consequently out of the question, and he gradually dropped from the national stage, remaining a local magistrate at Laon from the late 1580s to his death in 1596.

Bodin understood the existence of pragmatic limitations to thought and action. There was no point in creating a universal doctrine of state power that could cost him his head. So, for example, in discussing the issue of whether or not revolt and assassination are legitimate choices for subjects of a tyrant, he allows that in certain kinds of monarchies, where royal power is conferred by the subjects, the subject can remove a king. He includes the Holy Roman Empire as such a state, given that the emperor "is subject to the Estates of the Empire." He distinguishes between a ruler to whom "absolute power is given, pure and simple" because the people have stripped themselves of sovereign power, and those who have been granted authority by the action of the people. So:

> . . . if the prince is sovereign absolutely, as are the genuine monarchs of France, Spain, England, Scotland, Ethiopia, Turkey, Persia, and Muscovy—whose power has never been called into question and whose sovereignty has never been shared with subjects—then it is not part of any subject individually, or all of them in general to make an attempt on the honor or life of the monarch, either by way of force or by way of law, even if he has committed all the misdeeds, impieties and cruelties that one could mention.

He allowed that Calvin might have been correct in observing that officials who are appointed to protect the people against the arbitrary action of a sovereign might have a duty to resist royal authority, but that rule does not apply "in a proper monarchy." And, even in a place that was not "proper" (e.g., the Holy Roman Empire), random subjects could not simply decide that they didn't like the ruler. They could only act against him with the consent of the majority of the electors.

Bodin is a good deal more interesting when he turns his attention to states in which power is delegated to magistrates. Here, his vast command and astute reading of classical literature allows him to use well-chosen examples from the ancient world to make the point that the first prerogative of sovereignty is the power of giving law or commands. Hence, only "when the entire people was assembled" could an ancient Roman law code, drawn up by ten commissioners, be approved. A magistrate has some discretion in the way he might decide to interpret a law, provided that he takes care not to break it while bending it. Even if generals could decide on their own how to fight a war, it was up to the people first to declare the war. It is absurd, he writes, to assume that an official can transact business for someone without authorization.

For Bodin, so long as he is not dealing with "genuine" monarchs, much public business is modeled on contracts. Sovereignty is based upon principals derived both from ancient, especially Roman, history, and also from Roman law. It was a basic principle of Roman law, in which the theory of contracts was highly developed, that the power of the monarch was delegated by the people.

The view that a society was based on an implicit contract between its members was at odds with another contemporary approach to which Bodin briefly alludes when he states that a true monarch is bound by laws of God and nature, and that failure to follow these laws would result in rebellion. A more extreme version of the law of nature, much more clearly articulated in the next generation, was that there were rules of conduct that humans should follow if they were to obtain their true potential—that natural law should provide the touchstone for understanding right and wrong. The idea descended from a very basic proposition in classical philosophy according to which people had once lived at one with nature in a golden age.

In ancient thought, human societies emerged after the end of the golden age when humans, now in conflict with nature, needed to organize for their own protection. But what if mankind's best prospect was to live in accord with nature? Were there rules of conduct that could bring people to realize their true potential in the natural order? And, if that was the case, what should be done about people who defied nature's law? One answer, twisted from Roman thought, was that such people would then be "enemies of the human race," forfeiting the rights they would otherwise have as human beings. In Roman terms, such people tended to be pirates. That was also true in early modern theory, but the creation of a space in which humans could lose their rights for behavior judged not to be in accord with nature would have drastic consequences anon.

In the generation after Bodin wrote, the English Parliament went to war with its king, Charles I. The revolt stemmed from major changes in English society following a century of population growth. These were especially the rise of a greatly expanded class of county gentry, who had grown wealthy from commercial farms using wage labor; the struggles of peasants and workers for whom population growth meant scarcer land, higher rents, and lower wages; the growth of towns and cities, especially London, whose merchants, shopkeepers, professionals, artisans, and apprentices were stressed by the weight of royal taxes; as well as the uneven playing ground stemming from royal monopolies and the privileges possessed by royally charted guilds and companies.

Popular frustration and increased economic power made it possible for the House of Commons to stand up to a king who combined spectacular dishonesty with sheer incompetence and high-handed disregard for its power. Charles had justified his conduct with the assertion that he ruled by "divine right," a notion that had been enunciated in much less developed form when Henry VIII had split from Rome. In Charles' time, the theory had shaped a political discourse in which the king himself could do no actual wrong. Failures of government were the result of failures on the part of his advisers.

The years before the outbreak of war between the king and Parliament were dominated by royal demands for money and parliamentary impeachments of royal advisers. Once the war broke out, and in the years that followed, some on the parliamentary side, especially those on its radical Protestant fringe, began to explore the idea that all men were equal and equally deserving of rights and protections under the law that should apply to all.

Parliamentary claims to represent England's sovereign people had not hitherto been especially well articulated nor universally asserted, and they were not going to be in the war's immediate aftermath. When Charles was executed, it was not because his conduct had violated some well-articulated view of the duty of a monarch, but rather because he was a traitor. That charge was not unreasonable given that, after his surrender to Parliament, he had fomented a second round of civil war by encouraging a Scottish invasion of England. Indeed, the new regime was notably hostile to Protestant groups that advocated social leveling, and hardly democratic. Parliament replaced the king with Cromwell as lord protector. When Cromwell tired of what he considered parliamentary obstructionism, he dismissed Parliament and ruled through a cabal of his senior officers.

The civil war and subsequent Cromwellian dictatorship were not motivated by a desire for radical social change, and the enclosure of land, exacerbating the problems facing England's poor, picked up steam after Charles II was restored to the throne less than two years after Cromwell died in 1658. That said, the events surrounding Charles I's overthrow did stir major soul searching and an explosion of argument, from which Thomas Hobbes' *Leviathan* emerged as the most important contribution.

Hobbes did not love revolutionaries. Born in 1588, the son of a minor, and alcoholic, church functionary at Malmesbury in Wiltshire, he was soon recognized as being very bright. After a successful grammar school career, an uncle paid for his education outside of the regular college system at Oxford. Being a very good classicist, he was, immediately upon his departure from Oxford, taken into service as secretary to the branch of the Cavendish family, which provided the earls of Devonshire. He would remain in service to this family—usually to the earls of Devonshire, but sometimes to family members who were earls of Newcastle—for the rest of his life.

One of Hobbes' tasks as the earl's secretary was to take his children on the "grand tour" of Europe. In the course of these travels, Hobbes came into contact with a number of leading intellectuals, including, indirectly, the great astronomer Galileo, who was in hiding after having terminally offended the Catholic Church by publishing his view that the earth circles the sun (the two would not meet in person until 1648). Hobbes also became very familiar with works of political philosophy descending from the ideas of Niccolo Machiavelli, in which writers explored the techniques a person might use to survive in the treacherous political environments of the Italian city-states.

Machiavelli had most famously dealt with the perils of practical politics in a meditation he had published on the opening five books of Livy's history of Rome, a pleasing fantasy on the first several centuries of Rome's existence at first under kings and then as a republic. More recent writers, such as the Dutch thinker Justus Lipsius and the Frenchman Montaigne, had been more taken with what they saw as the more cynical approach in Tacitus' histories of the early imperial period as well as in Aristotle's vast philosophic oeuvre. Another author who was attracting attention at this point was Thucydides, the great fifth-century BCE historian of wars between the Greek states of Athens and Sparta. Hobbes' first major published work was an English translation of Thucydides.

Hobbes fled England in 1640, fearful that sentiments he expressed in a handbook on law, drafted for the earl of Devonshire, would provide grounds for his prosecution. While in France he mingled with French philosophers, including Rene Descartes, whose work he had once criticized, and ultimately took up the position of mathematics tutor to Charles II, the future king of England. Charles was in Paris because his father was busy losing the civil war with Parliament. It was at this point that Hobbes set to work on the *Leviathan*, his immensely influential contribution to political philosophy.

Before Hobbes set pen to paper to compose the *Leviathan*, there had been some changes in the way people thought about the state of nature. Increasingly, thinkers began to suspect that it might not actually have been the golden age of classical fantasy. The Dutch thinker Hugo Grotius, who wrote a book on the laws of war and peace, had envisioned the state of nature as being entirely hostile, escapable by humans only if they formed political associations, a view derived from thinkers like Plato and Aristotle.

Grotius' understanding of the state of nature would be critically important for Hobbes, who likewise viewed it as something dreadful, a state from which man escaped through the formation of civil society. For Hobbes it was obvious "that during the time men live without a common power to keep them all in awe, they are in that condition which is called war, and such a war as is of every man against every man." In "a time of war, where every man is enemy to every man" there was no culture, no science, no society and "the life of man solitary, poor, nasty, brutish, and short." Society arose when people agreed to "confer all their power and strength on one man, or one assembly of men, that may reduce all their wills, by plurality of voices, unto one will." "From this institution of the commonwealth are derived all the rights and faculties of him or them, on whom the sovereign power is conferred by the consent of the people." The people agree to abide by the decision of the majority or of the monarch; they are bound by the original agreement that formed their society and cannot make a new one among themselves, nor, if they are "subjects to a monarch" can they "without his leave cast off monarchy."

Given his association with Charles II at the time he wrote the *Leviathan,* it is perhaps not surprising that Hobbes took the view that no person with sovereign power could be justly executed; that the sovereign power sets social norms, has the right to decide disputes, and that there could be no secondary representative of the people's will (e.g., a parliament that could challenge a king in the name of the people). Hobbes has much to say about possible forms and constituent parts of government and the nature of crimes, punishments, and rewards. Throughout the work, he maintains that the only circumstance under which a person could cease to obey the authority of a sovereign was the failure of the sovereign to provide the protection that was the purpose for which a society had been formed. A society may fall because the original founding covenant was too weak, or because it is defeated in war. What cannot happen is for subjects to do as the Greeks and Romans did, which was to declare that a king was a tyrant and use that as justification for his overthrow.

According to Hobbes, it is the duty of the sovereign to ensure the welfare of the people, who are thereby enabled to pursue "contentments of life" through "lawful industry." Meanwhile, the all-encompassing state sees to defense, education, and law. Education will ensure that people understand the principles of their society, while "the safety of the people, requires further from him, or them that have the sovereign power, that justice shall be administered to all degrees of people . . . so as the great, may not have greater hope of impunity, when they do violence, dishonor or any injury to the meaner sort, than when one of these does the like to one of them."

There is much in the *Leviathan* to commend its author to monarchists. But there is one section that got Hobbes into a great deal of trouble. This is concerned with religion, which Hobbes saw as being a political entity. To write that "I find the kingdom of God to signify in most places of scripture, a kingdom properly so named, constituted by the votes of the people of Israel" outraged representatives of the Anglican Church. The observation that wars have stemmed "from a difficulty, not yet sufficiently resolved, of obeying at once, both God and man" did nothing to improve the situation, and suggested (correctly) that Hobbes was an atheist.

Hobbes was forced to depart Parisian society for England, where, fortunately for him, the earl of Devonshire had made his peace with the revolutionary regime. Hobbes lived out his days in the earl's household. He was protected from persecution after the restoration of Charles II to the throne in 1660 by the earl's friendship, and possibly by the fact that Charles simply thought he was odd.

In terms of the development of political thought, the crucial ideas that had emerged by this point were the conception of society as based on a contract into which people voluntarily arrived, and that there was an earlier state from which humans escaped when forming a civil society. Hobbes and Bodin were by no means the only people discussing things in these terms, but their work continued to be read. The printing press still governed the marketplace of ideas, and their work stayed in print more prominently than did that of others. Of one of Hobbes' contemporaries—James Harrington, who wrote a book about the utopian *Commonwealth of Oceana* (an idealized version of Cromwell's England)—one of Hobbes' most influential successors would write:

> Harrington in his *Oceana,* has also inquired into the utmost degree of liberty to which the constitution of a state may be carried. But of him, indeed, it may be said that for want of knowing the nature of real liberty he busied himself in the pursuit of an imaginary one . . . .

LOCKE, MONTESQUIEU, AND THE ENLIGHTENMENT

Bodin intimated and Hobbes asserted that a civil society is based on the agreement of the governed. The point would be made more forcefully by a younger contemporary with whom Hobbes was in periodic contact. This person was John Locke.

Born in 1632, the son of a lawyer who served as an officer in the parliamentarian army during the Civil War, Locke graduated from the Westminster School in London and arrived at Oxford at the age of twenty. He aspired to the study of medicine, which enabled him to take up a permanent position upon completing his degree at his undergraduate college, Christ Church. His position as a "medical student" (faculty member) was unique in the college because he wasn't required to take holy orders as a condition of employment.

In an era without the blessings of a Research Excellence Assessment (or an American style tenure review), Locke gave himself over to decades of experimentation in botany and philosophical speculation before developing his seminal work on human perception in the late 1690s. At that point, he suggested that all ideas come from sensation or reflection, either through reaction to sensation or the mind's ability to reflect "on its own operation within itself." The crucial conclusion that followed from these observations was that "the soul is material and mortal" and that humans were the intellectual creators of their own universes.

Before this, however, Locke had set his hand to works of political theory. Locke's first published work was *A Letter Concerning Toleration,* issued in 1689, in which he argued that governments should be concerned with issues such as life and property rather than matters of conscience. In the same year, he published the book he had written several years earlier. This was entitled *Two Treatises of Government.* It remains a seminal work of political philosophy.

Locke wrote his *Two Treatises of Government* in 1681/2, responding to a book whose overt imbecility betrays the severity of the crises at hand. Locke's target was authored by Sir Robert Filmore, a book published very posthumously in 1680 (Filmore had died in 1654) in which he defended the divine right of kings. At the point Filmore's book was published, English political society was in turmoil because Charles II was seeking to ensure the succession of his brother James. James was not only a devout Catholic, he was also devotedly interested in the principles of royal absolutism as practiced by his contemporary, Louis XIV, in France. Filmore's work could be taken as justifying absolutism on the grounds that royal power descended directly from God, who had made Adam the first monarch in the Garden of Eden.

Locke dealt with Filmore's arguments in the first of his treatises; in the second, he laid out his understanding of the principles upon which a proper society was constructed. For Locke, the state of nature was not so threatening as it was for Hobbes, and he expressly rejected Hobbes' equation of the state of nature with the state of war. Instead, it was "a state of perfect freedom" in which people could "order their actions and dispose of their possessions, and persons as they think fit," as "the natural liberty of man is to be free from any superior power on earth." The key word in the passage just quoted is "possessions," for Locke saw the purpose of the state as being the protection of inherent rights to property. He asserted that humans were justly endowed, in the state of nature, by "the rule of propriety," with as much land as a person needed for subsistence. The fact that there would originally have been more than enough land to go around was demonstrated, according to Locke, by the state of the Native American societies with which the English were in contact at the time. Differences in prosperity were explained by the "property of labor," which "puts the difference of value on every thing." Then, as "different degrees of industry were apt to give men possessions in different proportions," people invented money, which gave rise to greater inequalities.

The initial social group was, for Locke, the family. Power relationships were parental relationships; "the power . . . that parents have over their children, arises from that duty which is incumbent on them, to take care of their offspring, during the imperfect state of childhood." Just as parents and children have reciprocal responsibilities, and just as man and wife are joined by choice, so the creation of a civil society is a matter of choice, and the government of a society is characterized by the reciprocal responsibilities of governors and governed. "The only way whereby any one divests himself of his natural liberty, and puts on the bonds of civil society is by agreeing with other men to join and unite in a community." From this basic fact, it is obvious that absolute monarchy is inconsistent with civil society.

The biggest problem people faced in Locke's state of nature was conflict resolution "where men can be judges in their own case" and hence be moved to injustice through self-interest. Thus, in a civil society, it is important that subjects have "an appeal to law" and judges who will treat their cases fairly. The chief reason people agreed to put themselves under a government was the preservation of their property, which could only happen if there was "common consent" as to the standard of right and wrong. The legislative power in a civil society, which derives its power from a voluntary grant of the people, is therefore bound to govern by standing laws known to everyone. The legislative power may appoint an executive power to administer the laws, and it is implied, though nowhere explicitly stated, that judges will be independent of both the legislative and executive, for their impartiality is crucial to the system.

Locke's subordination of the executive to the legislative area of the state was revolutionary. Neither Hobbes or Bodin had ventured to say such a thing. Even more remarkable was Locke's view that people could dissolve a dysfunctional government. "Wherever law ends, tyranny begins," and tyranny is "the exercise of power beyond right." A person who exercises power in a way the community did not authorize does not have the right to be obeyed. Locke even quotes speeches of James I, both when he assumed the throne in 1603 and later in 1609, stating that a king must respect the right of the people if he is not to be a tyrant. Governments, Locke writes, are dissolved from within when the legislative power is changed; in cases where the government is dissolved, "the people are at liberty to provide for themselves, by erecting a new legislative."

It is no wonder that Locke did not publish these thoughts when he first wrote them. Absolute monarchy was then making a comeback as Charles II was grooming his brother James for the succession. Opponents of James' succession, such as Locke's friend the earl of Shaftesbury, were having to flee the country, usually to the Netherlands. Even though Shaftesbury died in 1681, that association made Locke suspect in the eyes of the king, who ordered Christ Church to deprive Locke of his position in 1684. Locke left Oxford for the Netherlands and never returned to his former institution, even though he came back to England in 1689. An invasion at the end of the previous year, led by William of Orange, ruler of the Netherlands, led to James' flight. Parliament declared that James had vacated the throne, and invited William, along with his wife Mary (James' daughter) to occupy the throne he had abandoned.

The timely publication of the treatises on government, and association with the English faction opposed to James, made Locke a suddenly powerful and influential man. In the fifteen years remaining to him he occupied positions in government while producing the works which, in addition to the treatises on government, made him one of the leading lights in the English tradition of rational thought.

Locke's influence extended beyond the English-speaking world, as his work was picked up with particular enthusiasm in France. One of his most influential readers, in the decades after his death in 1704, was a man born at Bordeaux in 1689 as Charles Louis de Secondat de Montesquieu. He studied law at the request of his uncle, and, on his father's death in 1713, he assumed the paternal title of Baron de Brède. He married his wealthy neighbor Jeanne de Latrigue, descended from a line of Calvinists (including a former doctor to William of Orange), with whom he had three children. In 1716, upon his uncle's death, Charles acceded to his title Baron de Montesquieu, and is thus commonly known simply as Montesquieu.

Montesquieu was phenomenally well read, and his early works included papers on a wide range of scientific topics, delivered to the Academy of Sciences at Bordeaux. His first published work in 1721, however, was a satirical novel, narrated through the letters of two

Persians traveling through France, who, at one point, observe that there is a magician known as the pope, who is able to convince people that three are one, that the bread they eat isn't bread, and the wine isn't wine. So much for the doctrine of the Trinity and the Eucharist. The idea of using outsiders to critique French society may not have been completely original—Montesquieu was well aware of an earlier book on the same theme composed by French-Protestant refugees in Amsterdam, a city that was a hub for the production of literature which could not be printed in France. And, in his critique of religion, Montesquieu's touch was lighter than that of another pair of refugees who had scandalized opinion with a book entitled *The Treatise of the Three Imposters*. The imposters were Jesus, Muhammad, and Moses, while God was actually the spirit of nature. Even the Dutch authorities were shocked and acceded to French demands to destroy all copies of the book (an ultimately unsuccessful endeavor).

The *Persian Letters* got a better reception, making Montesquieu a celebrity, opening many Parisian doors to him, and giving him a place in the society of the capital as he also began to travel extensively in Europe. It would be in Paris, nonetheless, that Montesquieu would ultimately settle, having sold the legal position he held in the government of Bordeaux in 1726. At this point, he had already begun what was to be his greatest work: *The Spirit of the Laws*.

Montesquieu's work ranges widely and at length, suggesting that creatures have laws appropriate to themselves. God has his laws, animals have their laws, and humans have laws of various sorts. Man is reminded of God (whom he might forget) by the laws of religion; he is reminded of himself by laws of morality created by philosophers; and he is prevented from forgetting his fellow men by political and civil laws, which are provided by legislators. Before the laws of society, though, there were the laws of nature. Montesquieu does not agree with Hobbes that the state of nature was a state of war; rather, he believes that humans would have recognized their weakness in the natural world, and the first law of nature would be peace. The next three laws of nature were need, attraction, and the ability to acquire knowledge, which led humans to form civil societies. It is the emergence of organized societies that leads to the state of war, which takes two forms: contests between states and between individuals. The purpose of civil law is to inhibit conflicts within society, while the law of nations ensures that states do as little actual harm to each other as possible, even in time of war. Hence "Law, in general, is human reason." Here ends the first of the thirty-nine books that comprise *The Spirit of the Laws*.

In the next several books, Montesquieu reviewed the three basic forms of government, which he termed republican, monarchical, and despotic. A republican form of government is a democracy when supreme power is lodged with the people, whereas it is an aristocracy when that power resides with a part of the people. In monarchies, the monarch is the source of all power, but that power is exercised through subordinate powers, chiefly the nobility and the clergy. There must also be a "depositary of the laws," which is comprised of the judges who make new laws and revive those that have fallen out of use. It is not a body that can consist of nobles, who are naturally ignorant and contemptuous of civil law. Despotic government is that of an individual. Montesquieu offers as examples the pope and the Ottoman sultan.

As he makes his way through many forms of government in the next several books, Montesquieu displays a vast command of classical literature, differing from Hobbes or Locke in his avoidance of reference to Christian scripture. He is also dismissive of Cromwell's government (it was his judgment on Harrington that closed the last chapter). He was less dismissive of contemporary English government and the thoughts of Locke when he arrives at his eleventh book, which takes as its subject laws that establish political liberty with respect to a constitution.

The key to the English constitution, according to Montesquieu, is that there are, as in every government, three sorts of power: the legislative, the executive with respect to those things that are dependent on the law of nations, and the executive that is concerned with civil law. The articulation of the separation of powers, while influenced by Locke, is far more explicit than anything Locke had published. In Montesquieu's view, "when the legislative and executive powers are united in the same person, or in the same body of magistrates, there can be no liberty," and "there is no liberty, if the judiciary power is not separated from the legislative and executive." Furthermore, he argued, people ought to be tried by their peers.

When it comes to legislative bodies, Montesquieu feels that they should consist of elected representatives who are able to discuss public affairs, "for the people collectively are unfit, which is one of the chief inconveniences of a democracy." In states where there are obvious differences in wealth, he feels there should be two representative bodies which can keep a check on each other. He favors a monarch as the supreme executive, noting that if a state is not a monarchy and "the executive power should be committed to a certain number of persons selected from the legislative body, there will be an end to liberty." Liberty required the checks and balances that could only exist if there were multiple branches of government.

Montesquieu delved deeply into classical texts and classical history, following the course set by Machiavelli and others. And, while writing *The Spirit of the Laws,* he composed an eloquent little book, *On the Greatness and Decline of the Romans,* in which he stressed the role of liberty in the empire's expansion, and of tyranny in its decline. That book would have considerable impact on a younger English contemporary, Edward Gibbon, who would adapt these ideas into his magisterial *Decline and Fall of the Roman Empire,* whose first volume would appear in the summer of 1776. Gibbon's argument that the rise of Christianity would contribute to Rome's decline led to accusations of atheism. The same charges were leveled (with equal validity, it must be admitted) at Montesquieu, and at the thinker whose works

Figure 4.1 This portrait of Rousseau by Quentin la Tour, who painted many of the era's celebrities, was deeply prized by Rousseau himself. An earlier, full-length version of the portrait in which Rousseau is seated in a wicker chair caused Diderot to remark that "all I see is the author of the 'Village Fortune Teller,' well dressed, well powdered and sitting ridiculously on a wicker chair."

would be attracting the most attention on both sides of the Atlantic in Gibbon's generation. This was Jean-Jacques Rousseau (Figure 4.1).

ROUSSEAU AND REVOLUTION: THE IMPACT OF LITERATURE

Rousseau was an appalling human being. His brilliance was matched by his cruelty, arrogance, and dishonesty.

Some of Rousseau's personal qualities might be attributed to the horrendous circumstances of his early life. Abandoned at an early age, he became an engraver's apprentice and then homeless in his mid-teens when he fled an abusive master, converted to Catholicism, and made for Turin. Taking a position as a menial servant, he remained in service for a year and a half, during which time he destroyed the life of a fellow, female, servant, before moving to southwestern France, where he found employment as a tutor for various subjects. Beginning an affair in his early twenties with a considerably older woman, Rousseau made use of his lover's resources to polish his credentials before moving to Paris. There he gained access to one of the great projects of the period, the *Encyclopédie,* edited by Denis Diderot and Jean d'Alembert, and attempted to cultivate France's leading free thinker, Voltaire.

The careers of Voltaire and Diderot reside at the heart of a developing crisis in French society. Dominated by the court and the Catholic Church, any thought—as we've already seen in the case of Montesquieu—that did not conform to Catholic doctrine or assert the propriety of the vertical structure of French society was bound to be condemned. Voltaire was accused of atheism more than once, and lived for many years in exile, even as his often-brilliant satires and philosophical writings enhanced his reputation. The inability of the French establishment to accommodate free thinking was effectively undermining its own authority. People turned not just to Voltaire but to other forms of "secret" literature for enjoyment and stimulation. Subtle criticism was the order of the day, as, for instance, was the case in the *Encyclopédie,* which offered a subversive description of human knowledge. Typical of the digs Diderot took at the establishment was a cross-reference in the article on cannibalism to that on the Eucharist, and an article on "political authority" which opens with the sentence, "no man has received from nature the right to command other men." Rousseau's task with respect to the *Encyclopédie,* in keeping with his periodic employment as a music tutor and composer, was to contribute articles on music. For a time, he and Diderot became close.

Diderot was not Rousseau's only important connection in these early Parisian years. Upon arriving in Paris, he began what would be a long-term liaison with a laundress named Thérèse Levasseur. Although the couple would never marry, they would have five children. Rousseau was responsible for the placement of all five children in Paris' foundling hospital, where the death rate was nearly 100%.

In 1749, en route to visit Diderot at Vincennes, where Diderot was incarcerated on a charge of impiety for six trying months, Rousseau got his break. He saw an advertisement for an essay contest—the subject was the role of culture—which he entered and won. His argument was that "as long as power is alone on one side, with enlightenment and wisdom alone on the other, learned men will rarely think about great things, princes will even more rarely perform noble deeds, and peoples will continue to be vile, corrupt and unhappy."

Victory turned Rousseau into an instant celebrity (he coined the term *célébrité* to describe himself). His literary output increased immensely in range and volume, though his most popular works in France were, by far, novels about sex and education. During this time, he broke from his typical fare to contribute an essay on "political economy" to the *Encyclopédie*. He then broke with the *Encyclopédie*'s authors, attacking their views on culture by asserting that morality could be protected by banning theatrical performance.

Rousseau's political theory, as it emerged from his discussion of inequality in his article on "political economy," provided the outline for his extensive discussion in *On the Social Contract*. Here, he differed from Montesquieu and Locke in seeing the state of nature, as had Hobbes, as inherently violent. But, while asserting the violence of the state of nature, Rousseau indicated that it could still be better than civil society, which corrupted the essential nature of mankind.

"Above all," as he had written in a work on the origins of inequality, "let us not conclude with Hobbes that because man has no idea of goodness he is naturally evil; that he is vicious because he does not know virtue . . . [w]ere he [Hobbes] to have reasoned on the basis of the principles he establishes, this author should have said that since the nature of the state in which the concern for our self-preservation is the least prejudicial to that of others, that state was consequently the most appropriate for peace and the best suited for the human race."

Rousseau's view of human nature was complicated. While sympathetic to the virtues inherent to the common man, he also observed that people "trample underfoot the most sacred duties and are faithful to the death to commitments that are often illegitimate." Political societies are composed of numerous smaller societies whose members have their own interests, and will place those interests ahead of those of the whole if given a chance. It is the duty of government to follow the general will (*volonté générale*), but to do this, a government must be able to distinguish the public will from the private. To achieve that end, it is necessary to "examine the motives that have brought men, united by their mutual needs in the larger society," and in doing so, a person "will find no other motive than that of securing the goods, life and liberty of each member through the protection of all." The good legislator is one who ensures that laws conform with the general will, and laws should be judged through their effectiveness rather than their harshness—a significant issue in France, where barbarous death sentences were still handed down—for people are what the government makes them. "Every prince who belittles his subjects dishonors himself by showing that he did not know how to turn them into something worthy of respect."

Rousseau's somewhat more positive view of the state of nature, as compared to Hobbes, was very much in line with other thinkers of his time, the result of greater study of other cultures. Voltaire, for instance, had approached what he saw as the problem of Christianity through comparison with Eastern religions, and exploration of the Pacific had introduced Europeans to peoples very different from the indigenous peoples of North America. The latter had been introduced to European readers, through the works of early travelers such as Samuel de Champlain, as being given to brutal confrontations with each other. Louis-Antoine de Bougainville's account of his visit to Tahiti gave people a very different impression of the state of nature. He had described the place as an earthy paradise.

The more genial view of the state of nature gave rise to what was still an undercurrent of thought, reinforcing views that certain humans could be characterized as "enemies of the human race," a Roman concept, that the worst people were at war not with each other but with nature, a concept that had already found its way into the work of Hugo Grotius. Diderot, who produced the article on "Natural Law" for the *Encyclopédie,* would write that "whoever refuses to look for truth renounces human status and must be treated by the rest of his species like a ferocious beast, and once the truth is discovered, whoever refuses to acknowledge it is foolish or morally wicked," and of a general will, which enlightened people as to the nature of their thoughts and desires. This "general will" could be discovered in "the principles of written law of all organized nations; in the social actions of savage and barbarous peoples; in the unspoken conventions held in common by the enemies of humankind even in the passions of indignation and resentment." The notion that one could be an enemy of nature and thus outside the bonds of the social contract would reemerge with subtle and brutal refinements at the end of the 1780s. For now, though, the key was still to understand the laws of civil society.

Rousseau published *On the Social Contract* in Geneva during 1762. A more substantial work than his previous efforts on political theory, it began with a revised view of the state of nature, arguing that war was something that could only take place between states, that the first law of nature is the preservation of liberty, that one's first duty is to look after oneself, and that the family is the prototype of political societies.

"Man is born free, and everywhere he is in chains." It is Rousseau's purpose, so he says, to discover the principles that will enable the alignment of justice with utility. The social contract is an "association that defends and protects with all common forces the person and goods of each associate, and, by means of which, each one, while uniting with one, nevertheless obeys only himself and remains as free as before." A corollary of this view was that slavery, a product of force, was illegitimate. Basing his approach heavily on his reading of Roman political institutions (and, to some degree, those of the ancient Greeks), Rousseau argued that people can delegate authority to an executive, but that once the sovereign people assemble, all other government is suspended.

Deeply suspicious of the notion that a political society should be based on the defense of property rights, and resentful of what he perceived as the snobbery to which he had been subjected (a reason for his split with Diderot had been Diderot's hostility to the humble background of his mistress, Thérèse Levasseur), Rousseau argued that "the better a state is constituted, the more public business takes precedence over private business." All people were capable of perfection, so he argued, no matter where they were born, and so, too, "since no man has natural authority over his fellowman, and force does not give rise to any right, agreements alone therefore remain as the basis of legitimate authority among men."

When it comes to law and justice, Rousseau differed significantly from predecessors such as Voltaire or Hobbes in allowing for the existence of a divine force that oversees human relationships. Although rejecting "the religion of the priest" as "a waste of time," he allows that there were two valid forms of religion. One was the "religion of man," which was "true theism," a recognition of the existence of a divine force. The religion of man could inform the religion of the citizen, which would "unite the divine cult with the love of laws" and be a positive thing, for "all justice comes from God; he alone is its source." The unification of divine providence governing the course of nature with the view that human laws left humans in chains, would prove immensely influential in asserting that radical change in the interest of freedom was in accord with the natural order. There was no "fundamental law that cannot be revoked, not even the social contract."

Crucial, once again, is the concept of "general will," which "is always right and always tends to the public utility" by representing the common interest of society. Sovereignty is therefore the exercise of the general will, and even the right to private property is subordinate to the community's right to all. The social contract therefore depends upon the proper operation of the general will, and if the contract is violated, "each person then regains his first rights and resumes his natural liberty." Crucially, then, there could come a time in the course of human events when one people might find it necessary to sever their bonds with another, and that would be in accord with nature.

On the Social Contract was banned pretty much as soon as it was published (beginning in Geneva, where the charge of atheism was leveled against the book). This ban was no more effective than other efforts on the part of the French regime to control the flow of ideas. Rousseau claimed everyone had read it. That would not be the case in France before the last years of his life. It did have a substantial English-language audience, however, and that raises the question of how seriously we need to take a claim on Voltaire's part that philosophy was no threat to the political order. In an essay on Locke, Voltaire wrote:

> If we divide mankind into twenty parts, it will be found that nineteen of these consist of persons employed in manual labor,

> who will never know that such a man as Mr. Locke existed. In the remaining twentieth part how few are readers? And among such as are so, twenty amuse themselves with romances to one who studies philosophy. The thinking part of mankind is confined to a very small number, and these will never disturb the peace and tranquility of the world.

Voltaire knew full well that he was regarded as a dangerous man because he questioned the institutions upon which French society was built. The romances he mentions discussed topics such as the sexual instruction provided by priests and the vast sums Louis XV spent on prostitutes. Fake news is still news. Stories condition the way people think. Even if a person didn't believe that Louis XV's sexual predilections were responsible for France's budget crises, the popularity of such works reveals the inherent unpopularity of the French regime. The French government was sufficiently worried about the impact of such books that it launched an effective crackdown on the circulation of salacious literature in the 1780s.

In the English-speaking world, it was one thing for American colonists to object to taxation imposed by British governments, but the articulation of those objections—the construction of a case that what England was doing was wrong—in such a way as to rally a continent depended upon the written word. The revolutionary movement depended upon values shared through print. One person who most certainly would have disagreed with Voltaire was George Washington. In the winter of 1776, he was facing times that could try men's souls. He needed a message to garner the support required to ensure the survival of the cause for which he had risked everything he owned. He found that assistance in a work published by a recent immigrant, Thomas Paine, whose *American Crisis* circulated in the fall of 1776. Paine's call to action, deploring "the sunshine patriot and summer soldier" who shrank from service to the country in a time of crisis, helped galvanize resistance to British forces that had been moving from success to success ever since landing in New York City at the end of the summer. "Tyranny, like Hell, is not easily conquered," he wrote. Washington rallied his troops to inflict sharp defeats on British forces in New Jersey at the end of 1776 and beginning of 1777.

AMERICAN INDEPENDENCE

War broke out between the government of His Majesty King George III and the Massachusetts Bay Colony on April 19, 1775. On that day, very few people could have anticipated the result of the conflict would include a new nation and a new form of government. Those who could imagine such a thing were on the outer fringe of the American political spectrum.

The conflict of 1775 was the result of poor planning, pathetic communication, and sheer stupidity on the part of His Majesty's Government. Britain had been the one true victor in the world war that had raged from 1746 to 1763, pitting it, Prussia, and some minor allies against a continental coalition including France, Spain, the Holy Roman Empire, and the Empire of Russia. While the bulk of the conflict had taken place in Europe, Britain had exploited superior naval power to seize effective control of French territory in the Americas and the Indian subcontinent.

The global reach of the Seven Years' War stemmed from Britain's alliance with the bellicose Prussian king, Frederick, whose armies had been heavily subsidized by the British. But the war had begun in North America with a pair of botched efforts to seize control of a French fort on the site of the modern city of Pittsburgh. George Washington had been a significant actor in both these military operations; he would subsequently gain the respect of his fellow colonists for his actions in the war and, when the situation in Massachusetts exploded, would be ready to serve.

The quarrels that led to the outbreak of fighting in 1775 stemmed from British efforts to recoup some of the costs of the Seven Years' War from the American colonists. They had, after all, started it. They had also benefited mightily from the expensive British expeditions which ended French control of Canada. The problem was that His Majesty's government had, at no point, consulted with the governments of the thirteen colonies about how it might collect this money. Taxation without consultation was a taking of property and a violation of what all understood was a fundamental aspect of the social contract that bound a society together.

With each failed attempt to enforce a new tax, and then with rather more effective efforts to restrict trade, punishing the Americans for their refusal to pay the new taxes, relations between the colonists and the crown worsened. Massachusetts, where the cousins Samuel and John Adams inspired resistance to the crown, was often the focal point for discontent. But it did not stand alone. In 1774, twelve colonies created an assembly to protest the British government's actions on behalf of all Americans (that is to say, all free white male Americans, the only members of political society at the time) by refusing to import a wide range of goods from English sources and by drafting a petition to the British government for redress of grievances. As news of the fighting spread in 1775, the Assembly reconvened. Observing that "government was instituted to promote the welfare of mankind, and ought to be administered for the attainment of that end," the Congress declared, on July 6, 1775, that the colonies were taking up arms to defend themselves against British aggression. "We have not raised armies with ambitious designs of separating from Great Britain, and establishing independent states," they said—the plural is significant, for no one yet imagined that the thirteen colonies would surrender their power to a single state. This was not a revolution, it was "defense of the freedom that is our birth-right, and which we ever enjoyed till the late violation of it—for the protection of our property." George Washington agreed to act as commander for the army that would now be sent forth by the colonies to protect Massachusetts.

The military situation of the colonists flourished and fizzled in the months following Washington's appointment. First, with the aid of canons snatched from Fort Ticonderoga on Lake Champlain, Washington compelled the British occupying force to withdraw from Boston in the spring of 1776. Then, in the late summer of the same year, the American army suffered a series of defeats around New York City and was forced, with ever dwindling resources, back into New Jersey and Pennsylvania. It had, in the meantime, acquired a new cause—independence—and that new cause was acquiring a fresh articulation upon which Washington was relying to rally his forces.

King George helped radicalize American politics in the autumn of 1775 when he refused to accept Congress' petition and declared that the colonists who opposed his officials were rebels. That encouraged more Americans to contemplate separation, but public opinion was decisively shifted by a book that Thomas Paine had published at the year's beginning. Paine's *Common Sense* was the first true bestseller in American history. A hundred thousand copies were sold within the first three months of its publication in February 1776, and as many as a quarter million within the first six months.

Paine argued that the British constitution was a farce, and now that the fighting had started, there was no way forward other than by declaring independence. He had a rosy view of the state of nature, noting that humans were "originally equals in the order of creation" and that kingship "was first introduced into the world by the heathens." England "hath known some few good monarchs, but groaned beneath a much larger number of bad ones," starting with

William the Conqueror, "a French bastard with an armed banditti" who established "himself king of England against the consent of the natives." As subjects of the monarchy, Americans were compelled to support British wars in Europe which were of no advantage to themselves. They needed to put their interests first. They should be confident in the resources available to them (Paine has some quaint views on how easy it would be for the colonies to equip themselves with a fleet that could take on the royal navy) and provided some advice on how they could better organize their political society. More importantly, he pointed out that the Americans could more reasonably apply to foreign nations for aid as an independent people than they could as rebels against their sovereign.

As spring turned toward summer, and as the British continued to build up their forces for the invasion of New York, the radical group in Congress, led by Massachusetts's John Adams, used the success of *Common Sense* to push Congress toward declaring independence, a step which Paine's work had made the central topic of discussion throughout the colonies. Previously reluctant groups—the Georgia legislature, which had not even sent representatives to the 1774 Congress—began to instruct their congressional delegations to consider the possibility. Virginia, a crucial colony given its size, introduced an independence resolution in June, and by the month's end, every colony other than New York had authorized its delegation to support independence. A committee was appointed to draft such a document.

Thomas Jefferson, a Virginian slave owner, was the principle author of the Declaration of Independence that the Congress adopted on July 4, 1776. Jefferson, well educated at the College of William and Mary, knew his Locke, and that civil government was based on a contract to protect the rights of property. So, he wrote, when it became necessary for "one people to dissolve the political bands which have connected them with another, and to assume among the powers of the earth, the separate and equal station to which the Laws of Nature and of Nature's God entitle them" that:

> We hold these truths to be self-evident, that all men are created equal, that they are endowed by their Creator with certain unalienable Rights, that among these are Life, Liberty and the pursuit of Happiness.—That to secure these rights, Governments are instituted among Men, deriving their just powers from the consent of the governed,—That whenever any Form of Government becomes destructive of these ends, it is the Right of the People to alter or to abolish it, and to institute new Government....

The problem with Voltaire's claim that great numbers of people did not read philosophy (and that therefore philosophy could not be dangerous) could not be more obvious. No great number of Americans may have read Locke's *Second Treatise on Government*, but they were familiar with the underlying idea that government depended upon the agreement of the governed, and that people had the right to rebel when government broke the social contract. Just as Luther had simplified existing theology, making use of the printing press to spread generally comprehensible versions of his thought, so did Paine simplify social theory, already familiar in outline, to set the parameters for the public discourse of rebellion. Theory created the framework within which a dedicated group of individuals could effect radical change.

A further issue in common between the Lutheran movement and the North American rebels was to what extreme they could go. The logic of the American position was that government was a bottom-up proposition. To what extent could the notion that authority derived from the popular will really work? The problem was similar to Luther's when he found himself confronted by John Calvin, and to groups such as the Anabaptists. He could not allow his movement to be drawn to ever more extreme positions if he was to remain an acceptable partner for Frederick and other German princes. So, too, when seeking to build a church that would satisfy Henry's conservative tendencies and continue to support royal authority, Cranmer had to avoid the more extreme tendencies in the Protestant movement. Some of the people who were devoted to more extreme forms of Protestantism had populated the New England colonies before the Civil War; others provided powerful support to the Parliamentarian cause in that dispute (and subsequently moved to America after the restoration of Charles II). A question that would persist through the end of the war that their descendants were now fighting for colonial independence was just how little government would be possible both to win the war and once it was done. Paine and Jefferson would stand at the extreme end of the anti–big government spectrum, but how would that work in practice? Could the attractive power of radicalism be tamed?

TOWARD A MORE PERFECT UNION

It proved easier for Congress to declare independence than to govern the new nation. Soon after the declaration, Congress had proposed the structure of a national government that would enable the independent states to "enter into a firm league of friendship with each other, for their common defense, the security of their liberties, and their mutual and general welfare." It took a year, however, before a final document could be drafted, and four more years before all thirteen states agreed to the articles. By then it was clear they were totally inadequate.

The Articles of Confederation did not create a functioning state. They did create a structure to appoint ambassadors to negotiate with foreign powers, and could provide a venue for discussion of matters that were of general interest. But the national government could not raise taxes, and it did not actually have an army. Articles six and seven made it clear that whatever armed forces there were would technically belong to the states from which units were raised, and the officers of those units would be appointed by the states. The crucial article eight, dealing with finance, merely stated that the costs of the war would be paid out of a common treasury to which the states would contribute, but that the states themselves would determine how they would raise the revenue necessary to make those contributions.

The financial side of the war effort descended from fanciful to shambolic. Initially, Congress issued paper money to cover costs. When people lost faith in the value of those notes, Congress essentially repudiated its own currency and began to instruct states to pay their contributions for the army's supply in kind, issuing certificates for future payment which the unhappy recipients then used to pay their taxes. As the threat of an English victory dissipated after Yorktown, and peace negotiations began in earnest, states lost interest in making any contributions at all. Even with an English garrison still in New York, payment to and for the army virtually ceased in 1782 and 1783. In March 1783, a group of army officers plotted with some members of Congress to take action that would force Congress to assert the power to tax states. The movement failed when Washington found out what was going on and convinced his officers to return to duty. He promised he would do his best to make sure Congress honored its obligations. That proved impossible.

Having declined to become the Cromwell of his country and replace Congress with a military dictatorship, and with the British having finally departed from New York on November 25, 1783, Washington returned to Virginia (Figure 4.2). He genuinely wished to retire from public life, but he also wished to keep up connections with his former officers, his army having disbanded at the end of the

Figure 4.2 Washington lays down his command. John Trumbull, who painted this scene, regarded Washington's decision to lay down his command as an exceptional moment, writing, "Beloved by the military, venerated by the people, who was there to oppose the victorious chief, if he had chosen to retain that power, which he had so long held with universal approbation?"

war. He did this through a group called the Society of Cincinnatus, named after a legendary Roman general who had retired to his farm after winning notable victories. Washington's relationship with his former officers was one reason why his retirement would not be anywhere as long as he wished.

The problems with the Articles of Confederation that had plagued the Continental Army in the last year of its existence were, if anything, exacerbated by the peace. States that had once needed to cooperate for common defense no longer had that need. Benjamin Rush, a Philadelphia physician who had signed the Declaration of Independence, summed things up when he wrote that there were four things wrong with the government. One was the lack of coercive power; the second was lack of control over currency (states were able to print their own paper money in addition to the money issued by Congress); third was the location of sovereign power in a single legislature (many states, including Pennsylvania, had bicameral legislatures); and fourth, the turnover of its membership was too rapid. He could have added that most members couldn't be bothered to show up to meetings, which might be understandable in light of Congress' lack of actual power over states, where the meaningful political action was.

The failure of national government was also causing concern in the nation's hinterland. There were many, living in states bordering the Appalachian Mountains, who felt the answer to all their problems might lie in settling the vast tract of land between the western slopes of the mountain and the Mississippi River, land that had been ceded to the new nation by Britain in the Treaty of London. But there were problems. Spain, which held the land at the river's mouth, was blocking access to the sea; also, the British had not fully withdrawn from the western lands. They maintained a base at Detroit through which supplies could be funneled to Native American tribes unhappy with the prospect of new settlers. Nothing could be done to protect settlers if there wasn't an army. There was also a nasty scare when efforts by Massachusetts' legislature to raise taxes, to pay the debts incurred during the war, caused a revolt in the western part of the state led by a man named Daniel Shays. In the end, the revolt was easily suppressed, but it attracted attention to the fact that the only way to deal with large-scale civic unrest was to summon the state militia.

The national government's inability to control commerce or raise taxes also meant it was soon in violation of terms of the peace treaty that required payments to expropriated supporters of the British crown who had fled the country. It also meant states were setting their own tariffs, which threw interstate commerce into chaos. It was to solve that problem that the Virginia legislature proposed a meeting of states at Annapolis in September 1786. Only five sent representatives, so nothing could be done.

The prospective failure of that meeting inspired one of the Virginia representatives—James Madison, a former officer in the Continental Army—to propose that a convention be summoned to fix the Articles of Confederation. The idea was taken up by another veteran of the war, Alexander Hamilton, who wrote to Congress saying "there are important defects in the system of the Federal Governments," a fact acknowledged by all the commissioners at Annapolis. They recommended that these defects be explored in a "convention of deputies from different states for the special and sole purpose of entering into this investigation, and digesting a plan of supplying such defects as may be discovered to exist." On February 21, 1787, Congress passed a resolution observing that the articles could be changed with Congress' agreement, and ordering the meeting of "a convention of delegates who will have been appointed by the several states" at Philadelphia "for the sole and express purpose of revising the Articles of Confederation" and reporting its recommendations to Congress. Congress would pass the recommendations it agreed with to the states for ratification. A critic of the events that followed upon the summoning of the convention noted that the states may have had no idea that they were authorizing a complete overhaul of the current government.

The war with Britain had started so American colonies could control their own destinies. It was an impractical dream, but at the core of this dream was the view, expressed clearly by Montesquieu and Rousseau, that democratic states had to be small, and that democracies were the best protection for the liberties of a people. A strong central government was antithetic to the principles upon which the Declaration of Independence had been based, and a core piece of Thomas Paine's argument in *Common Sense* was that the British system of government was too complex. The less government the better.

The direction of the new constitutional movement would be set by a group of men—the majority former officers in the Continental

Army, who had risked their lives to secure independence—who would create a new political order based upon a functional central government. Madison and Hamilton would be key players. But so too would be a man who would say virtually nothing at the meetings he chaired throughout the summer of 1787, but whose presence at the convention guaranteed its product would be taken seriously: George Washington.

Perhaps the single most important rule Washington imposed, one which the delegates to the convention were scrupulous to uphold, was that the proceedings should be completely secret. No outsiders were allowed into the room where the delegates met, and the delegates steered clear of members of the press. The drafting of the new constitution involved often intense debate to resolve serious differences with respect to the draft plan Madison had presented the convention when it assembled. Key issues were actualizing the principle of popular sovereignty; the power of the executive; and the relative power of large and small states. There was general concern with finding a way to prevent the new government from falling victim to factions, something which anyone familiar with the practice of democracy in colonial America would know a great deal about. Elections at the state level tended to go on for several days, and were fueled by generous distributions of food and alcohol from candidates who would quite often be running on openly "anti-government" platforms.

James Madison, and others, were deeply suspicious of direct democracy. He would later write that "a pure democracy, by which I mean, a society consisting of a small number of citizens, who assemble and administer a government in person can admit of no cure for the mischiefs of faction." The constitution was establishing a republic in which political power was delegated, and greater territory could be accommodated; the larger size of the republic made it difficult "for unworthy candidates to practice with success the vicious arts, by which elections are too often carried."

The solution, arrived at after long debate, was to create a bicameral legislative branch based upon proportional representation in the lower house, directly elected by all eligible voters, and an upper house with two members from each state, chosen by the legislature. Given that the legislative branch "alone has access to the pockets of the people," it was the most powerful branch of government. The division of that branch into two houses checked the power of large states, while at the same time it respected the sovereignty of the people. The chief executive (it took some time to devise a system where there would be a president and vice president) would be selected by electors chosen by the states in the same proportion as they provided members of the lower house and senate. This system, which replaced an earlier proposal that the executive be elected by the legislative branch, was felt to protect the executive from becoming the tool of factions within the legislative branch.

Throughout the Constitution of the United States runs a concern with preventing corruption on the part of the holder of the highest office. Hence the precision with which the impeachment process is spelled out in Article 1, detailing the responsibilities of the legislative branch, and in Article 2 on the executive branch. Likewise, treason is precisely defined in Article 3 on the judiciary (it had already been mentioned as grounds for impeachment). The president's oath of office, specifically that the president will "faithfully execute the Office of President of the United States, and will to the best of my ability, preserve, protect and defend the Constitution of the United States" is spelled out in Article 2.

In the debates that followed the publication of the proposed constitution on September 17, 1787—especially in the state of New York, which was dominated by a faction loyal to the governor, George Clinton (who later became vice president)—Hamilton and Madison articulated a vision for the constitution as ensuring a stable political order. Stability was necessary for prosperity. The amendment process, described in the constitution's Article 5, made it possible to update the document as needed (and it needed updating with a Bill of Rights in the first session of Congress).

What the constitution was not, was a document about fairness. States could determine who would vote, but only in New York, Pennsylvania, and New Jersey did it include property-owning African American men as well as the white propertied men who made up the rest of the electorate in those states and elsewhere. The widespread denial of equal voting rights to people of color was an aspect of the fact that the framers allowed that slavery was inherent to the economic system of the new nation. In Article 1, Section 2, it states that in determining population for congressional districts the count will include "free persons, including those bound to service for a term of years, and excluding all Indians not taxed, three-fifths of all other persons." In Article 4 (governing interstate commerce) it specifies that a person "held to service or labor" in one state will not obtain freedom through escaping to another state, and Article 1, Section 9 ensures that no action will be taken to prevent the importation of slaves for twenty years. This was not because some people did not realize slavery is evil—even Rousseau had made that very clear—but it was because, to the men assembled in Philadelphia, expediency was more important than justice.

The Constitution of the United States would be offered to the people of the United States as a model document, informed by profound understanding of the theory of government. To a large degree that was true, but at a crucial point, where theory ran up against entrenched self-interest in the case of slavery, theory lost. The relationship between theory and practice that underlay the Constitution was less overt, different from that which underlay the promulgation of the Declaration of Independence. But the idea that a state stemmed from the agreement of its citizens and was to function in the interests of those citizens shaped the thinking of members of the convention. In the times that tried men's souls, as Paine memorably described 1776, people needed ideas to fight for. In 1787, a nation needed rules to function. A very significant factor in the success of both the revolutionary and constitutional movements was that the people at the core of both knew and trusted each other—and they had showed up with a clear idea of what it was they wanted to accomplish.

FRANCE: 1787–1790

The Constitution of the United States was created by a small group of men who observed great discipline, had a history of association before the event, and were familiar with the actual workings of a democratic system of government. None of these things were true of the groups that would suddenly be coming to the fore when the royal government of France collapsed a few months after George Washington took up the presidency of the United States.

The process leading to the fall of the French monarchy and the emergence of a republic began with a fiscal crisis. The French government had financed its contribution to American independence by taking out large loans. In the summer of 1786, Charles de Calonne, Louis XVI's finance minister, explained to him that France could not pay its bills. The tax system was complicated, inefficient, and deeply embedded in French society. The bulk of the state's revenue was collected by a private corporation, the "General Farm," through a six-year contract. The corporation agreed in advance that it would raise a certain amount of money through its administration of the array of indirect taxes on goods transported between regions in France, as well as on imports from abroad. Any money that was collected above and beyond that agreed upon in the contract would be kept by the corporation, which also had the right to charge administrative fees.

It was a system that inhibited effective responses to the royal government's actual needs, enriched the tax collectors, and oppressed tax payers.

The tax collection system was further complicated by the process we glimpsed when we met Jean Bodin. This was the process by which new taxes could be imposed. Bodin had gotten himself into trouble as a member of a *parlement,* of which there were thirteen. A *parlement* was a regional court which had the power to register royal decrees (at which point the decree would become law in the part of France which the *parlement* served). If a *parlement* was unhappy with a royal decree, which was quite likely given that its members were drawn from the regional upper class that would most likely end up paying a new tax, it would issue a "remonstrance" complaining about policies that violated "fundamental laws of the realm." The king could override a *parlement*'s refusal to accept a degree by issuing a "*lit de justice*" (a "bed of justice"). But that took time.

Calonne proposed doing away with the traditional process and traditional taxes, replacing them with a property tax to be levied proportionally on all estates. As this would effectively raise taxes for the nobility, Calonne proposed that the king summon an "assembly of notables," including representatives from all three "estates"—the clergy, nobility, and commoners—to support the reform effort.

Calonne's assembly of the notables was a failure. When he revealed the extent of France's fiscal problem, members of the assembly were appalled. They also refused to approve a new system without some guarantee the money would be spent responsibly. Calonne, who had become embroiled in some financial scandals of his own, was dismissed. After his successor, who had tried to abolish the *parlements,* failed to effect any reform, Louis XVI recalled Jacques Necker, a previous finance minister, and asked him to solve the problem. This was in August 1788. Necker's solution was to summon an assembly known as the *Estates General,* a body that hadn't met for 175 years, to meet in May 1789. The nobility and the clergy were ordered to select members for this assembly, while local elections were held to select the representatives of the "third estate." These assemblies were also charged with developing lists of grievances for presentation to the Estates General, which would have 1,000 members.

Grievances were easy to come by. The months preceding the opening of the Estates General had been particularly grim. A massive storm in July 1788 had ruined much of the wheat crop. The following winter was the coldest anyone had experienced. While hypothermia joined starvation as concerns of the average person, prices for basic necessities went up. Rumors spread that merchants and bakers were hoarding grain to drive up prices. Riots broke out in many places. In the countryside, people heard stories of brigands. As this happened, the court lost any control it might once have had through censorship or containing public discourse. A wave of pamphlets began appearing, largely advancing far more radical views, often heavily influenced by Rousseau's theories of the state, than were strictly relevant to the fiscal crisis. As had been the case in the Reformation and the American revolt against Britain, extremist reforming voices got the jump on the "establishment" in public media and were able to center political discourse in a more radical place than Necker or others around the court would have expected.

It was against this background of suspicion and misery that the Estates General assembled. It seems not to have occurred to Necker, or to the king, that an institution that hadn't functioned in nearly two centuries might need some careful guidelines. One of the major differences between France and America was that the American colonies all had long traditions of representative government prior to the revolution. French *parlements* were in no way equivalent to elective colonial assemblies, and the exercise of direct democracy, which yielded the representatives of the third estate, delivered a group that came armed with lots of grievances and little experience of government. One result of this state of affairs was that leadership in the assembly rapidly fell to people with experience manipulating public opinion through the press—men like Honoré Gabriel Riqueti, Comte de Mirabeau. With many scandals in his past and a perpetual need for cash, Mirabeau was nonetheless an effective orator, well-practiced from his journalist career in advancing propositions for novel forms of government based on the theories of Rousseau and Diderot. Another man of similar views who was rapidly coming to the fore was the Abbe de Sieyès, who, despite his ecclesiastical office, had successfully sought a place with the third rather than the first estate, where he might otherwise have been expected to sit.

Given the absence of experienced leadership coming from people who had the interests of the crown at heart, and the abilities of those who were looking to advance a more radical agenda, it is not especially surprising the Estates General ran into trouble pretty much from the outset. The Assembly began on May 5, and the first issue was how it should meet. The first two estates were happy for the three estates to meet as separate bodies. The members of the third estate demanded the three groups meet as a single assembly. They claimed to be the true representatives of the nation. It was de Sieyès who had helped crystalize this view a few months earlier, when he published a pamphlet, *What is the Third Estate?*, in which he questioned the social value of the nobility, stated that its representatives had no mandate from the people, and that it was "foreign" to the nation and a tumor to be removed. Conversely:

> Who dares to say that the Third Estate does not contain within itself all that is needed to form a complete Nation? The Third Estate is like a strong and robust man with one arm still in chains.... Nothing can be done without it; everything would be infinitely better off without the other two orders.

On June 17, efforts to reconcile the differences between the three estates fell apart, and the third estate named itself the National Assembly. On June 20, Louis tried to shut things down by closing the hall where the Assembly was meeting. The result was exactly the opposite of what he had hoped. The members of the third estate assembled in a nearby tennis court and swore an oath not to adjourn "until the constitution of the kingdom is established." Less than a month later, tensions exploded in Paris.

There were rumors of conspiracy. Troops were gathering in Paris; the progressive Baron Necker had been replaced in the king's councils by arch-conservatives, and it was thought in some quarters that the king might use force to oust the National Assembly. On July 14, a mob stormed the Bastille, a notorious prison and armory, freeing the few prisoners still incarcerated there (including the Marquis de Sade, the leading contemporary advocate of sexual bondage and domination). Louis XVI appeared the next day before the National Assembly, which he now pledged to support, and restored Necker to his position.

There weren't any political institutions of national scope in France. Under royal government, public activity had been parceled out in a collection of local, regional, and overlapping institutions. The National Assembly could therefore claim that it was the only institution that could legislate for all of France.

Failures of communication gave rise to an atmosphere of fear and detestation. Rumor had sparked the storming of the Bastille; fresh rumors, a "great fear," now spread through the countryside, already unsettled by the previous year's climate problems. People believed that masses of armed men, brigands, were heading their way, seeking to steal what little they had left. Additionally, the fall of the Bastille had opened up even more space to the radical press, which increasingly shaped public opinion in Paris. Notable among these new publications were Jean-Paul Marat's *Friend of the People* and Jacques

Pierre Brissot's *French Patriot,* both newspapers, and pamphlets by Camille Desmoulins.

As violence took hold in the countryside, the neighborhoods of Paris were increasingly dominated by working-class associations wherein the king was generally loathed. In October, a mob of 7,000 women descended upon Versailles demanding the king solve the economic crisis that was threatening their lives and return with them to Paris. This he did the next day, becoming a virtual prisoner in his palace at the Tuileries.

The National Assembly also moved to Paris, having taken two significant steps in the month of August. These were the abolition of feudal rights and the publication of a stirring *Declaration of the Rights of Man and the Citizen.* As might be expected of a document in whose composition Mirabeau played a significant role, the *Declaration* emerged from the thought-world of Diderot and Rousseau. It opens by stating that "considering that ignorance, forgetfulness, or contempt of the rights of man are the sole causes of public misfortunes and the corruption of governments," the representatives of the French people have resolved:

> to set forth in a solemn declaration the natural, inalienable, and sacred rights of man, in order that such declaration, continually before all members of the social body, may be a perpetual reminder of their rights and duties; in order that the acts of the legislative power and those of the executive power may constantly be compared with the aim of every political institution and may accordingly be more respected . . .

All men are born free; social distinctions are only based upon general usefulness; the aim of political association is to preserve the inalienable rights of man; sovereignty resides in the nation; liberty is the power to do that which is not harmful to others, while the purpose of law, which is the expression of the general will, is to forbid actions that are harmful to society. No person should be detained except in cases determined by law, which may only establish penalties that are absolutely necessary; a person should be presumed innocent until proven guilty and should be free to express whatever views he wishes so long as he does not disturb the public peace. The preservation of the rights of the citizen requires the establishment of a "public source" that must be supported by taxation, which must be supervised by the representatives of the people. Public officials must be accountable to the public; a society in which the rights of man and the separation of power are not assured has no constitution, and no one may be deprived of property without due process. "Now everything will change, morals, laws, customs administration. Soon we will all be new men." So wrote one of those who voted on the declaration. He was absolutely right. Just not in the way he thought.

The contrast between the French and American processes could not be more obvious. Here, the National Assembly sets out a bill of rights without an actual constitution or an indigenous tradition of governance based upon democratic rights; the Americans had devised a political system drawing upon principles already inherent in their own practices, and then listed the rights that system would protect. Another difference was that the American constitutional movement began with a clear plan developed by a small number of people who knew how to work together. Despite the intellectual dominance of Mirabeau and his associates, there were very deep divisions with the National Assembly, which continued to be split between devout royalists who sat on the right of the meeting chamber and progressives who sat on the left. As would soon become very clear, without a structure of government, it is very difficult to maintain the rights of anyone. The National Assembly essentially declared the practice of government as it had existed to be at odds with the guiding principles of a government that did not yet exist.

Its most important acts were all negative: it dissolved the nobility, asserted government control over the Catholic Church, and stated that the previous system of taxation was to be abolished. The new tax system, administered by the Assembly, was no more efficient than the previous one had been.

THE END OF THE MONARCHY: 1790–1792

In the course of the two years after the promulgation of *The Declaration of the Rights of Man*, as the drafting of a new constitution took its course, the National Assembly introduced or debated many proposals that would transform society. One of these led to the decision to grant religious freedom to Jews. Another decision was to grant citizen rights to free blacks in the colonies as well as France. There was even discussion of equal rights for women (women having played an active role so far in the revolution). That did not pass. Other reforms had negative consequences, even if they were in accord with the spirit of the *Declaration*. The most important of these was the reorganization of France into eighty-three new departments, effectively decentralizing authority. In February 1790, local elections were held throughout France, which complicated matters even further as many people, especially peasants, were voting for the first time. Newly empowered, the still-poor and hitherto downtrodden attacked symbols of traditional authority in protests throughout the country. There was little the central government could do other than authorize the creation of "national guard" units at the local level. The result was the gradual militarization of the countryside and then of cities, especially Paris, where the National Assembly attempted to assert itself by reorganizing the city from sixty districts into forty-eight sections. The reorganization of the city did not alter the city's essential political institution, the Commune, which began acting as the city government shortly after the storming of the Bastille. If anything, the Commune became even more overtly political, and its leaders began to attach themselves to factions within the National Assembly which were often convening in "clubs." The most popular of these was the Society of the Friends of the Constitution, originally consisting of delegates from Brittany but now garnering widespread membership from professionals. Its members soon came, informally, to be known as the Jacobins, from their club meeting house in the Jacobin monastery in the Rue Saint-Honoré. Another potent association was housed at the Cordeliers convent, where the dominant voices were those of the radicals Georges Danton, a lawyer, and the journalist Camille Desmoulins.

Mirabeau was one of the most influential members of the Jacobin club, and he now assumed a crucial role as he worked to balance the interests of the National Assembly with those of the court, dealing, most importantly with the Comte de Lafayette. The one-time favorite of George Washington during the American Revolution now commanded both the royal army and the increasingly powerful National Guard. Although secretly on Louis XVI's payroll as well as that of the Austrian court, Mirabeau was able to maintain sufficient independence to convince Louis to accept the outlines of a constitution in which he and his ministers would serve as the executive branch of government. There would be an independent judiciary and a National Assembly—now to be elected only by "active," or propertied, citizens—to serve as the legislative branch.

Mirabeau did not live to see the completion of his constitution (he died in April 1791), which the king accepted after attempting a poorly planned and worse-executed escape from the virtual captivity in which he was being held. There followed his return to Paris under guard, and an act of stupid violence. Just after the king's return, the National Guard, commanded by Lafayette, opened fire on a mob, killing several people. "The Massacre on the Field of Mars" damaged

Lafayette's credentials as an ally of the revolutionary cause, with which he had hitherto been in high standing.

Having lost a crucial ally in Mirabeau, doubly discredited by his failed flight and the "Massacre," Louis had no choice but to accept the new constitution. The constitution's implementation was announced with great fanfare on September 18, 1791, and the National Assembly disbanded while elections were held for the new Legislative Assembly. In a substantial change from past practice, voting rights were limited to "active citizens," males who paid taxes equivalent to the local wages paid to a worker for three days' work, a provision that disenfranchised about half of the voters under the previous dispensation. Maximilian Robespierre (Figure 4.3), a radical member of the National Assembly from Arras, proposed that no member of the original Assembly could stand for election to the new Legislative Assembly. The motion passed, guaranteeing that the new assembly would be filled with people who had no experience of national politics. Coincidentally, it ensured the assembly would be dominated by members of the politically active clubs.

Perhaps the most significant aspect of the Legislative Assembly, whose 745 members took office on October 1, 1791, was its seating arrangement. It continued the system of the old National Assembly, whereby radical reformers sat on the left, conservatives on the right, and moderates in the center. The legacy of this seating arrangement remains with us today in our distinction between politicians of the "left" and "right."

With an elective presidency that changed every two months, the Legislative Assembly was more of a debating society than a governing body. The politically powerful groups (those meeting in the clubs) influenced the Assembly through members who came to their meetings, and assumed positions in alternative structures. Robespierre, for instance, became the public prosecutor for a few months and developed a strong relationship with units of Paris' National Guard.

Figure 4.3 Maximilian Robespierre. This bust was presented to the Jacobin Club in 1791 by Claude André Deseine. The portrait differs from others of Robespierre in offering an image of a thoughtful, somewhat welcoming individual while catching his fondness for elaborate clothing.

With a relatively ineffective government in place, made all the more so by Louis' constitutional capacity to veto its legislation, the situation facing the reformers became increasingly challenging as 1791 turned into 1792. Already in August 1790, Frederick William, king of Prussia, had issued a statement with Leopold—Holy Roman emperor, emperor of the Austro-Hungarian empire, and brother of the French queen Marie Antoinette—at Pilnitz, saying the rulers of Europe should come to Louis' rescue if he was further threatened. Such statements, reinforced by pronouncements from people who had emigrated that Paris would be subjected to "exemplary, never to be forgotten vengeance," only served to increase the tension, pushing the political situation ever more in the direction of extremists whose agenda included the end of the monarchy. Other members of the Legislative Assembly lost interest in their own institution. By August, only about 300 members were present at a crucial meeting.

In April 1792, France declared war on Austria with Louis' encouragement (he hoped the French would lose). The Austrian invasion of France moved at a deliberate pace, but was initially successful because French armies, riven by factionalism, could not offer a coherent defense. Failure, treachery, and desertion sparked greater suspicion in Paris. An English observer wrote, "the people are all armed and the government is feeble." On August 9, the Paris Commune fell under the control of radical Jacobins led by Danton, Desmoulins, and a popular journalist named Jacques Hébert. The next day, a mob, including many national guardsmen, burst into the Tuileries. The royal guard was slaughtered and the royal family only escaped by throwing itself on the mercy of the Assembly. Louis' reign was suspended by order of the Legislative Assembly on August 13. The Commune took the royal family into custody.

The suspension of the king made the constitution, which required his presence as an executive, unworkable. The Legislative Assembly declared that a new national convention would have to be elected to draft a new constitution, with an electorate now to consist of all male citizens. While awaiting the election, the Assembly essentially turned over power to a small executive committee headed by Danton.

The new elections were carried out in a highly partisan atmosphere, which turned off some voters—especially royalists, who largely boycotted the process. Turnout was roughly half of those eligible. But this time, a body of experienced legislators was returned with a distinctly more centrist outlook than the likes of Robespierre and Danton, who favored the abolition of the monarchy. The leader of this centrist group—currently inclining toward the constitutional monarchy enshrined within the current constitution—which controlled just under 53% of the seats in the assembly was Lazare Carnot. This number, taken with the 21.4% that went to Brissot's openly constitutional monarchist group, reveals the eccentricity of Robespierre's leftist party, which now controlled 26.7% of the seats.

One person who was both interested in the course of the revolution and elected to the National Convention was Thomas Paine. He had moved to France to experience the sort of social revolution that had been ruled out by the Constitution of the United States. As he took his seat in the convention, Paine was aligned with Brissot—another sign of just how far Robespierre's vision of populist control stood outside the mainstream of liberal thought.

The National Convention was governed by rules of the Legislative Assembly, in that the president was elected for a two-week term. Real power would again be determined from outside, again through the clubs, especially the Jacobins.

In the meantime, there was a war going on. The Prussians now joined the Austrians as invaders. Then news came that Lafayette, having failed to lead his army against the revolutionaries in Paris, had deserted to the Austrians. In September, just before the new convention took its seat, rumors of conspiracy led to yet another bloodbath as mobs burst into prisons, slaughtering 1,200 of the incarcerated, most of whom were apolitical.

Then, on September 20, a miracle occurred. The French army won a battle. This happened at Valmy, where the Prussians withdrew after a desultory attack. The French army greeted the event with vigorous singing. The Prussians, beset with logistical problems, returned to Germany.

In the meantime at Paris, details of the king's correspondence with the Austrians became public, pushing the centrist group in the direction of Robespierre's radicals. One of the first acts of the convention would now be the trial of the king. Conveniently, Dr. Joseph-Ignace Guillotin, a former member of the National Assembly, had just then introduced a new machine to the Legislative Assembly. He explained that his decapitation device was in accord with the *Declaration of the Rights of Man,* as it was designed to spare the victim the pain and humiliation of traditional forms of execution. It had come into general use by April.

THE TERROR: 1793–1794

Robespierre now moved to the forefront in Parisian politics. A member of an increasingly influential group on the left wing of the Jacobins, Robespierre was a man with a solid, traditional education, well read in the literature of the time. In light of what was to come, it is somewhat ironic that his first major speech argued against capital punishment. In it, he concluded:

> Free countries are those where the rights of man are respected and where, consequently, the laws are just. Where they offend humanity by an excess of rigor this is a proof that the dignity of man is not known there, that that of the citizen doesn't exist. It is a proof that the legislator is nothing but a master who commands slaves and who pitilessly punishes them according to his whim. I thus conclude that the death penalty should be abrogated.

How different the Robespierre who would say:

> Terror is nothing other than justice, prompt, severe, inflexible; it is therefore an emanation of virtue; it is not so much a special principle as it is a consequence of the general principle of democracy applied to our country's most urgent needs.

The key in getting from early Robespierre to the Robespierre of 1793/4 was the reemergence of theories based upon the state of nature, chiefly the point that nature's enemies were enemies of mankind and deserved no mercy. These theories reinforced Robespierre's own tendencies to distrust intellectuals and exalt the aspect of Rousseau's thought that saw virtue as inherent to common people. Robespierre's addresses to the Jacobins were increasingly accompanied with large claques drawn from his base in the Paris Commune, working-class men—the *sans culottes* ("without breeches," a reference to working-class dress in pantaloons rather than the knee breeches of the wealthy)—whose views were shaped by inflammatory communications transmitted through Marat's *Friend of the People*.

Antisocial though many found him to be, Robespierre had a powerful connection to the working-class base for whom he and his associates claimed the revolution was bringing back the golden age, the original state of nature in classical thought. For Robespierre, the new golden age was connected by the cult of the Supreme Being, which he launched in May 1794, to be France's civic religion. The underlying principle of the cult was that there was a god, but not the god defined by the Church. This god was the embodiment of reason. It was a view similar to the "Creator" whom Jefferson described as having endowed people with inalienable rights, and Rousseau's "divine being." Robespierre's divinity also represented the ideals of virtue that had come to reside in the new French republic.

Those who opposed Robespierre were thus enemies of reason and of nature; they were creatures of past corruption and, as such, should have no rights. Hence the law passed on June 10, 1794 (a few days after an attempt to assassinate Robespierre failed) offered a long list of enemies of the people who, upon being found guilty, were to be executed. Under this law:

> The proof necessary to convict enemies of the people comprises every kind of evidence, whether material or moral, oral or written, which can naturally secure the approval of every just and reasonable mind; the rule of judgments is the conscience of the jurors, enlightened by love of the Fatherland; their aim, the triumph of the Republic and the ruin of its enemies; the procedure, the simple means which good sense dictates in order to arrive at a knowledge of the truth, in the forms determined by law.

It is scarcely surprising that the rate of executions in the two months after the law went into effect would speed up. Nearly 800 people were guillotined in July alone. What Robespierre had convinced himself was a golden age was in fact the state of nature as Hobbes had described it.

The degeneration of the French revolutionary movement from chaotic constitutionalism to mass murder was the direct result of the collapse of the political center under the administration of the National Convention. The convention was rapidly hijacked by extremists whose rhetoric of moral purity was next to impossible to oppose with a rhetoric of common sense. Even earlier supporters of Robespierre who sought to draw back from his increasing extremism found themselves on the chopping block. Thomas Paine nearly shared their fate, as Robespierre found him overly sympathetic to the moderates and had him imprisoned. He remained there for eleven months.

Robespierre's rise to prominence had begun in 1792 as the leader of the left wing of the Jacobin club, where he was closely associated with Marat, Georges Danton, and Louis Antoine de Saint-Just, who had been the youngest member of the National Convention in the autumn of 1792. At the same time, he gradually expanded his connection with the increasingly radical Paris Commune, to whose governing committee he was elected the day after the storming of the royal palace (an event which he helped inspire by spreading false news of an alleged plot for the king's escape). In October, under attack by his rivals as a criminal and a monster, he replied that "only two parties exist in the Republic, the party of good citizens and the party of evil citizens, those who represent the French people and those who think only of their ambition and personal gain." When moderates, associated with Jean Pierre Brissot, leader of the "right wing" faction among the Jacobins, tried to prevent the execution of Louis XVI without asking the opinion of the people of France, Robespierre and his associates demanded the king's immediate execution if he should be found guilty. Saint-Just summed up the theory behind this course of action by arguing that "the sovereignty of Nature is above the sovereignty of the people." Robespierre said that "Louis must die for the fatherland to live," and carried the day with a substantial majority. The king was executed on January 21, 1793.

The vote for the king's execution damaged but did not eliminate the power of the moderate faction. That finally happened between March and May, when Robespierre ensured his rivals took the blame for a botched invasion of the Netherlands (followed by the desertion of the commanding general), which led to the creation of the Committee of Public Safety, dominated by radicals, among whom Carnot, former leader of the centrist block, could now be counted.

The Committee of Public Safety took charge of the war effort in March. At the end of May, the forces of the Paris Commune launched a coup d'état, which shattered the vestigial power of the moderates. Thereafter, the government of France was dominated by roughly 300 radical Jacobin deputies led by Robespierre, whom a former associate would describe as:

> Imperious in his opinions, listening only to himself, intolerant of objections, never pardoning those who wounded his vanity, never admitting mistakes, denouncing irresponsibly while taking offense at the slightest criticism of himself, always glorifying his own achievements and speaking of himself unrestrainedly, while assuming everyone was chiefly preoccupied with and persecuting him.

The Committee of Public Safety, which Robespierre rejoined after a four-month hiatus in membership in July, was now the effective government of France. Brissot, now accused of being a forger and police spy, went to the guillotine after a show trial on October 30; Marie Antionette had been executed on the 19th. The chief prosecutor in this case, as in many others, was a cousin of Desmoulins named Fouquier-Tinville. He would ultimately be responsible for some 2,500 executions during the 14-month reign of terror over which Robespierre presided.

Having disposed of many of their enemies, Robespierre's circle of close associates began to attenuate. Marat had been assassinated in his bath in July 1793. Hébert, Danton, and Desmoulins were decapitated with a number of associates in March 1794. That ultimately proved Robespierre's undoing. If Danton was not safe, no one was. When members of the Committee of Public Safety suspected Robespierre was planning to move against them at the end of July, they struck first. Robespierre was denounced before the convention on July 27. He, Saint-Just, and a number of others went to the guillotine the next day. The majority of his supporters in the Paris Commune followed within a few days, though Fouquier-Tinville, who survived the initial wave of arrests, wouldn't be executed until May 1795. In the course of his trial, which lasted fourty-two days (considerably longer than those which he had conducted before the Revolutionary Tribunal) he argued that he was just following orders, saying, "I had only acted in the spirit of the laws passed by a Convention invested with all powers."

The regime that replaced Robespierre lasted little more than a year, and designed yet another constitution before dissolving itself. The bicameral legislature created under this constitution passed executive power to a small committee, the Directory, one of whose leaders was Carnot. The architect of the regime's increasingly efficient mass armies, Carnot now took a young officer named Napoleon Bonaparte under his wing. That would prove the undoing for any future a non-autocratic government might have had, which wasn't much in any case. The Directory maintained its power for a number of years by suppressing the freedom of the press, executing the occasional extremist, and rigging elections to prevent royalists or more dedicated revolutionaries from forming a majority in the new legislature's lower house. So it was that, in 1799, lacking much in the way of popular support, the Directory fell victim to Napoleon, whose influence had been secured by a series of spectacular military successes, and his ability to hide the evolving catastrophe that would overtake an army he had abandoned in Egypt. Napoleon declared himself first Consul of the Republic, a title evocative of the annual magistrates who had governed ancient Rome into the first century BCE, and then, in a process which also mirrored the development of Rome, proclaimed himself emperor. Looking back again to imperial Rome, he would appoint a legal panel that finally replaced France's feudal traditions with a modern law code, albeit one whose principles could be discovered in the great Roman law codes of the fifth and sixth centuries CE.

THE SOVEREIGN PRINCIPLE

The idea linking the American and French revolutions was the notion that sovereign power derived from the consent of a citizen body. The theory banished political organization based upon the ordinance of a divinely appointed and traditionally sanctioned ruler. Although the theory of representative democracy could not perfectly reflect the will of the "people," however defined, it did allow for the development and actual implementation of concepts of human rights, though these were often slow to follow. Robespierre actually did what the framers of the US Constitution would not do. He obtained passage of a decree abolishing slavery in all French territories (Napoleon reversed this).

The idea that citizen rights were essential to the existence of the nation would prove to be the greatest inheritance of the two revolutions. Granted, this was a principle derived from ancient Greek and Roman political theory and practice, but its articulation by thinkers from Bodin to Rousseau gave it a currency that made it the obvious alternative to royal absolutism. The application of the theory to practice was a truly radical step, driven in both the French and American cases by fundamental institutional failure.

The American colonies were too prosperous to be denied any say in their own governance by the British parliament, which, in so doing, arguably violated principles of British government that had been in play since the overthrow of Charles I. The framers of the constitution were driven by the need to create an alternative to the system of government they had rejected. Their success stemmed from the clear understanding that while the new government had to respond to the principles in defense of which they had rebelled from England, it also had to work. It was not accidental that the framers of the constitution were mostly familiar with each other and had, in many cases, worked together in the past. They also had a leader in George Washington who commanded not only their respect, but the respect of the majority of the people in the country they were hoping to build. It remains an open question whether they failed to deal with the crucial contradiction inherent to their new form of government—the institutionalization of slavery—because they thought the problem would take care of itself, or because the majority didn't believe that all people are, in fact, created equal.

The French Revolution began with a functional breakdown of the royal government, a system long since compromised in the eyes of the king's subjects. The failure of the court to present a coherent plan of action to solve the financial crisis, followed by the failure of the various conventions to devise potentially workable systems of government, enflamed a political climate first dominated by hatred and mistrust directed at the monarch and then at fellow members of the political classes, as well as between classes within French society. Necker's biggest mistake was to think it would be possible to set an agenda for a group that had no practical experience of government. The failure to anticipate what could go wrong virtually ensured the collapse that followed. The failure of the institutional center opened the door to extremist factionalism and, in the end, mass murder. The result of the ensuing chaos was to replace a feudal monarchy with a more modern monarchy that derived power from what the new monarch, Napoleon, asserted was the will of the French people.

Stepping back from the course of events, the truly astonishing and transformational aspect of both the French and American experiences was the role of political theory in shaping political institutions. A state would henceforth not only be defined by shared institutions and beliefs, but also by shared rights and principles. It was not an easy juncture, and no one better described the complexity of basing practice on principle than the sixteenth president of the United States, when he said:

> Four score and seven years ago our fathers brought forth on this continent, a new nation, conceived in Liberty, and dedicated

> to the proposition that all men are created equal. Now we are engaged in a great civil war, testing whether that nation, or any nation so conceived and so dedicated, can long endure.

It was Lincoln's generation that finally confronted the issue that rights for "all men" had actually to be granted to all men. It would not be until fifty-five years after the end of the Civil War that "all men" could be extended to mean "all people," when women were given the right to vote under the 19th Amendment to the United States Constitution.

Chapter 5

Marx and Spencer

TRANSITIONS

Napoleon Bonaparte transformed Europe. He put an end to the Holy Roman Empire, leaving the Austro-Hungarian Empire in its place; his disruption of societies throughout Europe created revolutionary and nationalistic movements everywhere. Within a half-century of Napoleon's final defeat at Waterloo on June 6, 1815, a new Italian nation was in the process of formation, while the German state of Prussia was well on its way to building a "German Empire." France had finally rid itself of the monarchy that was re-imposed after 1815, English parliaments were now elected on the basis of broad-based (albeit all-male) voting, and the Civil War that had torn the United States apart on the issue of slavery was ending. Genuine participatory democracy was now contending with hereditary monarchy on a much more even playing field.

One of the signs that historians don't always make the best prophets is the statement, in the concluding section of the often-brilliant history of Rome written by Theodor Mommsen in the 1850s, that the southern American states would likely win any civil war against the northern. In Mommsen's view, this was due to the bellicose nature of the Southern aristocracy. He had missed the true importance of the other great transformation occurring in his lifetime. This was the industrial revolution, which had now spread from England to the European continent and the northern United States. The rise of capitalism based on factory labor would shape two of the most important ideologies of the second half of the nineteenth century. These were Marxism and "social Darwinism." Marxism is based on the view that the inequalities inherent to capitalism would ultimately give way to collective ownership of property in a future, socialist, state. "Social Darwinism" is a catch-all term encompassing a number of grotesque misinterpretations of evolutionary theory, giving rise to doctrines that included the pseudo-science of eugenics, the notion that it was possible to improve races through selective breeding; the idea that there is a hierarchy of races; and even the idea that war is a biological imperative.

Pseudo-evolutionary theory resonated with Europeans and Americans because of the other driving force of the nineteenth century: the equation of national power with the acquisition of empire.

As social Darwinists sought to assert the racial superiority of Western Europeans and the "threat" posed to "superior" races by "mixing," great changes were taking place around the world. In the decades after the fall of Napoleon, the spirit of nationalism sparked revolutions throughout Central and South America that led to the creation of new nations, independent of Spanish rule. In Asia, Japan and then China began to acquire the tools of the industrial revolution. The emergence of increasingly powerful non-Western societies, which proved the absurdity of social Darwinism, had the effect of enhancing the competitive neuroses of the governing classes of European states. Social Darwinism in its various forms provided the foundation for political conservatism in much the same way as Marxism inspired liberals.

The drive to power through empire, the need to assert national greatness in comparison to neighbors, drove governments to new levels of irrationality which led to the outbreak of war in 1914. The effect of the First World War was to destroy the balance of power that had come into being in the decades after the defeat of Napoleon. The collapse of the political center in Germany and Russia, the two states most responsible for the outbreak of war, opened the door to brutal extremism and the emergence of governments formed on the outer edges of political society. In one case, the government was based on theoretical constructs developed to oppose the dominance of capitalism that were associated with the thought of Karl Marx; in the other, they were directly influenced by social Darwinism. The fact so many people shared thinking that was similar to that of the former motivational speaker who became leader of Germany in 1933, and feared movements derived from Marxist thought, obscured the dangers of Nazism and the monstrosities it could bring with it.

The impact of social Darwinism did not end with Hitler's suicide in 1945. To this day, its various mutations provide the theoretical underpinnings for institutionalized inequity and racism.

THE STUDY OF SOCIETY AS A SCIENCE

Karl Marx's father was a lawyer. The descendant of generations of rabbis, Heinrich Marx converted from his ancestral faith to Lutheranism in order to pursue a successful career. Karl, who was born in 1818, disappointed his father's hope that he would follow him into the practice of law. He wished to become an academic.

After a year of excessive partying in the University at Bonn, Karl was sent by his father to live a more disciplined life at the University of Berlin. Here Karl thrived and soon aspired to receive a doctorate. Karl completed his thesis on atomic theory in classical Greek philosophy at the age of twenty-two.

The German philosophic world into which the young Marx entered was dominated by the thought of Georg Wilhelm Friedrich

Hegel. Hegel's great intellectual achievement was to design a system of "idealist" thought in which apparent conceptual differences—subject and object, for example—could be resolved. That said, Hegel believed reality could only provisionally be distinguished from thought, and that progress occurred through the negation of negation. He claimed the French Revolution illustrated this point because the revolution negated the monarchy, and was in turn negated by the terror that was negated by Napoleon.

Hegel's principle work, *The Phenomenology of Mind,* traced the development of human consciousness through a dialectic process. Thus, to use one of his own examples, if one person enslaves another, the result is an unstable relationship. At first the master would be all powerful, but, as the slave works and develops consciousness, the master becomes dependent on the slave, who then finds freedom. The result of the conflict is therefore the development of the weaker party into the stronger. Implicit in such an analysis is the idea that if the weaker party improves itself, it should become the stronger—a notion that would be very important to Marx as he developed his own theory of historical change.

By the time Marx reached the university, Hegel's thought, while preeminent, was by no means unchallenged (though one suspects Hegel would simply have pointed out that a philosophic movement defined by opposition to his thought simply proved the essential correctness of his approach). It was this group of critics, self-identifying as the "young Hegelians," that Marx found congenial. In time, his most important contribution would be to change the basis of the historical process from Hegelian abstraction or "idealism" to "materialism." Retaining Hegel's basic theory that progress occurs through negations, Marx would ultimately espouse the principle of dialectical materialism, the view that conflict between different interest groups drives progress in the real world, and that new forms of social organization arise from the resolution of contradictions inherent to past societies.

That would all, however, be very much in the future. But even now, Marx's views suggested his sympathies were much too radical for him to be allowed a position within the halls of German academe.

Unable to get an academic job, Marx entered the world of opposition journalism. Still finding his way, the Marx of 1841–1842 remained interested in critics of Hegel's understanding of religion, provided articles on philosophical subjects for a periodical known as the *Rhenish Gazette,* and married his childhood sweetheart, Jenny von Westphalen.

It was also at this time that Marx made the acquaintance of Friederich Engels, heir to an entrepreneur who operated textile factories in both his native land, the Netherlands, and at Salford in England. An unwilling capitalist, the younger Engels first trained as a soldier (it was at the end of his training that Engels had first met Marx). He then began penning critiques of what he termed "liberal" economic theory, that is to say, the theory of Adam Smith and his followers that wages and prices are set by the law of supply and demand, independent of government regulation. Marx saw this theory as justifying the brutal inequality of the early industrial age.

Marx's own contributions to the *Rhenish Gazette* came to include discussions of social and economic issues. One dealt with what he saw as the stupidity of a new censorship law; another one discussed a law forbidding small farmers from clearing brush from the property of large landholders. The result, in January 1843, was that the *Rhenish Gazette* was shut down, and Marx was ordered to leave the country. He and Jenny headed for Paris.

It was in Paris that Marx came seriously into contact with groups espousing views variously termed "socialist" or "communist." In essence, such people rejected the notion that the protection of personal property rights was at the core of human society. They envisioned a return to a state of nature rather like Locke's, in which people lived without hierarchy, holding property in common.

Marx would come to view these early socialists as "utopians," but he adopted their vision of an ideal future as his own. He would later write that the problem with such work was that their authors wrote when the industrial working class (Marx's *proletariat*) was "in a very undeveloped state," but they did contain "a critical element. They attack every principle of existing society." For Marx, the proper aim of the communist would be "abolition of private property."

The direct stimulation Marx could obtain from the Parisian environment was, however, short-lived. At the insistence of the Prussian government, he was exiled to Brussels in 1845.

It was in Brussels, between 1845 and 1847, that the vital components of Marx's political theory took shape. These included the labor theory of value and the view that society was progressing through capitalism to socialism. It is in the manuscript of a book he started with Engels (and never published) that Marx developed the view that humans "distinguish themselves from animals as soon as they begin to produce their means of subsistence, a step which is conditioned by their political organization." By producing their own subsistence, humans produce their material life. "The division of labor inside a nation leads at first to the separation of industrial and commercial from agricultural labor, and hence to the separation of town and country and to the conflict of their interests."

For Marx, societal development begins with "tribal ownership" in hunter gatherer societies, which gradually unlocks "the slavery latent in the family" as populations increase. The next phase of development is "communal ownership" proceeding from the union of several tribes into a city, which is accompanied by slavery. "The class relation between citizens and slaves is now completely developed," because "violence, war, pillage and murder" are the driving forces of history. It was in Rome that private property became significant for the first time, when the "plebeian small peasantry" was transformed into a proletariat. The decline of the Roman Empire destroyed its productive forces, and the conquering Germanic peoples developed a new form of social organization, feudalism. Expressly rejecting Hegelian "idealism," Marx wrote that "in direct contrast to German philosophy which descends from heaven to earth, here we ascend from earth to heaven." His thought proceeds from "real active men, and on the basis of their real-life process." The "multitude of productive forces accessible to men determines the nature of society" and thus the " 'history of humanity' must always be studied and treated in relation to the history of industry and exchange."

As he continued to refine his thinking, Marx concluded that workers sold their "labor power" to capitalists, and, as "the sole source of his livelihood is the sale of his labor power," the laborer is dependent upon the class of capitalists. The production of labor power amounted to "the cost of existence and reproduction of the worker," the price of which was represented by wages. Those wages reflected only a portion of the productive process, which the capitalist could expand by increasing a worker's efficiency without increasing wages. The "surplus value," the value created by the productive process on top of the capitalist's investment in labor and machinery, constituted the profits that enriched the capitalist.

The development of Marx's thought took place against an increasingly widespread background of discontent. Members of the working classes were organizing for improvement in their living conditions. Members of educated classes were impatient with the continued power of what they perceived to be the antiquated structures of traditional governments. In 1847, Engels introduced Marx to a workers' organization in London, the League of the Just, which changed its name, in the course of the summer, to the Communist League. In December, Marx produced a *Manifesto of the Communist Party* (now commonly known as *The Communist Manifesto*). Declaring that "the history of all hitherto existing society is the history of class struggles," Marx outlines the crucial division, as he saw it, between the dominant bourgeois class, which had played its "most revolutionary part" by overthrowing feudalism and was now due to be overthrown by the modern working class, the proletarians. So far, the organization of the proletarians into a class "and consequently into a political party, is continually upset again by the competition between the workers themselves"—but their time is coming, their power advances by stages: "the class struggle nears the decisive hour." He described the relations between the proletariat and bourgeoisie, and then the agenda for the proletarians (the abolition of private property), the differing understandings of socialism in the past, and finally the communists, who "everywhere support every revolutionary movement against the existing social and political order of things."

It was not Marx's intention to provoke an immediate revolution with his *Manifesto*, which, in any event, had at best a few hundred readers in its first edition. Revolution was, however, in the air, and various revolutionary movements broke out in Austria, France, Germany, and Italy.

The French revolutionary movement, largely a working-class revolt, got underway in the summer of 1847, with Engels as a keen observer. In February 1848 the monarchy fell, a new republic was proclaimed, and elections for a new Constituent Assembly were set for April, with all adult French males allowed to vote. The result was very different from what Parisian radicals expected. The government that took office in April was quite conservative. When riots broke out in Paris at the end of June, the government ordered troops into the city to suppress what was essentially a workers' protest. Marx would later write that "the Paris proletariat was forced into the June insurrection by the bourgeoisie. This sufficed to mark its doom." The battles of June constituted "the first great battle" between the two classes that split modern society.

The German movements, which took shape after demonstrations in March 1848, were led by members of the middle class and involved many intellectuals, including the aforementioned Theodor Mommsen and the famous composer Richard Wagner. The movements coalesced around a parliament in Frankfurt which issued a demand for the unification of Germany and the creation of representative government for the new German state (the demands in Vienna were roughly the same, though soon complicated by ethnic differences within the kingdom). It was with this group that Marx, expelled from Belgium in January, took a stand, moving to Cologne after a brief stop in Paris. He accepted an editorial position with the *New Rhenish Gazette*. Engels tried his hand at fomenting armed rebellion. All the German movements were suppressed by royal forces within a few months. In Austria, where the reform effort inspired nationalist revolts against the German monarchy, the situation was more serious, and Hungary briefly asserted independence before the army reestablished central government control. For Marx, the failure of these movements reflected the fact that "the June insurrection raised the self assurance of the bourgeoisie all over the continent, and caused it to league itself openly with the feudal monarchy against the people." The next revolution, the revolution in which the proletariat would take the lead, would change all this: "The revolution is dead!—long live the revolution!"

One result of the suppression of revolutionary movements was that Marx and Engels were *personae non gratae* throughout the European continent. Marx, who tried to return to Paris after the *New Rhenish Gazette* was closed, himself barely escaped being exiled to a malarial swamp in Brittany by removing himself and his family to England. He would remain there for the rest of his life, using the reading room of the British Library as his primary work space. He was supported in his endeavors by a combination of funds from Engels, family inheritances, payment for articles published in Germany, and weekly articles on European events, often connected with labor movements in England, for the *New York Daily Tribune*. The editor of the *Tribune* was the famous abolitionist (and socialist) Horace Greely; the man who drew Marx (see Figure 5.1) to Greeley's attention was Charles Dana, who interrupted his own career as a left-wing journalist to serve as Assistant Secretary of Defense under Abraham Lincoln.

Throughout the 1850s, during which time he was particularly hard up for cash, and the 1860s, when he was better off, Marx developed his economic theories, refining in particular his understanding of "surplus value," succinctly summed up by Engels as follows:

> It was shown that the unpaid laborer is the basis of the capitalist mode of production and of the exploitation of the worker that

Figure 5.1 Karl Marx in his London period.

> occurs under it; that even if the capitalist buys the labor power of his laborer at its full value as a commodity on the market, he yet extracts more value from it than he paid for it; and that in the ultimate analysis this surplus value forms those sums of value from which are heaped up the constantly increasing masses of capital in the hands of the possessing class.

In 1864, Marx accepted an invitation to a meeting of the International Workingman's Association. He was elected to the association's general council and soon became a dominant figure in the movement. Coincidentally, this also brought him a new stream of income, as the British government paid Marx for information on the association's doings. These payments were the result of pressure from Russia, which regarded the association, soon known as the First International, as a potential menace.

Most of the time, however, Marx was reading and writing, laying the foundation for what he saw as his great work, *Capital,* where he hoped to develop a scientific model for the working of the economy. He spent a great deal of time trying to develop mathematical models, and, when he realized that would not happen, he turned to other work in the hard sciences (he was particularly interested in chemistry). Finally, in 1867, Marx published the first volume of his great work. Massively learned, it did not make for light reading and only gradually came to be recognized as a seminal work of economic theory.

Perhaps the most important development in Marx's thought as he grew older was his rejection of the notion that revolution was necessarily violent. In articles for the *Tribune* he had allowed that the British were more suited for reforms than revolution, and that political revolution would be carried out through an election. In the 1870s, he allowed that in America and England (as well, possibly, as Holland) "workers can attain their goal by peaceful means." He looked ahead to a day "when the kings are forced to maintain their power with only moral influence and moral authority," at which point they would form "only a weak obstacle." Likewise, in his vision of a communist society, he would write that "after labor has become not only a means of life but life's prime want"—after productive forces have been increased through the all-round development of the individual—wealth will flow more abundantly for all. When the means of production are the property of the workers, distribution of production will change as well.

It was during the 1870s that Marx achieved his greatest notoriety. Although he never saw himself as the leader of a revolutionary movement, Marx was associated in the popular imagination with leaders of the Paris Commune in 1871. Some of these leaders did in fact communicate with Marx during the few months that elapsed before they were crushed by a French army that proved to be better at slaughtering fellow Frenchmen than fighting Germans. One point Marx made about the efforts of the Commune was that its leaders had not moved as rapidly as they might have to produce a new society.

As the decade progressed, Marx became the spiritual godfather to movements that described themselves as Social Democrats. These political parties claimed to represent the working class against the interests of the capitalist ruling class. As representatives of workers, these parties were thus "socialist" and were "democratic" in so far as they saw themselves in opposition to the establishment. The German Social Democrats, who pointedly excluded Marx from their formative conference in 1875 (he was still regarded as toxic in his native land), soon became a major force in German politics. This was despite the fact Otto von Bismarck, the guiding genius behind the formation of the German Empire, tried to ban them. Russian Social Democrats attracted Marx's special attention, as they made him think it would be possible to pass from an essentially feudal society to communism without an intermediate "bourgeois" revolution. Some Russians found this a very interesting idea. Their influence was, however, still quite limited while Marx was alive and in the years immediately following his death. He would die, at his writing desk, on March 14, 1883, a few months after the death of his beloved wife. He is buried in London's Highgate Cemetery. By the 1890s, he came to be included in lists of England's most influential thinkers.

What Marx envisioned as the ideal communist society is one in which class divisions evaporate when the means of production come under the control of workers. He did not envision a one-party state ratcheted into power by the application of mass terror. That would be the work of an intellectual heir of whom one suspects Marx would have disapproved quite strongly: Vladimir Ilyich Ulyanov (later known as Lenin). When Marx died, Ulyanov was thirteen years old.

Karl Marx was not the only person seeking a totalizing model to explain the human experience in mid–nineteenth century England. But, while Marx studied economics, others looked to biology. The most influential of these people, by mid-century, was Herbert Spencer, a man who went to work as an engineer for railway companies rather than attending a university, but became immensely powerful as a spokesperson for the spirit of his age. One of his specialties was importing scientific theories into the study of human populations. One of the most notable of these was the theory of evolution.

Although nowadays the name of Charles Darwin is most notably associated with the theory of evolution, that only gradually came to be the case in the nineteenth century. And even then, his extremely sophisticated analysis of natural selection was misread against the background of earlier evolutionary theorists. Spencer was, in fact, quite familiar with work that preceded Darwin's four-year cruise as the naturalist on the *HMS Beagle*. Among the authors whose work Spencer found most interesting were Jean Baptiste de Monet, Chevalier de Lamarck (hereafter Lamarck), and Thomas Malthus.

Malthus was a Catholic priest. In 1798, he published *An Essay on the Principle of Population*. Malthus stated that his purpose was to investigate causes impeding human happiness, and then to propose solutions to those problems. The big problem he saw was the "constant tendency in all animated life to increase beyond the nourishment prepared for it." Beginning with the natural world, he noted that "plants and irrational animals . . . are all impelled by a powerful instinct to the increase of their species," which is stemmed by lack of room to provide sufficient nourishment for their offspring. Humans are governed by the same instinct, and their population will naturally double every twenty-five years. Given that the world would not ultimately be able to support this increase, the check on population growth would be famine. What he saw as "voluntary measures" to restrict fertility results in "a promiscuous intercourse to such a degree as to prevent the birth of children 'that' seems to lower, in the most marked manner, the dignity of human nature" with negative impacts on men and women both. That said, the best way to avoid population disaster was sexual restraint.

Malthus lamented the fact that history tended to be written in terms of the governing class, obscuring data about populations and what he asserted was the constant cycle of expansion and contraction. The chief victims in times of contraction were members of the laboring classes, and, while he thought policy could be developed in the modern world to ameliorate the problem of overpopulation, in earlier times (he calls it "savage life"), "vicious habits with respect to the sex [sic] will be more general, the exposing of children more frequent, and both the probability and fatality of wars and epidemics will be considerably greater." He then moves on to a survey of populations across time, drawing upon parish records, when he can, to illustrate the effects of famine. For his readers the distinction between modern and "savage" populations would be of great importance, as would be his rhetoric describing physical degeneracy and the vicious competition for survival.

Lamarck was not directly concerned with human populations. Rather, he produced a massive *Natural History of Invertebrates* between 1815 and 1822. Lamarck's work was regarded as deeply controversial at the time (one contemporary said the appearance of each volume offered additional evidence of Lamarck's madness). Lamarck's particular madness took the form of insistence that life forms developed according to four laws. One was that life increased the body of every creature; another was that need drove the creation of new organs; the third was that organs developed through use; and finally, that parents passed their adaptations on to their offspring. Evolution was therefore the result of individually acquired improvements.

Darwin had familiarized himself with the work of Lamarck and Malthus when he returned in England in 1836, but he also read and was deeply influenced by the work of the geologist Charles Lyell. Beginning with the first volume in what would become his three-volume *Principles of Geology*, Lyell undermined the prevalent view that the Earth was shaped by periodic catastrophes (e.g., Noah's flood) by showing that the Earth changed gradually over time. In his view, "all former changes of the organic and physical creation are referable to one uninterrupted succession of physical events, governed by the laws now in operation." In a world where bishop James Ussher's "demonstration" that the world was created late in the afternoon of October 22, 4004 BCE was taken quite seriously, Lyell's observation that the world was hundreds of millions of years old was a radical statement. As Darwin himself would write, ". . . when Lyell first insisted that long lines of inland cliff had been formed, and great valleys excavated, by the slow action of coast waves. The mind cannot possibly grasp the full meaning of the term of a hundred million years . . . ."

Darwin spent twenty-two years after his return to England laying the groundwork for the publication of *The Origin of Species,* in which he adapted Lamarck's theories of development and announced his affinity to Lyell's principle that conditions operative in the past continued to govern existence, and he found himself unable to "accept any doctrine which implied a breach in the uniform course of natural causation." He also took account of Malthusian theory, as he writes of the tendency of each species to "increase inordinately in number" and that "new and improved varieties will inevitably supplant and exterminate the older, less improved and intermediate varieties."

While Darwin was at work, Herbert Spencer (Figure 5.2) produced his first two books, *Social Statics* and *Principals of Psychology,* in 1851 and 1855, respectively. Spencer's aim in life was to find "for the principles of right and wrong, a scientific basis." In *Social Statics* he took on the dominant "utilitarian" philosophy of the period, based on the principle that actions are right in proportion to the contribution they make to general happiness. He argued that it is very hard to know what is actually beneficial; that, as a result, limited government is the best form of government; and that change is the law of all things. Thus (and here, Lamarck's influence can be felt):

> Strange indeed would it be, if, in the midst of this universal mutation, man alone were constant, unchangeable. But it is not so. He also obeys the law of infinite variation. His circumstances are ever altering; and he is ever adapting himself to them.

Progress in this scheme is a necessity; civilization is a part of nature; "the modifications mankind have undergone, and are still undergoing, result from a law underlying the whole organic creation." Civilization itself is the development of "men's latent capabilities under the action of favorable circumstances." The result of the variability of the human condition is that the human condition cannot be used as a measure for moral truth. Instead, humans should submit to what Spencer calls "Divine Will." The notion of "Divine Will" is reconciled with science in Spencer's thinking because the premises governing morality follow upon each other in the same ways conclusions follow obviously upon themselves in a scientific demonstration.

Spencer's view that mankind is set on an upward trajectory comes through strongly in his second book, on psychology, and in his third, *First Principles of Sociology,* which appeared in 1862. It is in

Figure 5.2 Herbert Spencer in his early years.

this book that Spencer's views on evolution are stated more clearly than before, and were plainly unaltered by the fact Darwin's *The Origin of Species* had appeared three years previously. Unlike Darwin, Spencer was not interested in careful observation of fact; he was interested in the interpretation of "this Law of Progress, in its multiform manifestations, as the necessary consequence of some universal principle." To that end, he now ditched "Divine Will" and the notion of a "Creator" in favor of a universe governed by "the law of the continuous redistribution of matter and motion." These readjustments occur through the process of evolution, and hence "we see at once that there are not several kinds of Evolution having certain traits in common, but one Evolution going on everywhere after the same manner." Indeed, "all these processes by which organisms are re-fitted to their ever-changing environments, must be equilibrations of one kind or other." He further derived from Lyell the notion that no process could be operative in the present that had not also been operative in the past. "Evolution," according to Spencer, "is a change from an indefinite, incoherent homogeneity, to a definite, coherent heterogeneity through continuous differentiations and integrations."

Despite the coincidence in their reading matter on the subject, Spencer's understanding of evolution differed from Darwin's theory of natural selection. Darwin summed up the differences in their approach when he remarked to his friend, J.D. Hooker, "I have almost finished the last number of H. Spencer & am astonished at its prodigality of original thought. But the reflection constantly recurred to me that each suggestion, to be of real value to science, would require years of work."

Spencer himself drew attention to the differences between his approach and Darwin's in *The Principles of Biology*, published in 1868. Here again he explains that evolution must involve recalibration of "the equilibrium" and coins the phrase "survival of the fittest." He goes on to say that "this survival of the fittest, which I have here sought to express in mechanical terms, is what Mr. Darwin has called 'natural selection, or the preservation of favoured races in the struggle for life.'" While expressing a large measure of support for Darwin's work, Spencer slips in a Malthusian discussion of "modifications . . . which cannot have been aided by natural selection," such as "the diminution of the jaws and teeth which characterizes the civilized races, as contrasted with the savage races." Darwin finally adapted the phrase "survival of the fittest" from Spencer, and uses it sixteen times as a gloss for natural selection in the fifth edition of *The Origin of Species*. Darwin wrote that ". . . the expression often used by Mr. Herbert Spencer of the Survival of the Fittest is more accurate, and is sometimes equally convenient."

Although Marx and Darwin moved in very different circles, they were not unaware of each other. Karl Marx initially reacted ambivalently to Darwin's work. At first, he wrote to Engels that *The Origin of Species* "contains the basis in natural history for our view." He then decided that all Darwin had done was to apply Victorian social models to the natural world. By the time he wrote *Capital*, his view had changed again. He quotes Darwin with approval in a couple of places and even sent a copy to him with the inscription that it was from a "sincere admirer." Darwin opened the book, cut the first page, noticed it was in German, and sent Marx a polite note saying he thought that it was a great work but that he was an unworthy recipient, as he knew nothing of political economy.

Spencer's view of Marx (whom he mentions only once) was less collegial. He saw socialism as advocating bureaucracy. He thought that was bad. It is more than a bit ironic that when he died in 1904, he too would be buried in Highgate Cemetery. His grave site is a few hundred feet away from that of Marx. Few now know or care. That cannot be said of Marx's resting place.

GALTON, SOCIAL DARWINISM, AND EUGENICS

When he wasn't talking about equilibrations and such like, Spencer argued that the ideal state stayed out of people's way and allowed them to develop as their talents permitted. As early as *Social Statics,* he had asserted that the "arbitrary rule" of one human over another was becoming a thing of the past. The fact people felt they should be polite to their domestic servants was proof of this point. In his more developed work, *The Principles of Sociology,* he stated simply that "liberalism stands for the freedom of the individual against the state." A liberal regime was thus one which fostered free trade, an end to religious disabilities, freedom of the press, and the absence of foreign entanglements. Furthermore, given that the ultimate goal of social development was moral improvement, government should get out of the way and allow progress to take its course. People would learn to do better by learning from the painful consequences of their own failures.

Spencer's sociological theory was wildly popular in nineteenth-century England, dominated as it was by William Gladstone, whose four terms as prime minister between 1868 and 1892 followed two terms and a dozen years as chancellor of the exchequer between 1852 and 1866. Indeed, the tenets of Gladstonian liberalism, which, in its early form included low taxation, limited government expenditure, self-help, and freedom of choice, aligned very closely with Spencer's sociology. When it ceased to do so, Spencer complained bitterly.

Spencer's commitment to individualism would occasionally lead to confusion (or what, at the end of his life, he claimed was confusion) about what he actually meant by the "survival of the fittest." On the one hand, he said that people who learned from their mistakes would pass on the fruits of their experience to their children, thus making them better members of society. If being ignorant was the same as being wise, then no one would bother to become wise. People learned through suffering. That might be a hopeful message, and one influenced by Lamarck's belief (quite different from the randomness of natural selection) that progress was the result of generations of individually acquired improvements. But there was also an inherently pitiless side to Spencer's thinking, as appears in his statement about the victims of the Irish famine:

> For necessarily families and races whom this increasing difficulty of getting a living which excess of fertility entails, does not stimulate to improvements in production—that is, to greater mental activity—are on the high road to extinction; and must ultimately be supplanted by those whom the pressure does so stimulate. This truth we have recently seen exemplified in Ireland.

The sentiments expressed here repeat those implicit in his treatment of "poor laws" in *Social Statics,* where he said human progress will necessarily result in misery for some, and their misery is the price of progress. The language is that of Malthus, who had written that "poor-laws as a general system are founded on a gross error."

Spencer's version of Malthusian theory is even more pronounced when he discusses race. Malthus had asserted that "savages" who were malnourished tended to physical deformity as a result. Spencer went much further than this when he stated (this is in 1862) that "In proof of the first of these positions [that humans had become more heterogenous] we may cite the fact that in the relative development of the limbs, the civilized man departs more widely from the general type of the placental mammalia, than do the lower human races"—an ongoing process, as "in the Anglo-Americans, [there is] an example of a new variety [race] arising within these few generations."

Spencer united biology with social theory, an approach which Marx rejected despite his interest in Darwin; he had always found

Malthus despicable. Even before *The Origin of Species* appeared, he and Engels had written that hûmans distinguished themselves from animals as soon as they began to produce their own means of subsistence. This distinction between Marx and Spencer would become ever more significant as others leapt upon the Spencerian bandwagon. In the first instance, the most important of these people was Francis Galton, a cousin of Darwin. Galton, a friend of Spencer, took Spencer's theories in support of racial and economic discrimination in a new direction.

Galton's first incursion into the area of population studies was a book entitled *Hereditary Genius*, published in 1869 (Figure 5.3). Galton's argument fell into three parts. In the first, Galton produces a scale of "mental values" to serve as the basis for classifying intelligence ranging from a–g and A–G (lower case is below average in the category, upper case is above average), with "a" at the low end of the scale. He then asserts that "the four mediocre classes a, b, A, B, contain more than four-fifths, and the six mediocre classes more than nineteen-twentieths of the entire population." Mediocrity is also location-specific because "it defines the standard of intellectual power found in most provincial gatherings, because the attractions of a more stirring life in the metropolis and elsewhere, are apt to draw away the abler classes of men, and the silly and the imbecile do not take a part in the gatherings." He then enters into a study of family relationships and finds that people who are regarded as of distinguished intellect are often related to each other, thus proving the proposition of the book's opening sentence that "a man's natural abilities are derived by inheritance, under exactly the same limitations as are the form and physical features of the whole organic world." Finally, he discusses the way the descent of talent can be interrupted, and a consideration of the natural ability of nations (if this sounds a bit like Malthus, it is no accident). His argument will end up with the proposition that Malthus' view about delaying marriage so as

Figure 5.3 Francis Galton in the 1850s.

to prevent overpopulation needed to be amended so the "prudent" should marry young and have more babies, while the "imprudent" should marry later.

When it comes to his analysis of race in the third section of the book, Galton determines that the best "race" was that of the ancient Athenians (by which he means the Athenians of the fifth and fourth centuries BCE). They declined, he thinks, because

> Social morality grew exceedingly lax; marriage became unfashionable, and was avoided; many of the more ambitious and accomplished women were avowed courtesans, and consequently infertile, and the mothers of the incoming population were of a heterogeneous class. In a small sea-bordered country, where

> emigration and immigration are constantly going on, and where the manners are as dissolute as were those of Greece in the period of which I speak, the purity of a race would necessarily fail

These comments, revealing Galton's ignorance of Athenian history, are typical of his sweeping commentary across time and space, to say nothing of his brutal commentary on what he regards as the intellectual properties of Africans. His message to his contemporaries is that the vast expansion of Anglo-Saxons across the planet was creating a need for more ability than was currently available. It "may seem monstrous," he allows, "that the weak should be crowded out by the strong, but it is still more monstrous that the races best fitted to play their part on the stage of life, should be crowded out by the incompetent, the ailing, and the desponding." His work encouraged others, leading to the foundation of a "Neo-Malthusian League" in 1877.

Galton himself returned to the subject in 1889 with a book entitled *Inquiries into Human Faculty*. Here, he introduced the concept of eugenics. He explained that:

> . . . in Greek, *eugenes*, namely, good in stock, hereditarily endowed with noble qualities. This, and the allied words, *eugeneia*, etc., are equally applicable to men, brutes, and plants. We greatly want a brief word to express the science of improving stock, which is by no means confined to questions of judicious mating . . . the word eugenics would sufficiently express the idea."

The sorts of conclusions for which Galton claimed "statistical support" include the notion (stemming from Lamarckian theory) that women display "[c]oyness and caprice . . . together with a cohort of allied weaknesses and petty deceits, that men have come to think venial and even amiable in women, but which they would not tolerate among themselves"; and that "[t]he ideal criminal has marked peculiarities of character: his conscience is almost deficient, his instincts are vicious, his power of self-control is very weak, and he usually detests continuous labour;" and that "[i]t is . . . easy to show that the criminal nature tends to be inherited." He maintained that "[t]he hereditary taint due to the primeval barbarism of our race, and maintained by later influences, will have to be bred out of it before our descendants can rise to the position of free members of an intelligent society." He argued these and other cases while at the same time admitting that there was not enough data to provide a clear path for the "evolution of a higher humanity."

Darwin objected to Galton's line of reasoning. In *The Descent of Man,* published in 1871, Darwin stressed physical adaptations through natural selection that enabled humans to surpass other species—hands, feet, the development of the pelvis to allow for bipedalism—and others that eliminated redundant features such as a tail. He noted that the "slight corporeal strength" of humans was offset by intellectual developments that enabled them to become tool-using. Humans were able to learn the values of cooperation and developed the moral sense upon which societies were founded. Humans could not abandon their sympathy "even at the urging of hard reason, without deterioration in the noblest part of our nature." In private, he wrote to Galton telling him his genetic theories were "utopian." Darwin died seven years before Galton published his *Inquiries.*

Galton, Spencer, Darwin, and those who discussed their work did not form a coherent intellectual movement. Indeed, the term *Darwinisme social* was coined by a French journalist named Émile Gautier in 1880 to characterize what was essentially Spencer's insistence on fierce individualism. It was a Russian who applied the French term to interstate relations in the 1890s. By that time, Spencer's influence was rapidly declining in England, where his opposition to imperialism set him at odds with the prevailing politics of the later

Gladstone administration, and university faculties began to professionalize along lines already established in German universities. Galton's eugenic theories likewise remained outside the mainstream of British thought until the early twentieth century. It would be elsewhere that Spencer or Galton would ultimately have their most profound impact. The United States would prove far more fertile ground for their thoughts, as would Germany and the newly emergent power of Japan.

In the United States, Spencer's sociology aligned closely with the ideology of the "Gilded Age." In a land where the railway baron James J. Hill could exclaim that "the fortunes of railroad companies are determined by the law of the fittest," Spencer developed a powerful following. This included two of the world's wealthiest men, John D. Rockefeller and Andrew Carnegie. When Spencer first visited the United States in 1882, the trip included a meeting with Carnegie in addition to a tour of Niagara Falls and a fancy dinner at Delmonico's in New York. A former Secretary of State took the occasion to proclaim Spencer "the smartest man in the world," a Union general said that his thought could have prevented the Civil War, and the president of Columbia proclaimed him "the most capacious and most powerful intellect of all time." Spencer responded with a somewhat ill-judged speech suggesting that he was not actually all that keen on American capitalism.

Spencer's eccentricity did not dampen American enthusiasm for his thinking. His statement in *Social Statics* that slavery was a feature of a savage stage of existence won him many friends in the northern states, and various public intellectuals twisted his words into something definitely acceptable to an American audience (chiefly this meant making him seem more Christian than his post–*Social Statics* writings were). Popular magazines in the 1870s and 1880s often contained discussions of Spencer's latest writings. Then he was taken up by William Graham Sumner, who held the chair of political economy at Yale.

A former Episcopal minister from New Jersey with minimal formal training in economics, Sumner was a powerful figure on the Yale faculty. He was also possessed of a substantial journalistic presence (he shared Spencer's dislike for "big government"). Like Spencer and Galton, Sumner's theories owed far more to Malthus than to Darwin. His principle argument was that human society was based on the ratio of people to productive land, and that survival stemmed from strength, success from virtue. In a world where the governing class was increasingly removed from physical activity, he recommended that young men find ways to test themselves. A student in his classes was a young man named Walter Camp. He was inspired by Sumner to promote virtue through sport, selecting as the ideal activity a game that was then played only on elite college campuses. That game was football. Walter Camp laid the foundation for collegiate football and ultimately the National Collegiate Athletic Association, which was founded to keep young men from killing each other on football fields.

Sumner was primarily interested in Spencer, but the prominence of his pseudo-biological thought opened the door for eugenic theory, which flourished in the United States in ways that it would not in the United Kingdom. As early as 1877, a man named Richard Dugdale had written a book purporting to study six generations of a family called the Jukes, who were prone to criminal conduct. Such nonsense did not go unopposed. No less a figure than Alexander Graham Bell objected to the notion that humans could be bred like animals. But that alone could not stem the tide. Selective breeding reemerged as a cause (linked with prohibition) in Boston in the 1880s, and remained the cause of various intellectuals until the turn of the century when the work of Gregor Mendel on heredity in plants suddenly began attracting widespread attention. Armed with Mendel's work, eugenicists now claimed that "socially defective" individuals should be prevented from having children.

In 1912, the eugenics movement got a boost when Henry Goddard published *The Kallikak Family,* which purported to show how a man had initiated two biological lines: one from a "respectable" woman whom he had married, the other through a woman he had impregnated in a tavern. The descendants of the "respectable" woman were all themselves respectable; those of the other woman were all criminals. Eugenic theory of this sort reinforced the systemic racism imposed by the Jim Crow laws which undid the protections created by the 14th Amendment to the United States Constitution, guaranteeing due process and equal rights to all citizens.

Books like *The Kallikak Family* inspired efforts to mandate eugenic sterilization of "criminals." Initially, efforts to pass such laws were opposed on religious grounds and thwarted by the courts. There was also a very strong racial aspect to these proposals, whose proponents quoted passages from Galton which painted extremely hostile pictures of African populations. Good people, according to this theory, were white Protestants, and their supremacy needed to be protected. Ivy League schools notoriously restricted non-white and Jewish admissions. New immigration laws were passed, requiring a literacy test in 1917 and, in 1924, restricting immigration from southern Europe, Asia, and by Jews. In 1927, the Supreme Court of the United States upheld a Virginia law passed allowing eugenic sterilization of people judged to be mentally deficient. The victim in this case was a woman named Carrie Buck. She was neither promiscuous, as was charged, nor a "moron," as she was described. Her child was the product of a rape, and she was certainly not of "below average" intelligence as those charged with protecting her welfare claimed. The decision has never been overturned, and some 60,000–70,000 eugenic sterilizations have been carried out into the twenty-first century. Most of the victims have been African American and Latinx.

The triumph of eugenic theory accompanied the emergence of a mythology reshaping the history of the recently concluded Civil War, so that armed rebellion in defense of slavery became a romantic "lost cause" that sought to preserve the true spirit of the Revolution, defined as resistance to centralized government. Confederate generals became heroes, and statues of men who tried to destroy the United States were erected by organizations such as the United Daughters of the Confederacy and United Confederate Veterans Association. Public statues were accompanied by the growth of a violent racist organization, the Ku Klux Klan, mythologized by the 1915 film, *The Birth of the Nation*, a movie which, in turn, encouraged the erection of even more statues of Confederate generals. Contrary to what was said, Spencer's theories would not have prevented the Civil War, but they were, along with Galton's, useful to those who would reverse the result.

One person who found American legislation on eugenics very interesting was the man who became chancellor of Germany in 1933. He said he studied these laws with care. He must have had help—Adolf Hitler didn't read English.

Hitler was not the first German to take an interest in eugenics. Racial theories of various sorts had been common in Germany before the First World War. Among particularly German developments was the notion that the cell could be a metaphor for social and psychological life: popularizers like Ernst Haeckel argued that history and archaeology were extensions of biology (a view which could easily be derived from a casual reading of Galton); others claimed that each race was an organism within the greater organism that was humankind. One prominent thinker stated that "state and nation must develop organically;" another, Friederich Meinecke, a leader of the German historical profession who became famous for a book on the history of nationalism, was anti-Semitic and violently anti-Slavic. He claimed Slavs represented a threat to the German race. He was not alone. It was commonplace to assert that Slavs had required "civilizing" by Germans since the Middle Ages. Prior to 1914, Germans could assert both that Russia's defeat by the Japanese in the Russo-Japanese War of 1904–1905 was a sign of the fact that Russia was in a state of "Asiatic barbarism" and that "Pan-Slavism," the doctrine that all Slavic peoples had common interests, lay at the root of Russia's problems. This doctrine, which had originally developed as a reaction against German nationalism in the Austro-Hungarian Empire, was widely popular in Russia, where public opinion favored the notion that Russia was the natural guardian of Slavic peoples everywhere. Germans regarded Pan-Slavism as a "thoroughly hostile instinct." Educated German opinion also held that Russian hostility to the Austro-Hungarian Empire was the result of the clash between the Slavic and German races.

Not all social-Darwinian accounts of contemporary politics had to be tinged by the overt racism of Pan-Germanism and Pan-Slavism. In 1911, a member of the German general staff, Friederich von Bernhardi, wrote that war would be a biological necessity for the German people. His book, translated into English in 1914, was entitled *Germany and the Next War*. In von Bernhardi's view, if Germany was to achieve its destiny to become the world's greatest power, it would have to go to war with the United Kingdom. He was not alone in believing that war was the ultimate test of a nation's psychological resolve and discipline, the test that would establish its rightful place in the world.

On a more academic level, eugenic and social Darwinist notions could be projected into the distant past to provide "lessons" for the present. Thus, for instance, Otto Seeck, a historian of the Roman world, claimed the Roman Empire had been fatally weakened because the "Italian" stock that had acquired the empire had degenerated through intermarriage with people from the eastern Mediterranean. It then fell victim to German immigrants, a superior people. No professional historian would take Seeck's explanation of the failure of the

Roman Empire seriously today. But bad history, like bad science, can take on a life of its own. Seeck's theory was revived in 2016 by the president of the Netherlands with reference to the European Union's response to mass migration from Africa and the Middle East.

Good history also has its fans. Seeck was a student of Theodor Mommsen, whom we have met at various points in this chapter. Mommsen very much disapproved of Seeck's interest in eugenics and fought against the creep of social Darwinism into the University of Berlin. In 1902, he was awarded the Nobel Prize for literature. The person who finished second that year was Herbert Spencer.

THE TSAR OF ALL THE RUSSIAS

In July 1914 Tsar Nicholas II of Russia faced a dilemma, largely of his own making. Franz-Ferdinand, heir apparent to the throne of the Austro-Hungarian Empire, had been murdered by a Serbian terrorist on June 28. The Austro-Hungarian regime was preparing to avenge itself upon the government of Serbia, which it accused, with some justification, of having masterminded the assassination. It was generally believed that the Austro-Hungarian army would crush the Serbian. That would be an embarrassment to Russia, Serbia's most prominent ally, and alienate the Pan-Slavic public.

The tsarist regime that was going to start the First World War was having trouble working with the modern world. The problem was not that the system of government was autocratic—the twentieth century was going to see a great deal of autocratic government—the problem was that it was an old-fashioned autocracy which depended upon the stability of relationships that were centuries old. It didn't help that Tsar Nicholas himself was a man of limited intellectual attainment, and that the principle for which he lived was the preservation of the traditional regime which he would pass to his heirs.

He even claimed that he had sworn to uphold the tradition of tsarist autocracy. (In point of fact he hadn't actually sworn such an oath in so many words, but his wife, Alexandra, liked to tell him that he had.)

Most of the institutions upon which the tsarist autocracy had long been based were in a state of flux as the economic conditions of Russia changed in the decades before the war. Indeed, perhaps the only one of the state's five fundamental institutions that was functioning properly was the interior ministry, which ran the highly proactive secret police. The other four groups were the state bureaucracy, the army, the landholding gentry, and the church.

The state bureaucracy was not a major factor by the time Nicholas II had taken the throne. It was too small and largely non-existent in many regions of the country. In areas where the state bureaucracy was dysfunctional, power had devolved upon a combination of local elective groups, zemstvo, and traditional peasant cooperatives, which ran the villages where property was still largely held in common.

The traditional landholding gentry, which had primarily been based on estates worked by serfs, had also fallen on hard times. After Russia's defeat in the Crimean War (1853–56), Tsar Alexander II had emancipated the serfs. This was in 1861. At that point, the gentry had already been in financial trouble, which meant it had been in no position to resist the decree. They were somewhat mollified by "redemption payments" from their former serfs for the land they were given upon emancipation, and the right to continue to charge for the use of "common lands" such as forests, roads, and rivers.

The result of the emancipation was fully satisfactory to neither the peasantry nor the gentry. The peasants wished to take over the common lands and to end redemption payments. Members of the gentry found that they could no longer support their traditional lifestyles—many were by this point little better off than rich peasants—and moved to cities. By the time war threatened in 1914, less than half of the gentry still possessed a rural base.

Many members of the gentry joined the developing professional classes in the cities and participated in the "zemstvo movement." Zemstva (the plural of zemstvo) were created by Alexander II in 1864. They were elected from five classes (large landholders, small landholders, rich townspeople, less well-off townspeople, and peasants). Their primary responsibilities involved education and economic development; their existence had given people a taste for non-autocratic administration. By the beginning of the twentieth century, they functioned in all provinces of the Russian Empire other than those in the west, where the majority non-Russian populations of Ukrainians, Poles, Jews, and Germans were regarded as suspect by the tsarist regime.

Of the remaining branches of tsarist power, the agents of the Interior Ministry were widely loathed, the army was inadequate, and the essentially medieval Church had little sway among the educated classes. These educated classes were expanding as Russia began to join the industrial revolution in the second half of the nineteenth century. New industries required people with technical skills, and the Russian educational system began to provide them. Enrollment in schools increased by 400% between 1880 and 1911, while the literacy rate for the population as a whole increased to nearly 30% (albeit far more so in cities, where the literacy rate was 45%, as opposed to the vastly more populous countryside, where the rate was just over 17%).

Unfortunately for the tsarist regime, people encountering the world of Western ideas soon became hostile to the autocracy. Universities became hotbeds of anti-regime thought and launching pads for various radical groups. One member of an extremist group, a group that held that regime change could be provoked by acts of terrorism (a peculiarly Russian belief at the time), was Aleksandr Ulyanov. He was hanged on May 20, 1887 for his role in a failed conspiracy to assassinate the tsar. That would cause some difficulty for his younger brother, Vladimir.

Figure 5.4 Vladimir Ilyich Ulyanov Lenin in 1920. Vladimir Ulyanov adopted the name Lenin, possibly derived from the Siberian river, Lena. He is here shown with the implacable image he favored at the height of his power.

The Ulyanov boys were sons of a local school inspector, and, at the time of his brother's execution, Vladimir (Figure 5.4), who had excelled as a student of classical languages, had earned a place at Kazan University. Already suspect to the regime, he was soon expelled for subversive behavior. It was only with a great deal of help from his mother, and many apologetic letters on his own part, that Vladimir Ulyanov was readmitted to Kazan University a year after his expulsion and obtained his law degree.

After a few years of country living, and continued contemplation of the works of Karl Marx and other modern thinkers whose work he had encountered at Kazan, Ulyanov moved to St. Petersburg. Now thinking, as result of his reading, that change in Russia would stem not from terrorism but rather from the fulfillment of the historical process which would lead to a proletarian revolution of Marxist theory, Ulyanov became involved with the Russian Social Democratic Labor Party, organizing workers in the belief that they would make common cause against the "autocracy" with the "liberal bourgeoisie." Soon after his marriage to fellow radical Nadezhda Krupskaya in 1897, he and she were exiled to a reasonably salubrious part of Siberia for organizing a strike.

Released in 1900, the revolutionary couple moved abroad to continue their participation in radical politics, joining the Liberation of Labor, a Swiss group connected with the Russian Social Democrats. Ulyanov took up an editorial position in its Russian-language paper *Iskra* (*Spark*). At this point his study of the Russian labor movement convinced him that, if left to its own devices, it would fall short of forming the revolutionary proletariat required by Marxist theory for the establishment of a socialist society. What he saw (correctly) was that a labor movement tended to acquiesce with capitalism if it was granted a greater share of the profits.

Having spotted a legitimate problem with conventional theory, Ulyanov now began gaining a reputation as a major theorist in his own right. In 1902 he published a pamphlet, using his new pseudonym, Lenin, entitled *What is to be Done*. In this work he developed his perception about labor movements to argue the autocracy could only be overthrown by a group of professional revolutionaries who would inject socialism and revolutionary fervor into the workers. In his view, "the theoretical doctrine of Social-Democracy arose quite independently of the spontaneous growth of the working-class movement, it arose as a natural and inevitable outcome of the development of ideas among the revolutionary socialist intelligentsia." It was for this reason that "class political consciousness can be brought to the workers only from without." The way forward was through an organization of revolutionaries "who make revolutionary activity their profession."[1]

Following the publication of *What is to be Done,* Lenin practiced what he had preached by seizing control of the extremist wing of the socialist movement at the Second Congress of the Russian Social Democratic Labor Party, held in 1903 in Brussels, calling his supporters the Bolsheviks, or "majoritarians." The losing faction came to be known as Mensheviks or "minoritarians." Given that there were all of fifty delegates in attendance, this might not seem like a particularly earth-shattering event. The fact it would become one was largely Nicholas' fault.

Lenin's experience was at the extreme end of the spectrum, but most well-educated people, who were not recruited into government, remained contemptuous of the regime. The result of this situation was that the state was effectively at war with what became known as Russia's liberal intelligentsia, as well as the radical fringe. The increasing success of Russian industrialization—industrial productivity increased by an astounding 129% during the 1890s—also meant there was an expanding class of factory workers. For these people, the result of their labors was not an improvement in their living conditions, which quite often remained squalid. As late as 1920, 42% of homes in St. Petersburg had no plumbing.

TEN YEARS OF TENSION AND TWO YEARS OF DISASTER

The collapse of the traditional regime began in 1904/5. The emergent empire of Japan launched a surprise attack on Russian holdings in northern China and Korea in 1904. The subsequent failures of

1. The parallel between Lenin's theory and the model of change presented thoughout this book is fortuitous.

the army led to rallies in the capital of St. Petersburg, culminating, on January 9, 1905, in a mass demonstration upon which the army opened fire, killing hundreds. As news from the front went from bad to worse (including the destruction of the Russian Baltic fleet, which had been sent around the world to join the fight), there were strikes, mutinies, peasant revolts, and further mass shootings.

Various groups emerged to put pressure on the government. Zemstva members formed a zemstvo congress; socialist radicals, meeting initially in Paris, formed a Union of Liberation demanding a constitutional monarchy, the right of self-determination for non-Russian minorities, and the right to vote for all (male) Russians. In May, the even more radical university students formed a Union of Unions, largely representing white-collar workers and, like the Union of Liberation, demanded expanded voting rights; unlike the liberals, this more radical group demanded a parliamentary democracy and the abolition of private property.

The major difference between the "liberal" and "radical" wings of the Russian opposition was that the former looked to reform the tsarist government, the latter looked to destroy it. Leaders of the liberals like Peter Miliukov and Peter Stuve saw themselves as people who could modernize the tsarist regime. What they would not countenance was an appeal to terrorism to bring the regime down. On this point they differed from the radicals, who were well connected with Russia's vigorous terrorist organizations. This is where Lenin's critique of social democratic movements is particularly important, for, in *What is to be Done*, he wrote:

> He who does not close his eyes cannot fail to see that the new "critical" trend in Socialism is nothing more nor less than a variety of opportunism . . . the freedom to convert Social-Democracy into a democratic party of reform, the freedom to introduce bourgeois ideas and bourgeois elements into Socialism.

Further, he had written of his bitterness toward Social Democrats who disgraced the calling of a revolutionary. This was shared by others who saw themselves as revolutionaries in his terms, and who saw themselves as shaping the workers into a revolutionary force. They became stronger than the Social Democrats in the streets precisely because they developed better relationships with the workers, whose views they saw it as their purpose to reform. So it was that when, in October, workers in St. Petersburg organized the first elective committee, or Soviet, to coordinate anti-government activities, one of their leaders was a radical Menshevik named Leon Trotsky.

Faced with war in the east and riots in the streets, Tsar Nicholas bowed to pressure from his ministers, announcing what appeared to be a comprehensive program of political reform. This was on October 17; the tsar's decree included a guarantee of civil rights for Russia's people and the creation of a national assembly, or Duma, which would have the power to approve legislation.

In some quarters the October decree garnered approval. Elsewhere it created even more chaos. In rural Russia, peasants saw that strikes were going unpunished in the cities. They decided they needed to get in on the action, taking what they saw as justice into their own hands, which meant trying to force landlords to sell up and move away. This violence, largely directed against property because the landlords were absent anyway, was ultimately met with extreme violence, directed against humans, by the state.

As violence spread in the countryside, the tsar undermined whatever goodwill (there wasn't a lot of it) had accrued as a result of his decision to summon the Duma. A logical conclusion that could have been drawn from the October decree was that Nicholas was creating a constitutional monarchy. That was not how Nicholas understood himself. He saw the Duma as a consultative assembly to his continuingly autocratic self.

The result of what appeared to members of the liberal intelligentsia as the tsar's prevarication was that the divisions continued to fester. The first Duma, elected in 1906, was almost immediately dissolved for being too liberal. A second Duma, also elected in 1906, was also dissolved for excessive liberalism (it was chock full of socialists). When a Duma that was marginally acceptable to the tsar took office in 1907, the leading parties were conservative. These parties were dominated by landowners with close connections to zemstva. They believed private property rights provided the foundation for modern civilization and were strongly nationalistic, wishing to see Russia as a dominant power in the Middle East and the chief protector of Slavs everywhere. They tended to be deeply suspicious of the Germans, whose assumption of racial superiority they deeply resented. The most liberal group in the Duma (aside from a few socialists) were people linked to urban and industrial groups. The ministers who formed the tsar's effective government met with the Duma, and while there was a chair who ran the Duma's meetings, Nicholas rather than the Duma appointed the ministers.

The complicated politics of the earlier Dumas had left severe splits pretty much everywhere. Left-wing parties loathed the tsar, whom they felt had betrayed them by not living up to the promise of a constitutional monarchy. Socialists loathed the liberals, who, they thought, had betrayed them by dealing with the tsar. They also tended to hate each other. In 1912, eighteen Bolsheviks, meeting in Prague, formally split from the Social Democrats. The most important things liberals and radicals had in common were the beliefs that workers could overthrow the state and that the tsar was evil. Just for good measure, the court continued to loathe the professional classes.

Beyond the walls of the Duma, the peasants, whose hopes for massive land distribution had been enflamed by the revolution of 1905, saw their hopes quashed by the conservatives, and workers did not feel they had gained much of anything. Conservatives, who regarded Russia's Jews as potential revolutionaries, took advantage of their power to foment mass murders of the Jewish population (pogroms). The depth of these divisions was lost on Nicholas as he contemplated leading Russia to war.

Although Russia's military had been modernizing at a good clip in the wake of the catastrophe of 1904/5, it was still far from complete functionality in the event of a major war. This was not lost on the government, for when tensions erupted with Turkey over the appointment of a German general to the senior post in the Turkish army, Russia had contemplated war. At that point, Peter Durnovo, a former interior minister, had published a memorandum in which he pointed out that:

> The quantity of our heavy artillery . . . is far too inadequate, and there are few machine guns. The organization of our fortress defenses has scarcely been started. . . . The network of strategic railways is inadequate. The railways possess a rolling stock sufficient, perhaps, for normal traffic, but not commensurate with the colossal demands which will be made upon them in the event of a European war. Lastly, it should not be forgotten that the impending war will be fought among the most civilized and technically most advanced nations. Every previous war has invariably been followed by something new in the realm of military technique, but the technical backwardness of our industries does not create favorable conditions for our adoption of the new inventions.

On all points he was correct, as he was when he predicted that the government would be blamed for disasters and that:

> In the legislative institutions a bitter campaign against the Government will begin, followed by revolutionary agitations

> throughout the country, with Socialist slogans, capable of arousing and rallying the masses, beginning with the division of the land and succeeded by a division of all valuables and property. The defeated army, having lost its most dependable men, and carried away by the tide of primitive peasant desire for land, will find itself too demoralized to serve as a bulwark of law and order. The legislative institutions and the intellectual opposition parties, lacking real authority in the eyes of the people, will be powerless to stem the popular tide, aroused by themselves, and Russia will be flung into hopeless anarchy, the issue of which cannot be foreseen.

Durnovo died in 1915 just as what he wrote here was proving to be completely correct. For, even though a settlement was reached with Turkey, the salient facts he outlined were shoved under the carpet when tensions erupted in the Balkans following the assassination of Franz Ferdinand.

Russia's government was not alone in behaving irrationally in the summer of 1914. The Austro-Hungarian regime was given to magical thinking, as was the government of Serbia. But it was Russia's government that started the war despite the deficiencies that had been noted earlier that year. The German government, which had encouraged the extremely aggressive Austro-Hungarian response to the assassination, was awash in Social Darwinist fantasies about the greatness of imperial states. This made it possible for the chief of the German general staff to assert that it was better to start a "preventative" war (his term for a war that would begin with the all-out violation of the sovereignty of a peaceful state) sooner rather than later, because Russia would complete rearming within two or three years. That would make the "inevitable" two-front war between the Germans, the French, and the Russians much more dangerous. Also, there was a well-developed tendency in German thought to regard extreme violence as logical when deployed in the interests of the state. Civilians, in the German view, were no more protected by international conventions than were states, if "reality" dictated otherwise in the event of war. Hence the German Chancellor Theobald von Bethmann Hollweg's genuine surprise when England responded to the invasion of Belgium by declaring war, and his infamous comment that he could not believe Britain would enter the war because of a "scrap of paper" (the treaty obligating it to come to Belgium's defense in the event of an invasion).

The one thing all the governments had in common, hastening into the war that would destroy them, was the belief the war would be short. They had no plan for what would happen if an offensive through Belgium, depending in part on the physical conditioning of reservists (not good), should grind to a halt at the Marne; or if the aggressive offensive into the Rhineland, lacking proper artillery support, should be blown to smithereens. On all sides, long-standing expectations of a future "great war" that would reshape the balance of power, linked with "all or nothing" military planning, had created a situation in which freedom of diplomatic maneuver was restricted.

Brutal as the losses were on the western front, the biggest disasters were those suffered by the Russians in the east. Offensives against the pitifully equipped and worse led Austrian army in what is now western Ukraine were successful, but two armies, sent into Germany on an accelerated schedule per France's request, were annihilated. The year 1915 was even worse for the Russians. While the war in France and Belgium sputtered along as a bloody, mud-soaked stalemate, the German army launched an all-out offensive into Poland. Russian armies, which had not been adequately equipped—men were routinely sent into the front lines without rifles—were pummeled. Demoralized soldiers surrendered en masse. Around a million Russians became prisoners of war, more than the number of soldiers still under arms in September 1915. When the Germans ended their offensive, they had occupied more than 10% of Russia's prewar territory.

Nicholas' response to the disasters of 1914 and 1915 completed the destruction of the monarchy's vestigial authority. In January 1915, Nicholas prorogued the Duma for seven months. When it reconvened in July, with the army in full retreat, liberals and conservatives joined forces in attacking the conduct of the war. A leading figure was now a man named Alexander Kerensky; a leading topic of discussion was the need for the Duma to take charge of affairs from the now-discredited bureaucracy. There was no actual plan for this, but the tsar didn't like all the negativity. He prorogued the Duma again in August. This made the creation of a unity government that would include himself an impossibility. Then, also in August, Nicholas sacked his uncle, also Nicholas, the titular commander of the army since the outbreak of the war. Nicholas assumed command, which meant all future failures would be blamed on him, and disasters would happen even though Mikhail Alekseev, the new chief of staff, was actually a competent person.

The previous war minister, Sukhomlinov, was another casualty of the 1915 campaign. His replacement, a man named Polivanov, was stunningly competent. Joining with leaders of industry he solved the production problems that had disarmed the army in the previous two years. He was so good at his job that Nicholas sacked him in March of 1916 (he would later assist Leon Trotsky in creating the Red Army). Otherwise, Nicholas was visibly under the influence of his wife Alexandra, whose loyalty was suspect since she was German by birth; and aristocratic society was appalled by the influence exercised through Alexandra on Nicholas by a man named Rasputin. Rasputin had gained influence with Alexandra by claiming that he could cure the hemophiliac crown prince (in fact all he did was hypnotize him from time to time). Rasputin had advised Nicholas not to go to war, but now that the war was on, he supported Alexandra in her efforts to toughen Nicholas' resolve.

The war went better for Russia in 1916. Polivanov's reforms meant soldiers went into battle with weapons and the artillery had shells. The Germans were largely distracted by their offensive against the French fortress city of Verdun and by the British offensive on the Somme. Russian armies could thus turn on the hapless Austrians for much of the summer, which they did. The Germans only intervened to halt Russian progress at the summer's end. By that time there were new problems. Chief among them was the food supply of major cities.

The peacetime rail system was geared to shipping grain south to the Black Sea for export. It could not be easily redesigned to ship the large quantities of food needed by the army and urban populations largely located in the north. The transport issue was further complicated by bureaucratic issues. The large estates which provided most of the surplus for the market were hard hit by the recruitment of their workers into the army; common peasants, who were less well connected with the export market, found little reason to sell their grain when inflation seemed to be pushing their potential returns higher. They might as well hold on to their grain, and there wasn't much for them to do with whatever money they might get. With production shifted to the war effort, there were few consumer goods on the market. Also, the production of anything was hampered by problems in delivering coal to major cities, where there were factories to be run and buildings to be heated. By the end of 1916, Moscow and Petrograd were getting only a third of the food they required. The Duma, which was still meeting in December, expressed ever-increasing frustration with the regime. And, on the evening of December 16–17, right-wing aristocrats assassinated Rasputin. The assassins thought they could save Russia by removing his banal influence from the court that even they no longer trusted. It made no difference.

More serious were the morale issues afflicting the mass of the population. Peasants recruited into the new army and sent into rear areas for training were worse off than peasants who stayed at home with their food. Also, with much of the professional officer corps either dead, captive, or at the front, the process of re-professionalizing the reservists who made up the bulk of new draftees fell into the hands of officers who were badly outnumbered even when, as some were, they were competent. By the winter of 1916/17, Petrograd (as St. Petersburg was now called) was filled with hungry, unhappy soldiers. There were more than 150,000 men stationed there in barracks built for 20,000. To make matters worse, the weather turned really foul. Such was the situation in February 1917, when the Duma was scheduled to reconvene. Durnovo's dire predictions were about to be realized.

LENIN TRIUMPHANT

February 14, 1917 was the beginning of the end for Tsar Nicholas. The date in the rest of the world was February 27; the tsarist refusal to adopt the Gregorian calendar was emblematic of the regime's problem with modernity.

On February 14, 90,000 workers marched through Petrograd's streets protesting shortages. On the 20th, rumors spread that rationing would be introduced. On the same day the tsar decided it would be a good idea to leave Petrograd to visit the general staff at Mogilev, 500 miles to the south, in what is now Belarus. On February 24, there were further demonstrations, with crowds numbering into the hundreds of thousands. Nicholas sent orders (against the advice of Alexandra, who had stayed in Petrograd and was the object of vigorous protest) for the garrison to shoot protestors. This they did on the 26th, killing about forty people.

The revolution began in earnest on February 27 (March 12). Petrograd's garrison, regretting its actions of the day before, mutinied. At the same time, socialist agitators summoned workers to elect a new Soviet. The Duma, led by a "provisional committee," declared it would be forming a government of its own. The result was that Petrograd now had two self-authorized administrations. In the course of the next eight months, they would evolve into a two-headed government. The conversations between these two heads were usually strained.

On the night of the 27th, Nicholas' prime minister sent him a telegram recommending a new government be formed with ministers chosen by the Duma (precisely the step that had already been initiated by the Duma). The tsar wrote back ordering the Duma's dissolution and decided to return to Petrograd, taking a detour through Moscow so he would not slow the advance of troops he had dispatched to restore order in the capital. He would not make it home as tsar.

On the evening of March 1–2 (March 14–15), the Provisional Committee of the Duma and the Petrograd Soviet reached an agreement for a government that would last until a Constituent Assembly could be called to shape a new constitution (the terminology was self-consciously borrowed from the French Revolution). On March 2, the Duma committee was officially proclaimed the "Provisional Government." It was headed by Prince Lvov; the old liberal Paul Miliukov served as Foreign Minister, and the radical Alexander Kerensky became Justice Minister. The previous evening, Nicholas' train reached Pskov, a town about 250 miles south of Petrograd. There he met the commander of the northern army group, who told him that the path ahead was blocked by hostile soldiers and urged him to accept the Duma cabinet. Then there arrived a message from chief of staff Alekseev, saying there was no way to halt the revolution in the capital. The chair of the Duma sent a message telling

Nicholas that he might want to consider abdication. After a sleepless night, Nicholas was confronted by a fresh message from Alekseev and a personal appeal from his uncle Nicholas, who he had fired as commander of the army, and some other generals. They all pressed him to resign. Alone and exhausted, Nicholas agreed. He passed the throne to his brother Mikhail, who promptly refused to accept it. The events of March 2–3 (15–16) marked the formal end of the Romanov dynasty.

The government of Russia had fallen apart in the face of a poorly organized military coup d'etat, riots in the capital, and a rebellious legislature with no formal power. These groups were neither coordinated nor individually capable of running the country. Worse was yet to come.

Arthur Zimmermann was a German diplomat who liked interfering in other countries' affairs. He is perhaps most famous for the ludicrous telegram he sent to Mexico, urging the Mexican government to seize the territories forming part of the southern border of the United States. That helped precipitate the United States' entry into the Great War. Equally destructive was what he did with information passed upstream by a Marxist businessman, active in Zurich, that Vladimir Lenin was living there. Zimmermann arranged for Lenin's return along with that of a number of associates, including both his wife and his mistress, to Russia. On March 24 the train left Zurich for the port of Sassnitz where the travelers took ship for Sweden and a new train that would take them through Helsinki to Petrograd. In the evening of April 3, the train reached Petrograd's Finland Station. Lenin greeted the Bolsheviks and other socialists who gathered to meet him with a speech attacking the Provisional Government.

Before Lenin's return, Bolshevik leaders, chiefly Lev Kamenev (Trotsky's brother-in-law) and Josef Stalin (a bank robber), both of whom had returned from Siberia, had looked to cooperate with the Provisional Government and reunite with other socialist parties.

Lenin put a stop to that. Three weeks after his arrival, the Bolsheviks were organizing riots against the regime and recruiting "Red Guards," thugs to attack their enemies. In May, Leon Trotsky, who had been in New York when the February revolution broke out, arrived back in Russia. Reconciling earlier differences, Trotsky would become Lenin's invaluable agent, without whom the Bolshevik revolution could not have succeeded. British intelligence had briefly detained Trotsky in Canada, then let him continue his journey at Miliukov's request. That was a huge error on the part of the Provisional Government.

Lenin's plan was to use the Petrograd Soviet as a base from which to pressure the Provisional Government into collapse. Trotsky would be the point person for putting the plan into action. In plotting his revolution, Lenin was aided by a series of errors on the Provisional Government's part (aside from not shooting him on sight).

The Provisional Government was an unelected entity whose members had taken over from the tsar. Unlike members of the Central Committee of the Petrograd Soviet, who were elected to their positions, the leadership of the Provisional Government could not claim any sort of popular mandate. As the Provisional Government delayed seeking a mandate, soviets were springing up all over Russia—seven hundred by the spring of 1917, and labor unrest increased. The Provisional Government's first error was therefore the failure to immediately seek a popular mandate. The Constituent Assembly was pushed off until January. The Provisional Government's second error, arguably as serious as the failure to seek a mandate, was agreeing to General Order Number 1. This was issued on March 1 (13) by the governing committee of the Petrograd Soviet, addressed to the garrison of Petrograd. Among other things, it required the election of soldiers' committees which would provide members for the Soviet; that the garrison was politically subject to the Soviet; that the Soviet could countermand orders of the Provisional Government; that off-duty soldiers should have the same rights as civilians; and that officers, who were not to be rude to their men, were no longer to be addressed by their titles. General Order Number 1 undermined the discipline of the whole army and deprived the Provisional Government of the ability to control the capital. General Order Number 1 also made the continued prosecution of the war effort deeply problematic. The third error was not ending the war as soon as possible. Instead of ending the war, the Provisional Government insisted it would honor existing agreements with the allies.

It was in the context of the continuing war that Kerensky's tendency to dress in a military uniform and claim that he would be the Carnot of the new regime caused concern. At a time when people across the political spectrum were contemplating parallels between what had happened in France during the 1790s and what they were experiencing since the overthrow of the tsar, there was concern that what Kerensky really wanted to be was not the architect of a people's army, as Carnot had been, but rather a new Napoleon.

The Provisional Government rapidly lost credit. The continuation of the war, on the grounds that it was necessary for the nation's honor, alienated the garrison in Petrograd, which remained the ultimate power broker. But all was not yet lost. In June and July, the garrison was unready to abandon the Provisional Government for the unknown quantity of the Bolsheviks. The failure of a riot, which he inspired, to gain traction with the garrison caused Lenin to flee to Finland. Kerensky, proactive for once, saw to it that "details" of massive payments from the German government to the Bolsheviks were published in Petrograd newspapers. Lenin would not return to Russia until October, and then it would be in disguise.

Working from his Finnish base, Lenin instructed his followers to issue a simple message: "Bread, Peace, Land." Kerensky, who became Russia's virtual dictator after the failure of the Bolshevik agitation in July, meanwhile, alienated whatever support he might have expected from the army outside of Petrograd. In August he suppressed a nascent coup being planned by General Lavr Kornilov to suppress the Bolsheviks. In doing so, Kerensky alienated the military's leadership and was left pinning his hopes on the elections to the Constituent Assembly, which was still not due to assemble in Petrograd until January. A Congress of Soviets was scheduled to assemble in October.

Lenin once again sprang into action. Taking advantage of the fact Kerensky had now alienated the Petrograd garrison as well as the general staff, and anticipating the convening of a Congress of Soviets, Lenin ordered a coup against the Provisional Government for the evening of October 23–24. By the morning of October 25 the Bolsheviks had seized control of Petrograd, Kerensky had fled the scene, and the last defense of the Provisional Government, by a battalion of female soldiers stationed in Petrograd's Winter Palace, ceased. The Bolsheviks, although still a minority party, secured ratification for their seizure of power from the Congress of Soviets. A few days later, again employing armed force, the Bolsheviks took control of Moscow. From these two bases they would gradually develop the capacity to govern Russia. As important as Lenin's leadership was Kerensky's failure to build any sort of coherent opposition to Bolshevik extremism. He had no answer for the slogan "Bread, Peace, Land." His inherent suspicion of tsarist institutions, honed by years of antagonism between the tsar and the Duma, made it impossible for him to build an effective coalition with which to suppress the growing power of what had been, in February 1917, truly the oddball fringe of the Russian political spectrum. Bolshevism was so outside the mainstream that many of its leaders, among those who were not incarcerated, had not lived in the country for years.

Lenin had crushed the hollow Provisional Government. The next challenge was building an actual government of his own. The structure that rapidly evolved, by which a single party took over the institutions of a state, bore an eerie similarity to states imagined in the historical past, such as the vision Theodor Mommsen (whose *History of Rome* Lenin had read) had offered of the government of Julius Caesar, who "retained the deportment of the party-leader" while building a new Roman state after 48 BC. Even more important for Lenin was the French experience of the 1790s. He had eighty-seven books on French history in his library, most of them on this period; his enthusiasm for the Jacobins had led to colleagues and rivals comparing him to Robespierre as early as 1903. Now, with an actual coup to run, Lenin often turned his thoughts to the events of 1793 and 1794. Despite analogies people drew, Lenin didn't think he was Caesar or Robespierre. But he was very aware of what happened to them, and he had no intention of falling short of total success.

The Constituent Assembly which convened in January was suppressed after only a day, and a new government took shape under Lenin's guidance in March with two elements: the party, which renamed itself the Communist Party so that it could not be confused with the German Social Democrats (whom Lenin despised); and a Council of People's Commissars, which would serve as the executive committee of the Congress of Soviets, the governing body for the state that was now known as the Russian Federative Socialist Republic. Lenin served as president of the Council of People's Commissars.

On the party side, the key elements were the Politburo, or the administrative committee for the party's central committee, which was elected by party members. Lenin chaired the Politburo, which initially had five members—in addition to Lenin these were Leon Trotsky, Josef Stalin, and two men who had been exiled to Siberia when the war broke out, Kamenev and Nikolai Krestinsky, a law professor and friend of Trotsky.

Lenin's thinking about the way Russia could be governed was not a sudden development of 1917/18. It was based on his own study of history. The key thing Lenin added to existing models of one-party states was the direction provided by dedicated revolutionaries. He was the champion of the proletariat, which would learn that wholehearted devotion to him was the path to an ideal world. Deeply hostile to peasants, private property, and pretty much anyone including fellow socialists who disagreed with him, Lenin now employed the Bolshevik party to build the workers' state (whether the workers wanted it or not—the Bolsheviks remained a minority party in 1918). To accomplish this, he needed peace with Germany. The difficulty the Bolsheviks had in securing this peace probably belies Kerensky's claim that the movement was a subsidiary of the German government. Negotiations broke down more than once, as what was left of the Russian army disintegrated. Peasant soldiers went back home to await the great distribution of land they expected as the result of the end of tsarism. They were in for a nasty surprise.

Lenin achieved his desired peace with Germany in March, handing over the western provinces of the Russian state, chiefly Poland and Ukraine, to German control. In his view this would be a temporary state of affairs, because he expected the workers of the world to unite and overthrow capitalism, at which point national boundaries would become irrelevant. The Germans expected the troops they could now move to the western front would strengthen the final great offensive that would win the war. That proved to be a false hope.

Lenin needed peace with Germany to gain the space he required to impose his vision of a new society. Opposition newspapers were banned, private property was abolished; supplies of food for the starving cities were expropriated from peasants. A new army was formed to suppress the resistance movements beginning to take shape in various parts of Russia, and a new secret police force began to round up domestic opponents. Lenin drew direct analogy to the Terror of 1793/4 which he saw as essential to protect a revolution from counterrevolutionary forces.

In December 1917 Lenin announced that what the Bolsheviks needed was their own Fouquier-Tinville—the prosecutor under the Terror. He found his man in Felix Dzerzhinsky, who rapidly built upon a secret police force, the Cheka. In June Lenin added regicide to his resume, ordering the assassination of the tsar and his family, though he could not do so through a public trial. The imperial family was murdered in secret. Lenin lied about what he had done for fear that the Germans would be unhappy with the assassination of Alexandra and her children. Through his study of history, especially that of the events of 1793/4 in France, Lenin had determined that any means could be used to secure what he believed to be a virtuous end, and that history required drastic action if it was to arrive at the conclusion that Marx had predicted, the creation of a communist state.

Lenin provided the theory, Trotsky the operational capacity. It was Trotsky who built up the Red Army in the face of the resistance movements that began to develop in the summer of 1918, largely consisting of former tsarist army officers. These groups did not, however, have a monopoly on the service of former officers, and Trotsky made use of the service of many thousands, often men of humble backgrounds who had been recruited into the officer corps to replace officers who had been killed in the course of 1915 and 1916. These men were convinced that, if nothing else, the communists had a vision for the future, while the best their opponents could offer was a vision of the past. In this view they were joined by the vast majority of peasants who, although finding little to love in the communist tendency to expropriate their harvest, found even less to love in the resistance armies, which also took their food and promised to restore prewar property regimes. These had collapsed in the course of the revolution as peasants occupied land that had formerly belonged to absentee landlords.

It took several years of brutal warfare and equally brutal economic exploitation in the interests of "war communism"—the nationalization of industry and private property—before the communists defeated their opponents and suppressed the peasant revolts that followed upon the defeat of the conservative resistance movements. With victory secure, Lenin shifted course, allowing for the existence of private property to rebuild the economy war communism had shattered or driven underground. Pretty much nothing that Marx would have recognized as his vision of a post-revolutionary socialist paradise of proletarian joy took shape at any point. What did take shape was a society in which the class system of the past was eradicated and replaced by a new aristocracy based on party affiliation. That said, there were far more opportunities for women to advance (albeit with a firm glass ceiling), which was unique in a world where the right to vote was only gradually being accorded to women elsewhere. And there were far more opportunities for people not born to wealth to achieve prominence and, for a while, exceptional economic advancement under the New Economic Policy, essentially a system of capitalist production under communist supervision that replaced war communism.

FROM LENIN TO STALIN

Lenin would not live to see much of the post-revolutionary world, though he was worried the New Economic Policy was introducing a "Thermidorian" period, rolling back the radical economic changes of the civil war period. He had been badly wounded by an assassin in 1918, and suffered the first of a series of strokes in 1922. He was almost completely incapacitated by a third stroke in March of 1923—he was taken to a dacha at Gorki, outside of Moscow, where he was tended by his sister, his wife Nadya Krupskaya, and a small staff (the cook was a man named Spiridon Putin, whose grandson is Vladimir Putin).

Before falling ill, Lenin had promoted Josef Stalin to the position of General Secretary of the Communist Party. The promotion was in recognition of Stalin's powerful work ethic and organizational ability—Stalin was largely responsible for the transformation of the Russian Federative Socialist Republic into the Union of Soviet Socialist Republics on December 30, 1922. The position of general secretary, which Stalin would retain until his death in 1953, gave him the ability to stock the upper echelons of the party apparatus with loyalists—something that would prove decisive in the long succession struggle that followed Lenin's death on January 21, 1924.

When Lenin died, Trotsky was on his way to convalesce from an illness of his own. He therefore missed the grand funeral that Stalin organized on January 26. It was the first of many miscalculations that would cost Trotsky any chance to emerge as Lenin's successor. Additionally, although Trotsky was popular with his contemporaries—men and women like himself who were well educated—he alienated the new generation of communists whose origins lay outside the old tsarist intelligentsia.

Stalin came from a humble background and built a powerful faction of people like himself, the most important of whom would be Vyacheslav Molotov, another pre-1918 Bolshevik without a university education. Stalin also presented himself as Lenin's loyal student, the keeper of true Leninist doctrine. It was Stalin who arranged for Lenin's body to be embalmed and laid to rest in a massive mausoleum in Red Square.

It was well known that Trotsky, who had been a Menshevik until 1917, had often quarreled with Lenin—and, for all that their partnership had been crucial to communist success in the civil war, he was suspect to true believers. The only thing hindering Stalin's rise to supreme power was a document circulated before Lenin's death by Nadya Krupskaya in which Lenin was recorded as criticizing six members of the Politburo (including Trotsky), warned of the possibility of a factional struggle between Trotsky and Stalin, and recommended that Stalin be removed as general secretary because he was too "coarse." The document was made public within the party in May of 1924, but bungling on the part of Grigory Zinoviev, another influential pre-war Bolshevik who was now on the Politburo, and Kamenev, who were themselves lukewarm to Trotsky, prevented the document from destroying Stalin.

By 1928 Stalin had become all-powerful within the party, Trotsky had been expelled and would be sent into exile a year later. Stalin now began implementating the first "five-year plan" that would roll back the New Economic Policy and begin the total reformation of the Russian economy through the forced collectivization of agriculture and enhanced state control over production. Millions would starve to death in the first years of collectivization, thanks to the general incompetence and brutality with which the process was carried out. People who had been successful under the New Economic Policy now became social enemies, with kulaks (rich peasants) or NEPmen (capitalists) to be rounded up and shipped to labor camps. The expertise to build a new Soviet industrial economy was largely imported from abroad. The Ford Motor Company, for instance, oversaw the construction of what would become a famous tractor factory in the city of Stalingrad. The justification for the process was that the Soviet Union needed to catch up with the West, that it was encircled by enemies who threatened its very existence. That line was repeated in 1936 when Stalin carried out a murderous purge to eliminate "Trotskyite" opposition.

Stalin abandoned the line, dear to Lenin, that the Russian example would inspire Socialism around the world. For Stalin, the Socialist experiment would be a Russian experiment. The USSR was surrounded by enemies, and needed to be constantly vigilant. There were traitors everywhere. Stalin's paranoia permeated the nation, setting colleagues against each other, with denunciations for treason leading to mass torture and death. Stalin became Russia's teacher of terror as he constructed a new party, obedient to his will.

Stalin's collectivized and mechanized Russia depended upon external technology to survive—home-grown experts had been annihilated in the purges, charged with conspiring to wreck the economy. Industrial production shifted increasingly to military hardware, and still people went hungry. Agricultural production was below 1914 levels in 1940.

Stalin's forced collectivization and purges form a second phase of the revolution that broke out in 1917. Russian society would be completely transformed into a dystopian mirage of Marx's image of a communist society.

There was nothing inevitable about Stalin's triumph, which was as much a product of the bungling of his adversaries as it was of his own genius. But, like Robespierre, Stalin had a knack for creating an image of counterrevolutionary threats that could only be routed out through organized terror. Stalin's own paranoia contributed to the scale and brutality of the massacres he oversaw, but it was his control of Soviet media that made it possible to build the bogus image of threat that ensured support for his brutality.

As Stalin purged his party of "traitors," he had his eyes turned to Germany, whose leader fascinated him. It was in part because Stalin misunderstood the actual menace posed by Adolf Hitler that Hitler had come to power. It would then be the treaty Stalin had Molotov strike with Hitler in 1939 that encouraged Hitler to launch the attack on Poland that started the Second World War.

HITLER AND WEIMAR GERMANY

Adolf Hitler was an Austrian who moved to Germany after failing to gain a place in a Viennese architecture school. Arriving at Munich, he lived in a men's hostel while he continued the process of self-education which had so far failed to yield results. He read works of extreme German nationalism (with a strongly racist, anti-Semitic tenor) and attended operas by Richard Wagner. He supported himself by painting postcards. Like many Germans with similar views, he saw Jews as invaders from the east, and indeed, many of the Jews he would have met had fled the right-wing pogroms raging in Russia after 1905.

Also like many Germans of his generation (and more than a few of his fellow Austrians), Hitler was thrilled by the outbreak of the war in 1914. He signed right up and served throughout the conflict. His role was as a messenger for regimental headquarters; he was wounded twice, promoted to corporal, and received a couple of medals. He was in the hospital when the final allied offensive shattered the German army and, again like most Germans, was unaware of the shenanigans of the general staff on September 29, 1918. On this day, Erich Ludendorff, quartermaster general and effective director of the war effort nominally led by Paul von Hindenburg, chief of the general staff, informed the kaiser that the war being lost, Germany needed to seek an immediate armistice. The kaiser agreed and appointed a new chancellor, who invited the Social Democrats into government. To Lenin's disgust, they had initially supported the war effort before splitting into pro- and anti-war factions in 1916.

When Germany's initial peace feeler was greeted with a demand for unconditional surrender, the German government sent a note to allied governments offering to negotiate a treaty on the basis of the Fourteen Points Woodrow Wilson had announced as the war aims of the United States when it entered the war. The most important of these points would prove to be national self-determination and the formation of a League of Nations. After some initial hesitation, Wilson replied that he would accept the German proposal on two conditions: the immediate end of submarine warfare, and that the German high command negotiate an immediate armistice. He would add a further demand, the kaiser's abdication. In a stunning parallel to what had happened in Russia nineteen months earlier, Hindenburg convinced the kaiser to do this, and Germany was soon the last of the central powers standing. Turkey had signed an armistice on September 29, and the Austro-Hungarian empire signed one on November 3. On November 11, Germany did the same.

The German decision to seek an armistice came as a total surprise to the vast majority of Germans, who had been routinely informed that victory would reward their sufferings. The suddenness of the war effort's collapse promoted a myth that the virtuous army had been "stabbed in the back" by civilian traitors. Hindenburg and Ludendorff stood behind this lie.

In the wake of the armistice and the kaiser's departure, German politics fell into chaos. The left wing of the Social Democratic Party, the wing that had come out against the war in 1916, renamed itself the Communist Party in December. They pressed for a new revolution. More traditional Social Democrats were appalled, fearing that the leaders of the communists, Rosa Luxemburg and Karl Leibknecht, would follow Lenin's policy of abolishing private property and instituting a Red Terror of their own. They therefore aligned with conservatives in organizing a paramilitary force, the Free Corps, to resist a communist takeover. Members of the Free Corps were often ex-soldiers for whom the myth of the "stab in the back" by "November criminals" rang true. They were quite happy to slaughter the communists when they lifted the banner of rebellion in Berlin during January 1919. A few months later in Bavaria, two short-lived communist regimes seized power, inspired by the also short-lived communist coup in Hungary. In May, the Bavarian communist experiment was crushed by heavily armed members of the Free Corps. Memories of these events ensured that the Communist Party and the Social Democrats would never be able to coordinate their activities, even when confronted by a new threat from the right. Right-wing propaganda stressed connections between communists and Jews, the beginning of what would become a powerful lie.

In the meantime a Constituent Assembly was elected, which, meeting in the town of Weimar in July, approved a new constitution to provide a federal government for the twenty-one states which had made up the German Empire since 1871 (hence, although Berlin remained the capital, the new state became known as Weimar Germany). Under this new constitution, the central government controlled foreign policy, trade, the currency, the postal service, and the army. This government would be headed by a ministry selected from the majority party, or a coalition forming a majority in the lower house of the parliament, the Reichstag. The leader of this government would be chancellor, and he would serve at the discretion of the president, who would be elected for a seven-year term. The lower house of the new Reichstag was elected on the basis of a very liberal extension of voting rights to all adult Germans, male and female. Police power was left in the hands of the constituent states, which also provided representatives to the Reichstag's upper house. The single biggest weakness of the new constitution was that it reserved enormous power to the president who could dismiss a chancellor even if that chancellor had a majority in the lower house, and then rule by decree.

The chaos preceding the formation of the new national government, especially the Bavarian civil war, created a new career opportunity for Corporal Hitler. In June 1919, he was signed up by his superior officers for political education. He was such a good student, with some genuine ability as an actor, that in August his superiors made him an instructor. It was here that the man of many failures came into his own. He proved an excellent speaker for audiences of poorly educated men. His ultra-nationalism and increasingly vehement anti-Semitism aligned with the mood of the moment, and he became a star speaker for the newly formed German Workers Party. In March 1920 Hitler left the army to become a full-time employee of the Party. An early witness to one of his rallies wrote of "hypnotic mass excitement," another that "he knew how to rouse and carry away those crowds," and that he succeeded "in putting people into a trance like a primitive tribe's medicine man."

While Hitler was progressing up the political ladder, two things happened that would have a profound impact on German politics in the next decade. The first, in 1919, was the Peace of Versailles. It had not been understood, when Germany agreed to an armistice and then to negotiate a treaty on the basis of Wilson's Fourteen Points, that the allies would keep up the wartime blockade, strangling Germany's economy while the country fell into political chaos. Nor had it been understood that allied governments would feel entitled to impose peace terms which, while not as vindictive as those imposed by Germany on Russia, were devastating. Germany was stripped of 10% of its population, all of its gains in the east, and was forbidden to unify with Austria. The principle of national self-determination that was applied to the peoples of the former Austro-Hungarian Empire, laying the foundation for today's Central Europe, was not applied to Germans. In addition, according to the treaty's Article 231, Germany accepted all guilt for the start of the war and thereby responsibility to pay huge reparations to the allies.

The short-term impact of the reparations payments, along with the separation of economically productive portions of southern Germany, was to cause a period of hyper-inflation which discredited the government that had negotiated the treaty. The long-term impact of the reparations agreement was to prevent Germany from putting the war behind it. That meant that the "November Criminals" remained an ever-present issue.

The Versailles Treaty was the making of Hitler's political routine. He recalled the excitement in the streets when Germany went to war in 1914 and the shock of the armistice when Germany had not lost the war. He would tell people:

> . . . old Prussia and the former Reich was unquestionably the best administered country in the whole world. No other state had such honest and principled civil servants as the former Germany,

> no other nation possessed an army in which the highest regard for personal honor had become a tradition. This applied both internally and externally. Twenty-six states tried to defeat this Reich but in a struggle that lasted for four years they failed, a proof of the power and strength of this Reich.

The German people had not been asked what they thought about the treaty of Versailles; the German people were treated like colonized Africans (Hitler's language was more blunt). Essentially, his message was "Make Germany Great Again." In 1921, Hitler had ousted his former employers to take control of what was now called the National Socialist Workers Party. In 1924, while the Weimar government under the leadership of the new foreign minister Gustav Streseman was beginning to take effective steps to end the period of hyperinflation that had begun in 1922 and lasted into 1923, Hitler became embroiled in a Bavarian conspiracy to overthrow the national government. As others faltered, Hitler took matters in his own hands. He seized the leaders of the Bavarian government at a public meeting in a beer hall, and marched with Ludendorff at his side through the streets of Munich on November 9, 1923. His demonstration was ended in a hail of police bullets. Arrested two days later, Hitler was tried for treason.

Hitler's trial, the occasion of the speech quoted above, linked with that of other conspirators (including Ludendorff), was a farce. Ludendorff was acquitted; Hitler was sentenced to five years in prison, where he was treated as a celebrity inmate, and allowed regular visitors and the resources he needed to write a book entitled *Mein Kampf* (*My Struggle*). Here, Hitler spelled out more clearly than before his anti-Semitic agenda and his belief that Germany needed more "living room" to realize its greatness. None of this was new—"living room" to the east had been a guiding principle of German annexations in the treaty with Russia in 1918. And anti-Semitism was hardly a new aspect of German thought. But (albeit with the aid of an editor) Hitler put the combination of national grievance, hatred, and nostalgia together as a plan. The book became a bestseller.

Hitler himself was released after barely a year in prison. According to his parole, he was banned from speaking in public until 1927, and from entering Prussia until 1928. The end of his political career could have been in sight. The ultra-nationalists were pummeled in the 1924 elections, and the Weimar government, dominated by Streseman, was shaped by a coalition of centrist parties including the Social Democrats and the Center Party, which represented Catholics.

Despite his legal situation and the unpromising political environment, Hitler would not give up on political organizing, the one thing in his life at which he had been successful. Reelected as leader when he left prison, he set to work behind the scenes. His aim was to expand the reach of the Nazi Party, which he managed to do through Gregor Strasser, a skilled political organizer and sometime rival, as well as some new allies, of whom the most significant were Joseph Goebbels, a skilled liar, Martin Borman, Henrich Himmler, and Karl Röhm. Röhm was responsible for developing the party's paramilitary wing, or *Stürmabteilung* (SA). The SA was the Nazi response to the armed gangs of thugs that filled the streets on behalf of other groups. These included the Red Front Fighters employed by the Communist Party, the *Reichsbanner,* who fought for the Social Democrats, and the Steel Helmet, a group supporting other right-wing groups.

In the later 1920s, an increasingly important feature of Nazi identity was as a party devoted to defending "German values" against communists and other undesirables. Hitler gradually weaned the party of the "socialist" aspects of national socialism, such as a call for state ownership of major corporations. He concentrated on demands to tear up the Versailles Treaty, for the reacquisition of territory in eastern Europe, and the creation of more "living room" to house ethnic Germans. At this point the Nazi message was essentially prewar social Darwinism with a strong dose of anti-communism thrown in for good measure.

In the late 1920s, the Communist Party, led by Ernst Thälmann, posed a serious threat to any German government and was a far more potent force than the Nazis. Whereas Hitler's followers were concentrated in small-town Germany, the communists drew their support from workers in the cities. The division between communists and Nazis overlay deeper cultural divisions within German society. Elite German culture was experimental and extremely liberal. Women not only voted, many also worked; corruption and murder were favored themes in literature and the increasingly important film industry; music was dominated by modernists like Schoenberg and Hindemith. Berlin had a reputation for being open to a wide variety of lifestyles. Those who subscribed to the value system of the largely traditional Lutheran north of Germany were appalled. The culture war didn't turn people into Nazis, but a combination of cultural discomfort and fear of communist violence made them receptive to Hitler's message. But that still would not have been enough to turn the Nazi Party into anything more than a fringe conservative group, especially if the Weimar government could build on some real successes as Streseman negotiated Germany back into the international fold. Then, in 1929, Streseman died; two years later, the Depression struck.

Just as there would not have been a Russian Revolution if it had not been for the world war, Nazi Germany would not have existed without the Great Depression. The Depression reversed the Weimar government's baby steps toward construction of a viable political society and opened the door to an extremist regime. It was not immediately clear what form that would take. In 1931, a moderate conservative would wonder if, when the government fell, would it be Hitler or Thälmann who would take power.

THE NAZI SEIZURE OF POWER

The reparation payments imposed by the Versailles Treaty were, as intended, a major impediment to the German economy. Even after it had solved the problem of hyper-inflation by placing Germany on the gold standard in 1923, the government had trouble balancing the budget. It cut public services and fired government servants, some of whom, feeling they had been betrayed by the centrist parties and allergic to communists, drifted toward the Nazis. In 1930, the government had renegotiated the payment schedule for reparations, stretching it into the middle of the century, which promised some extra cash. Most of this was loaned by American banks.

The stock market crash of 1929 initiated a series of bank failures across the United States, and, desperate for cash, US banks began to call in international loans. That had a particular impact on German industry, which depended on those investments. German unemployment shot upward. Chancellor Brüning followed current economic theory in seeking to cut domestic consumption to make German products cheaper on the international market. It was an improbable solution, given the fact that the target export markets were all in decline. Worse was to come. Starting in July, the government began reducing unemployment benefits even as its policies were throwing more people out of work. When German banks began to fail, foreign banks were, not unreasonably, unwilling to lend more money, although at the urging of the United States, reparations payments were suspended. Brüning took Germany off the gold standard and continued his deflationary policies. This was all in the face of signs the government was in serious trouble. New elections to the Reichstag had been held in 1930. Of the 577 seats available, the Nazis won 107, up from 12 in 1928 (the communists had raised their total number of seats to 77 from 54).

With Brüning having established himself as the most unpopular chancellor since the end of the war, Hindenburg, now eighty-four years old, approached the end of his seven-year term as president. After failing to get himself reappointed without an election and fearing a communist takeover, Hindenburg decided to run for another term. Hitler ran against him (acquiring the necessary German citizenship along the way).

Hitler campaigned with extraordinary energy, hiring a plane—something hitherto unheard of in German politics—to fly around the country giving speeches at giant rallies. "The German farmer is impoverished. The middle class is ruined. The social hopes of many millions have been destroyed. One-third of all German men and women of working age is unemployed, and thus without income," Hitler said in his standard stump speech of this year, and:

> If the established political parties seriously want to save Germany, why have they not done so already? If they really wanted to save Germany, why has that not happened? If the leaders of those parties had honest intentions, then their programs must have been deficient. If, however, their programs were correct, then either their intentions were not sincere, or they were too ignorant or too weak.

Hitler promised a government by:

> A faithful community of people that is resolved to take up the fight for the preservation of our people, not because it is made up of Bavarians or Prussians, or people from Württemberg or Saxony, or because they are Catholics or Protestants, workers or civil servants, middle class or salaried workers, and so forth, but because they are all Germans.

He gave some version of this speech forty-six times during the election campaign. His energy level invited immediate contrast with that of Hindenburg. He also learned to vary his message according to his audience. In talking with German industrialists, he would play up anti-communism and play down anti-Semitism. Hitler understood that people didn't mind being lied to if it made them feel safe. As with Lenin in 1918, or Robespierre before him, or Luther before them both, Hitler understood that consistency and simplicity of message, combined with the willingness to exploit current technology to the fullest possible degree, was the key to success. Once the opposition was forced into reactive mode, it could not readily recover the initiative.

Still, Hindenburg was a war hero and Hitler was an ex-corporal. Hindenburg won 53% of the vote, Hitler came second with 37%, and Thälmann ended up with 10%. Hitler was now a major factor. Would it be possible to govern without his support? Hindenburg tried to bring him into the cabinet in a subordinate role. Hitler insisted on being made chancellor. Hindenburg, who found Hitler socially, though not politically, repulsive, turned to Franz von Papen. Working with General Kurt von Schleicher, Papen tried to win Hitler's support by lifting a ban Brüning had imposed on demonstrations by members of the SA. The SA now flooded the streets looking for communists to beat up. After a particularly bloody encounter, Papen dismissed the state government of Prussia, a major bastion of the Social Democrats, for its inability to maintain the law and order he had just undermined. At a time of massive unemployment, the Social Democrats were unable to call a general strike, something that would otherwise have been a tool to resist Papen's act. Goebbels would observe that "the reds have missed their big chance."

Papen's attack on the Prussian government came in the midst of yet another election. With the left appearing ineffective and the Nazis pounding on the themes of the "November criminals,"

Jewish "wire-pullers," and murderous communists, the election was a disaster. The Nazis won more than 200 seats in the Reichstag, more than the Social Democrats and Communists combined; support for centrist parties evaporated. Hitler was again invited to join the government, Hindenburg telling him that he had "no doubts about your love for the Fatherland" but warning him against the excesses of the SA, which he threatened to suppress. Hitler insisted again upon the chancellorship, saying that he wanted "victory for a nationalistic Germany, and annihilation for its Marxist destroyers and corrupters." After a no-confidence vote in the Reichstag, which thwarted Papen's plan to dissolve the body and rule by decree, new elections were called for November. This time Hitler lost ground and the Nazis were outnumbered by the Social Democrats and the Communists. More significant, however, was the fact that, even with the Nazis losing seats, an increase in the number of seats held by communists meant that for the second straight election the majority in the Reichstag had gone to parties opposed to democracy, and violently opposed to each other.

With violence increasing in the streets, Schleicher told Papen that he was out as chancellor and took over. But he offended Hindenburg, in large measure because his planned economic reforms would have had a negative impact for Hindenburg personally, and his son. Hindenburg worried that the decline in Nazi vote totals meant the party was failing, which could strengthen left-wing parties. Rumors of a military coup spread. Schleicher saw the best way out of the crisis would be to give in to Hitler's demand for the chancellorship. Hindenburg agreed, and agreed that Hitler could be controlled. On January 30, 1933, Hitler became chancellor. He obtained the office because other right-wing politicians saw him as the solution to their problems. They also believed they could control him. Papen told a friend, "We have hired him. In a few months we will have pushed him so far in the corner that he will squeak."

Less than a month after Hitler entered office, Marinus van der Lubbe, a homeless construction worker from the Netherlands, set fire to the building that housed the Reichstag. Despite rumors the fire was a Nazi plot, it appears Hitler was genuinely surprised. That does not mean he wasn't ready to take full advantage of the event. On the morning of February 28, Hitler brought Hindenburg an emergency decree suspending personal liberties guaranteed by the constitution (Figure 5.5). This decree, presented as a temporary measure required for the suppression of terrorism, was still in effect when Hitler committed suicide twelve years later. And there was more to come. The Nazis created a power of "preventive detention," which allowed the police to detain individuals on suspicion they might commit a crime and ship them off to concentration camps without trial.

Figure 5.5 Adolf Hitler and Paul von Hindenburg. The two stand on the steps of the Potsdam Garrison Church on March 21, 1933. In bowing to von Hindenburg, Hitler is assuming the role of servant to the German state. He could afford the pretense, given the passage of the Reichstag decrees three weeks earlier.

At first, the most violent acts of oppression targeted the communists and others deemed "criminals" (largely the homeless). Nazis promised "social discipline," and soon it was not just those deemed criminal but also those deemed socially deviant who were targeted. This appealed to the cultural antagonism felt by many Nazi supporters for the free and easy ways of Berlin society. And it involved the active persecution of Germany's Jewish population. After a misfire when the order to boycott Jewish businesses on April 1, 1933 elicited more sympathy for their owners than Hitler had anticipated, he backed off somewhat, but still went ahead with a "Law for the Restoration of a Professional Civil Service" to eliminate "Marxist and Jewish" influence from all levels of government. Jewish children were persecuted by their classmates; Jewish professionals lost their jobs. By the end of the year, Hitler was more popular than ever.

In 1934 Hitler cleaned house. He had already driven Gregor Strasser, who had threatened his domination of the party, into exile. Now he went after Röhm, the less than sycophantic leader of the SA. Hitler was building a parallel organization, now allied with state police forces, known as the *Schutzstaffel* (SS) or Protection Squadron. He unleashed the SS against the leadership of the SA on June 30, 1934. Röhm was murdered along with much of his team. Another victim was Shleicher. Himmler, who advertised himself as a policeman rather than the homicidal thug he was, now took charge of the administration of what was called justice.

Nazi vigor replaced the inaction of the old regime. Hitler set guidelines his followers interpreted in their own ways as they worked "toward the Führer." He set the tone by ridiculing his opponents and creating an alternative reality within which to work. The world watched while Hitler reneged on reparations payments, remilitarized Germany, and sought out conservative elements elsewhere.

Nazi scientists, for instance, reached out to American eugenicists, strengthening existing moves toward enforced sterilization. By the beginning of the 1940s, before the mass murder of Europe's Jewish population began, German doctors would be overseeing the slaughter of the mentally ill. They were a burden on society (a view shared with eugenicist groups elsewhere). After the issuance of the overtly racist Nuremberg decree banning sexual relations between Jews and Germans in the autumn of 1935, and the reoccupation of the Rhineland, which had been declared off limits to the German army by the treaty of Versailles, in March of 1936, the world met in Berlin to celebrate the Olympics. When many organizations proposed boycotting the games, Avery Brundage, head of the United States Olympic Committee, ensured widespread participation. Not only was Brundage violently anti-Semitic, he argued that there wasn't much difference between Nazi racial laws and the "Jim Crow" laws which banned intermarriage and created "separate but equal" schools for African Americans and Whites. This was true. Americans could celebrate the amazing achievements of Jesse Owens after the games, but he had been denied campus housing by the Ohio State University, and American immigration laws had been rewritten in the 1920s to favor applicants from the "better" (northern European) races at the expense of southern Europeans, Jews, and Asians. Nor were Americans likely to focus on the fact that the program had been rigged so that German athletes could win the bulk of the medals. Anti-communism was more important than racism. "Law and order" were more important than the violation of human rights.

With each improbable success, Hitler grew ever more enamored of what he now believed was his own genius. By the time the Olympic flame was extinguished in Berlin, world war was three years away.

TYRANNY AND IDEOLOGY

Tsarist Russia and Weimer Germany were failing states before either Lenin or Hitler came along. But that does not mean their victories were forgone conclusions. Neither man had ever run anything; their immediate supporters hadn't either. Powerful slogans and mass demonstrations were more important to their campaigns than the capacity to point to any active achievements in public policy (of which there were none). Theory was more important than reality. That should not have been a recipe for success.

Lenin and Hitler were obsessed with power, but they appeared to their followers as representatives of recognizable schools of thought. Even though Lenin perverted Marxian theory into a doctrine of tyrannical dictatorship, he got his start by theorizing the fate of the bourgeoisie at the hands of the proletariat; he presented himself as the champion of class warfare. The Bolsheviks were at one end of a spectrum of Marxist thought that ended with social democratic parties in Russia as well as Germany. Hitler's party was no more mainstream at the beginning than Lenin's, but, like Lenin, he was able to outflank his closest opponents. In Lenin's case these opponents were focused on the continuation of the war, and in Hitler's, the threat of communism.

The theoretical underpinnings of both movements stemmed from movements that had achieved success on their own, albeit in very different ways. While Marx theorized the rise of the dispossessed, Spencer justified the status quo. The best people were in charge because they were the best people. He misused the good science developed by Darwin to create the image of a society perpetually in conflict with itself, one in which the winners had to keep winning. Galton made matters far worse by introducing a further bogus science. While Marxist theory was ultimately one of hope for a better future, Spencer and Galton presented a vision of competitive failure and social ruin unless corrective action was taken. Hitler's message of social discipline and racial purity took the theories of Spencer and Galton to logical extremes. His language was recognizably close to mainstream conservative thought deriving from their influence.

Lenin and Hitler faced incompetent and unwary opponents. But before either could succeed, the central institutions of Russian and German society had to be profoundly shaken. The challenges each faced did not, however, make either the Bolshevik or Nazi revolutions inevitable, Germany might have had a communist revolution if the Nazi Party had not come along, and even though the tsar was not coming back from his abdication, it was just possible a parliamentary democracy could have emerged in his place. The tragedy was that the blindness of Kerensky and Hindenburg closed off paths to different futures based on compromise rather than dictatorship.

Ideological correctness is a moral hazard. As had Robespierre, Lenin and Hitler created environments in which obedience to the party line precluded basic human decency. The same is true of religious partisans in the sixteenth century. According to no definition of humanity is the public incineration of the ideologically disobedient a reasonable act. Nor is stealing food from the people who produce it, a fundamental tenet of "war communism," or murdering people because it represented revolutionary vigor, a feature of Robespierre's terror as well as war communism. The people who actually kept Lenin in power were not the few professional revolutionaries with whom he spoke, but the former tsarist army officers who joined up with the Red Army either through fear or because they thought it represented "the future." Lenin naturalized violence as a path to that end. Stalin took advantage of the identification of violence with revolutionary fervor in his dystopian reinvention of communism.

The vicious political world of Weimar Germany naturalized the thuggish brutality lurking beneath the facade of Hitler's public performance. What would soon become the Nazi war on alternative thought, as well as alternative race and physical condition, made no one safer. It could only be accepted in a state where people were willing to terrorize their neighbors because they believed this was the way to greater security. The illogic of such a view is obvious. Or it is obvious until its proponent has a gun.

The tenets of social Darwinism, dividing the world between "winners" and "losers," between "successful" and "unsuccessful" races, created a "scientific" justification for mass murder more deadly than doctrines of class warfare derived from the thought of Karl Marx. In the hands of social democratic parties, Marxist doctrines provided the foundation for workers' rights, gender and racial equality. The cause of economic justice is not necessarily violent. The cause of racial superiority and nationalist self-assertion is inevitably so.

Epilogue: January 6, 2021

On January 6, 2021, a mob invaded the Capitol building in Washington DC. Members of this group, coming from an event at which Donald Trump and his allies had repeated lies about the result of the election for well over an hour, intended to disrupt congressional certification of Joe Biden's electoral victory. For some hours they succeeded. Several members of the group were carrying firearms, some had zip ties with them. In the summer of 2020 a group of extremists had plotted to kidnap Michigan's governor, Gretchen Whitmer, and "try" her for "crimes" against the people. Those "crimes" included taking steps to protect the people of Michigan against the spread of Covid-19 and insufficient deference to Donald Trump. Was that a dry run for an effort to try congressional leaders? As Donald Trump's second impeachment trial unfolded, various media outlets uncovered extensive connections between the groups which stormed the capitol and extremist internet conspiracy theorists.

For much of 2020, when not facing trial in the senate for abuse of power and contempt of Congress, or impeding the nation's response to the Covid-19 pandemic, Donald Trump had been promoting fantasies about the forthcoming election and encouraging violence by members of extremist groups. These groups included overt white supremacists, various conspiracy theorists, and members of a white evangelical Christian movement who consider the increasing diversity of American society a threat to "traditional values." The sources of information for these groups was largely provided by Internet sites and Donald Trump's Twitter account.

In the course of the summer, some members of right-wing groups were recruited by the Department of Homeland Security, against the wishes of local authorities, to join a response to protesters for racial justice in Portland, Oregon. Taken with efforts on the part of the Republican Party to pack the courts with pliable judges, and efforts by Donald Trump to involve the military in the suppression of largely peaceful protests, and to discredit traditional media, events in the summer and early autumn of 2020 suggested planning for a coup d'état was in progress. Then more Americans showed up to vote for Joe Biden than had ever voted for a presidential candidate in the history of the country, and two months later voters in Georgia ousted two wealthy Republican senators in favor of a young documentary film maker of Jewish descent and an African American pastor. The results of that election were announced hours before the mob stormed the Capitol.

Despite the strength of Joe Biden's support, the intransigence of Donald Trump's supporters is a sign of deep divisions. The divisions in American society are all the more troubling because they are shared with other liberal democracies. The autumn of 2020 saw the end of the British departure from the European Union. The so-called "Brexit" process threatened decades of work developing strong European institutions that followed upon the collapse of Soviet domination in Eastern Europe in the late 1980s. Even though the final withdrawal agreement underscored the European Union's strength and delivered far less "independence" than Boris Johnson had promised, the Brexit movement itself had eerie similarities to the situation in the United States. The original 2016 campaign in favor of Brexit was notable for the extraordinary combination of dishonesty—for instance, false claims about the positive impact that Brexit would have on funding for the National Health System—combined with nostalgic nationalism, tinged with racism. An "advantage" of Brexit would be that the United Kingdom could shut its borders to immigrants from the European Union, which was experiencing a crisis of large-scale migration as a result of the destructive Syrian civil war and economic trauma in sub-Saharan Africa.

The strong sense among Brexit voters was that the rise of economic globalization had left them behind, that labor market protections and living standards were better protected before the fall of the Soviet Union. The prosperity experienced by those at the top of the economic food chain was not widely shared. That is a feeling shared with nationalist groups throughout the European Union.

Boris Johnson's Tory victory was not only a victory for Brexit, but a massive repudiation of the campaign run by his Labour opponent, Jeremy Corbyn. Corbyn responded to the extremism of Johnson's Brexit position with an extremist campaign of his own. Instead of staking out middle ground where voters of various political persuasions could come together, Corbyn ran a campaign based on extreme socialist principles, turning many traditional Labour voters away, opening the door to strategies designed by Johnson's advisor, Dominic Cummings (like Johnson, another able, if unprincipled, student of Greco-Roman antiquity in his younger years). As both parties moved to the extremes, the center disappeared. Similar forces lay behind the election of Donald Trump in 2016, and the earlier Tea Party movement in the Republican Party. Donald Trump's open contempt for government and openly racist rhetoric harks back to the anti-immigrant and eugenicist rhetoric of earlier generations, painting new immigration as a threat to the cultural heritage of the previous immigrants who had shaped American society. The power of his message was reflected in the debate over his first impeachment, where the passionate defense of his actions recalled the fears of the framers of the Constitution about the perils of faction in the national government.

The decades leading up to the elections of Donald Trump and Boris Johnson have seen the most radical global economic transformation since the Industrial Revolution of the nineteenth century. As was the case in the nineteenth century, new technology is the chief driver of change. The rise of the digital economy is now accompanied by an ideology of disruption. Originally it was not so. Some of the most important early developments in computing were connected with the code-breaking efforts of British intelligence, inspired by Alan Turing, in the Second World War. The government of the United States funded large-scale computing during and after that conflict to develop the atomic bomb, enhance radar, to support the space program and delivery systems for intercontinental ballistic missiles. In the private sector an important step was taken even before the war, when two Stanford graduate students, Bill Hewlett and Fred Packard, founded a powerhouse firm specializing in electronic testing and measurement devices—the most famous early product was an audio oscillator that Walt Disney used to test sound in theaters showing *Fantasia*. They moved into the computer business in the 1960s.

In the post-Vietnam era, the US economy stagnated, and traditional industries faced new challenges from foreign competitors. Post-industrial Massachusetts reinvented itself as a hub for electronic innovation, with a good deal of help from the incubator offered by federally funded research at Harvard and MIT. Tech was something Americans could do better, and to a country suffering through a decade of doubt, that was comforting. It was in this environment that people began experimenting with the possibility that computers could be something other than the giant mainframes which dominated the industry, and which was associated with unpopular governmental bureaucracies. What if you could have your own machine and make it do what you wanted it to do around the house? Could people make gadgets that would make their lives easier? A couple of high school students in Seattle named Paul Allen and Bill Gates had figured out how to make a device that would measure local traffic flow even before Richard Nixon was forced from office for corrupting the presidential election of 1972. The first personal computer, called an Altair 8080, came on the market in 1975 from a company called Micro Instrumentation and Telemetry Systems (MITS); reading about this in *Popular Electronics,* Gates and Allen called MITS telling them they could develop a program that would make an Altair run more efficiently. They did, and on April 4th they established their company dedicated to writing software. A year later, in the Palo Alto area, another pair of Stanford graduate students, Steve Wozniak and Steve Jobs, developed their own machine and founded their company, incorporated as Apple Computer, in 1977.

Up to this point the development of the digital economy depended on the exceptional technical capacity of a few individuals. There was no plan for the future; the key was an environment that allowed people to experiment and test their ideas in the free market. Until the end of the 1980s there wasn't even much contact between the high-tech community and Washington. This would change with the third phase of high-tech development as attention turned away from computers per se to the way they could be made to talk to each other. The birth of the Internet in the course of the 1990s transformed the transmission and processing of information. And this was the point where the federal government, which had provided the Internet's initial infrastructure, dropped the ball.

The culture of Silicon Valley and Seattle was inherently libertarian; tech companies were the product of individual inspiration and not government planning. So long as they competed with each other, that was fine. The Internet, however, put tech companies in competition with the traditional economy, where understanding its possibilities was often slow to percolate. So it was that in 2001, a bookstore chain called Borders made an arrangement with a tech company that had been founded six years earlier in Seattle to sell books online. That company was called Amazon, and Borders essentially slit its own throat by turning over its online selling to Amazon, undermining a business model that was based on luring customers into generously sized stores with various amenities (e.g., coffee shops) to help them enjoy their shopping. If you could place an order from home and make your own coffee, why bother going out? By the time Borders' executives realized what was going on and ended their agreement (in 2007), their company was in headlong decline.

The failure of Borders could be seen as an example of "creative destruction," the overthrow of inefficient companies by the efficient. In many ways that is true. Borders was inefficiently run, and Amazon was not the only problem it faced. That said, Borders' failure was just one feature of a process through which a predatory monopoly took shape, unregulated by the federal government, which had adopted policies to limit monopoly power in the interest of workers and consumers for more than a century.

The rise of Internet shopping was joined, in the early 2000s, by social networking. Bitter regional divisions were becoming increasingly evident by the time of the hotly contested presidential election of 2000, and these were being exacerbated by ever-increasing number of news outlets. Americans could choose who they wanted to talk to, who they wanted to hear from, and, while doing so, they were increasingly turning over their personal information to large tech companies—the new kids on the block, Google and Facebook, as well as the companies that powered the ever more ubiquitous cellphones. The message now was not "this is cool because it works" but rather "move fast and break things," the mantra of Facebook's founder, Mark

Zuckerberg. The problem is, when you break something how do you know if you can fix it? Disruption is not the same thing as creation.

The product of the disruption introduced by Zuckerberg is surveillance capitalism, the commodification of personal data for the purpose of profit. Surveillance capitalism preys on the populations it has made dependent upon itself by placing the consumer in a box and making sure that he/she stays there. It reinforces the separation between communities, disables discourse, and increases distrust of institutions. It opens the door to governments, and even private enterprise groups, who seek to sway public opinion by steering people to specific sources of (dis)information.

The corollary of the cult of disruption is that government regulation of any sort is a bad thing. Government stood aside as the virtuous aspect of creative disruption that gave rise to the digital era surrendered to ever more monopolistic behavior by giant corporations looking to snuff out competition. Despite the public assertion that government regulation damages innovation, major tech companies are all too willing to partner with the federal government when its suits their mutual purposes.

Surveillance by private companies has risen hand in hand with mass data collection by governments, and not just governments of totalitarian states. In the United States, the terrorist attacks of September 11, 2001, led to the passage of the Patriot Act, which created an intimate bond between the National Security Agency and technology companies whose capacities were increasingly supported by the federal government in an unholy alliance of surveillance—the one dedicated to collecting data for sale to advertisers, the other dedicated to the false belief that mass surveillance will prevent terrorist attacks. If anything, mass surveillance has made the United States less secure than it was before, as the sad tale of mass shootings in the last decade, very few of which can be associated with people identified as "terrorists," has shown.

The effect of institutionalizing fear of "terror" has had the coincidental effect of militarizing the "war on crime." The "war on crime" has a class rather than party affiliation. The phrase originated with a Democratic president—Lyndon Johnson—and continued as a "war on drugs" under the Republican Ronald Reagan and the Democrat Bill Clinton, culminating in the 1994 passage of the brutal crime bill. The "criminals" who are the enemy in this war are not white-collar workers; they are residents of inner-city America. An impact of the "war on crime," which allows for the imposition of long prison sentences for drug-related and other non-violent offenses, mostly on people of color and others who cannot afford high-powered legal representation, is to deepen the divide between communities on the basis of wealth as well as race. Identifying areas with large nonwhite populations as being "high-crime" areas contributes to the impoverishment of these communities when the dependence of educational and health care resources upon property values has created a vicious cycle whereby struggling neighborhoods cannot support the institutions that serve (and enhance property values in) wealthier areas.

Since 2001, the "war on terror" has reinforced the negative impact of the "war on crime" with its accompanying transfer of military technology to local police departments on the theory that it would be needed in the event of a terrorist attack. The transfer of equipment has increased violence on America's streets, as it is used not against foreign terrorists but rather against American citizens, especially at moments of protest against racially charged injustice such as the 2014 shooting of Michael Brown in Ferguson, Missouri, or the public murder of George Floyd by a Minneapolis police officer in 2020. Those instances have called attention to the fact that an economic system designed to keep people in place will inevitably harden the lines of institutional racism.

The state that turns its resources against its citizens in the cause of maintaining the status quo is less good at regulating the large corporations with which it has allied itself in the interests of "security." Most notable in the past year has been the health care system's ability to assert a false correlation between public health and the fiscal well-being of the manufacturers of drugs and other tools of the trade. Perhaps the most obvious instance of disruptive monopolization is the failure of the US government's Project Aura, begun in 2008 to develop low-cost ventilators. When Newport Medical Instruments—which was developing the ventilators at 30% of the standard rate, with a government contract—was acquired in 2012 by Covidien, a much larger medical device company that already sold ventilators, Covidien quietly dropped the project. The catastrophic result of this failure to enforce a government contract aimed at protecting the public because it would hurt the corporate bottom line became obvious when the Covid-19 virus struck in 2020.

Although as a member of the European Union, the United Kingdom was protected from some of the worst abuses of surveillance capitalism, it was not protected from the same policy trends that helped drive members of the American public into their information rabbit holes. The financial crisis of 2008 resolved itself in favor of those who had done the most to cause it—the wealthy have seen their incomes climb; members of the middle class have not. Austerity budgets, introduced following the financial crisis in the United Kingdom and elsewhere in the European Union, have damaged the public services and increased basic costs for populations where labor's share of national wealth has shrunk. Lack of investment in public goods such as higher education has increasingly turned great public universities from the engines of social mobility that was their mission into credentialing services for the children of the well-to-do.

Despite claims that government regulation wrecks innovation, it can otherwise be seen as a crucial aspect of Locke's notion of a social contract whereby government remains responsible for the well-being of all people within a society. The failure of governments to observe that contract, allowing the widespread impoverishment of the working classes, the weakening of labor organizations, failure to provide accessible health care, viable public transport, and other goods, gives rise to powerful movements seeking to undercut "the system." Such movements reject the principles of liberal democracy and reinforce social Darwinist "truths," especially those connected with race, to claim public welfare is undercut by immigration, that good jobs are being taken from the deserving and given to outsiders. As nationalist parties have expanded, they are increasingly looking not only inward but also outward to challenge the international institutions that governed the post–Cold War world.

The traditions of liberal democracy face a crisis of confidence fueled by the increasing isolation of communities overseen by surveillance capitalism. The power of attraction toward the extreme, which we've seen so often in this book, means that the more outrageous the new "truth" the more believable it is. Audience development enabled by surveillance capitalism makes it possible for extremist groups—groups such as QAnon which emerged in the wake of Donald Trump's election as president—to peddle lies and absurdist fantasies (such as one that Bill Gates devised Covid-19 or that Trump is defending the world from an international cabal of pedophiles) that disrupt rational efforts of government. Thus, even though the professionalism of the judicial branch snatched away the diaphanous veil coating Trump's naked effort to disrupt the 2020 electoral process, many elected leaders of the Republican Party supported increasingly ludicrous efforts to prove widespread voter fraud, refusing to treat obvious lies as such. The result is a spectacle in which the leadership of an avowedly conservative party is at war with the legitimate functioning of the United States Constitution. The widespread support for these efforts among the party's rank and file, operating within the echo chambers of partisan information networks, underscores the nature of political discourse shaped by the substitution of "information" for truth in an "information age" wherein most Americans are stuck in place.

The decision by Facebook and Twitter to shut down Donald Trump's accounts in the wake of the assault on the Capitol raises even more fundamental questions about the relative power of monopoly capitalism and governments. The claim that Internet providers are merely offering platforms to others rather than acting as publishers was belied by this action. Kate Ruane, writing for the American Civil Liberties Union, reasonably noted, "it should be a concern when companies like Facebook and Twitter wield the unchecked power to remove people from platforms that have become indispensable for the speech of billions—especially when political realities make those decisions easier."

Senator Richard Blumenthal of Connecticut has said it is time for Congress to "reform big tech's privileges and obligations." The repeal of section 230 of the Communications Decency Act of 1996, which freed tech companies from responsibility for material published on their sites, would be a start. If the United States would also join with the European Union in regulating the economic impact of big tech, the result could help repair fractured societies.

The case studies in this book show that the collapse of central institutions can lead to extraordinary results. In times of crisis, people will react to the immediate challenge rather than the long term; if something sounds plausible it can become possible. Responsible leadership, for instance that provided by members of the constitutional convention, by Frederick of Saxony, Constantine, and 'Abd al-Malik can transform revolutionary ideology in constructive ways to rebuild confidence in institutions that are on the verge of failure. Robespierre and his colleagues, to say nothing of the two twentieth-century examples we've seen, remind us that this is not inevitable.

What remains is a clear choice. Will the institutions of liberal democracy that have dominated Western politics since the end of the Second World War escape the clutches of monopolistic capitalism and once again work to serve the interests of working people? Will compromise and rational discussion displace absurdity and extremism to build a better future? Or will the institutions of liberal democracy be subject to a disruption to which an obvious end is not in sight but is unlikely to be the betterment of the human condition. Disruptions first and foremost serve the ends of the disrupters.

REFERENCES

Introduction

For important discussions of economic factors behind change, see D. Acemoglu and J.A. Robinson, *Why Nations Fail: The Origins of Power, Prosperity and Poverty* (London, 2012); C.M. Christensen, *The Innovator's Dilemma: When New Technologies Cause Great Firms to Fail* (Boston, 1997); and B. Moore, *Social Origins of Dictatorship and Democracy: Lord and Peasant in the Making of the Modern World* (Boston, reprint, 1993). For historians' reluctance to embrace sociological models of change, which I share, see K.M. Baker and D. Edelstein, *Scripting Revolution: A Historical Approach to the Comparative Study of Revolutions* (Stanford, 2015).

Chapter 1: Constantine and the Christian Church

13 **Christians under Trajan:** see Pliny, *Letters* 10.96–97.

JESUS AND HIS FOLLOWERS

Transformation of Rome: D. Potter, *The Origin of Empire* (London, 2019); for Jesus' message see Fredriksen, *When Christians Were Jews* (New Haven, 2018).

14 **For the date of the birth of Christ adopted here:** see G. Vermes, *Jesus the Jew* (New York, 1973): 21 on the basis of Luke 3: 23. This is a significant statement because Luke did not recognize the fact that it was contradicted by the date he

selected for the birth of Jesus (6 CE), which probably means that it reflects an earlier tradition about Jesus' career.

15 **Census of Quirinius and chronological issues:** R. Syme, "The *Titulus Tibertinus*," in R. Syme, *Roman Papers* 3 (A.R. Birley, ed.) (Oxford, 1984).

16 **Junia:** see *Rom.* 16.7.

17 **Narratives of the crucifixion:** F.G. Millar, "Reflections on the Trials of Jesus," in F.G. Millar, *The Greek World, the Jews, and the East* (H.M. Cotton and G. Rogers, eds.) (Chapel Hill, 2006): 139–163.

THE SPREAD OF CHRISTIANITY

The most efficient summary of the development of Christianity remains Fredriksen, "Christians and the Roman Empire in the First Three Centuries," in D. Potter, *A Companion to the Roman Empire* (Oxford, 2006): 587–606; for pagan thought, see S. Ahbel-Rappe, "Philosophy in the Roman Empire," in D. Potter, *A Companion to the Roman Empire* (Oxford, 2006): 524–540; more generally, see R.J. Lane Fox, *Pagans and Christians in the Mediterranean World from the Second Century AD to the Conversion of Constantine* (London, 1986).

18 **Household of Narcissus:** *Rom.* 16.11. For the possibilities see *Prosopographia Imperii Romani*, 2nd ed. N 23–25.

18 **Peter and Paul:** see the debate between B. Shaw, "The Myth of the Neronian Persecution," *JRS* 105 (2015):73–100 and C. P. Jones, "The Historicity of the Neronian Persecution: A Response to Brent Shaw," *New Testament Studies* 14 (2017): 146–152.

19 **Gladiators and athletes:** D. Potter, *The Victor's Crown: How the Birth of the Olympics and the Rise of the Roman Games Changed Sport Forever* (London, 2011): 78–88; 258–272.

20–21 **Development of the Christian canon:** B. Metzger, *The Canon of the New Testament: Its Origin, Development, and Significance* (Oxford, 1987); **for suggestions of a later date for Luke,** see D. Billings, *The Acts of the Apostles and the Rhetoric of Roman Imperialism* (Cambridge, 2017). For Christians and other intellectual groups, see K. Eshleman, *The Social World of Intellectuals in the Roman Empire: Sophists, Philosophers and Christians* (Cambridge, 2012) and J. Secord, *Christian Intellectuals and the Roman Empire: from Justin Martyr to Origen* (State College, 2020).

21 **Tertullian:** *Apology*, 40.

21–2 **Christian martyrdom:** G.W. Bowersock, *Martyrdom and Rome* (Cambridge, 2010); D.S. Potter, "Martyrdom as Spectacle," in R. Scodel, ed., *Theater and Society in the Classical World* (Ann Arbor, 1993): 53–88.

22 **Christianity in the third century:** D. Potter, *The Roman Empire at Bay 180–395*, 2nd edition (London, 2014): 308–317.

CRISIS AND TRANSITION

The discussion here is based on D. Potter, *The Roman Empire at Bay* 2nd edition (London, 2014). Since the publication of that book, the most important advances have come through the publication of new fragments of the contemporary historian Dexippus. I also was unaware that the site of Decius' defeat has been discovered; see the excellent study in G. Radoslavova, G. Dzanev, and N. Nikolov, "The Battle of Abrittus in AD 251: Written Sources, Archaeological and Numismatic Data," *Archaeologia Bulgarica* 15, 3 (2011): 23–49.

23 **Persians overrated:** Dio 40.14.2–3.

24 **Grant of citizenship:** J.H. Oliver, *Greek Constitutions of Early Roman Emperors from Inscriptions and Papyri* (Philadelphia, 1989), n. 260–262.

25 **Decius' edict on sacrifices:** see now the evidence collected in D. Potter, "Decius and Valerian," in D.P.W. Burgersdijk and A.J. Ross, eds., *Imagining Emperors in the Later Roman Empire* (Leiden, 2018): 21 n. 11.

26 **Paul of Samosata:** see Eus. *HE.* 7.30 with F.G. Millar, "Paul of Samosata, Zenobia and Aurelia: The Church, Local Culture and Political Allegiance in Third-Century Syria," *JRS* 61 (1971): 1–17.

DIOCLETIAN AND THE CONVERSION OF CONSTANTINE

For issues covered in this section, see, in general, D. Potter, *Constantine the Emperor* (Oxford, 2012).

29 **Documents from Cirta:** see Optatus of Milevis, *Against the Donatists,* appendix 1, readily accessible through M. Edwards, *Optatus: Against the Donatists* (Liverpool, 1998).

29 **Bishop acting against imprisoned Christians** is in the *Acts of the Abitinian Martyrs,* for which see M. Tilley, *Donatist Martyr Stories* (Liverpool, 1996): 25–50.

31–3 **Historiography of Constantine's conversion**: D.S. Potter, "Writing Constantine," in E. Siecienski ed., *Constantine: Religious Faith and Imperial Policy* (London, 2017): 91–112.

CREATING IMPERIAL CHRISTIANITY

For issues covered in this section, see, in general, D. Potter, *Constantine the Emperor* (Oxford, 2012).

34 **Bishops with Constantine in 312**: W. Eck, "Eine historische Zeitenwende: Kaiser Constantins Hinwendung zum Christentum und die gallischen Bischöfe," in F. Schuller and H. Wolff, *Konstantin der Große. Kaiser einer Epochenwende* (Lindenberg 2007): 69–94.

NICAEA

For issues covered in this section, see D. Potter, *Constantine the Emperor* (Oxford, 2012).

36 **Constantine's Good Friday sermon**: H.A. Drake, *Constantine and the Bishops: the Politics of Intolerance* (Baltimore, 2000): 292–305.

38 **Text of the Nicene Creed:** see Socrates, *Ecclesiastical History* 1.8.4.

CHRISTIAN AND NON-CHRISTIAN

See, in general, A. Cameron, *The Last Pagans of Rome* (New York, 2010); E. Watts, *The Final Pagan Generation* (Berkeley, 2015).

39 **Constantine's Letter to Sapor** is in Eusebius, *Life of Constantine* 4.9–13.

40 **Acclamation of Constantine**: see *Theodosian Code* 7.20.2.

40 Augustine, *Confessions* 1.13 (Dido); see also S. MacCormack, *The Shadows of Poetry: Vergil in the Mind of Augustine* (Berkeley, 1998).

41 **Closing temples**: Eusebius, *Life of Constantine* 3.55–56.

41 **Letter to Orcistus**: P.R. Coleman-Norton, *Roman State and Christian Church: A Collection of Legal Documents to A.D. 535* 1 (Eugene, 1966): 95–98.

41 **Letter to Spello (ancient Hispellum)**: N. Lewis and M. Reinhold, *Roman Civilization* vol. 2, 3rd edition (New York, 1990): 579–580.

42 I. Sevchenko and N.P. Sevchenko, *The Life of Saint Nicholas of Sion* (Washington, 1984).

42 **Death of Hypatia**: E. Watts, *Hypatia: The Life and Legend of an Ancient Philosopher. Women in Antiquity* (New York, 2017).

Chapter 2: The Rise of Islam

All quotations from the Koran are taken from M.A.S. Abdel Haleem, *The Qur'an* (Oxford, 2004). The understanding of Muhammad in the text leans heavily on J. Cole, *Muhammad: Prophet of Peace Amid the Clash of Empires* (New York, 2018).

THE WORDS OF THE PROPHET

47 **The first vision**: *Sura* 97.

47 **Treatment of orphans**: *Sura* 93.9–10.

48 **Manuscript in the Mingana Collection**: see https://www.birmingham.ac.uk/facilities/cadbury/birmingham-quran-mingana-collection/birmingham-quran/index.aspx.

48 **Manuscript in Yemen**: B. Sadeghi and M. Goudarzi, "Ṣanʿā' 1 and the Origins of the Qur'an," *Der Islam* 87 (2012): 1–129.

49 N. al-Kaʿbi, *A Short Chronicle on the End of the Sasanian Empire and Early Islam: 590-660 A.D.* (Piscataway, 2016).

49 **Meaning of *jihad***: see Cole, *Muhammad*, 3, 76, 146.

50 **Imperial structures**: M. Whittow, *The Making of Byzantium, 600-1025* (Berkeley, 1996): 36–37.

ECONOMIC DISLOCATION

For the Roman Empire, see especially M. Whittow, *The Making of Byzantium, 600-1025* (Berkeley, 1996). For the state of the Persian Empire, see (despite its title) M. G. Morony, *Iraq after the Muslim Conquest* (Piscataway, 2005).

51 Procopius, *History of the Wars* 2.22.10–11 (apparitions), 2.22.34 (recovery for no obvious cause), 2.23.5–10 (Theodore); W. Witakowski, *Pseudo-Dionysius of Tel-Mahre,* Chronicle, *Part III* (Liverpool, 1997): 83 (town on the Egyptian border), 95 (death toll in Constantinople), 97 (death during transaction), 100–101 (Theodore), 102 (house filled with the dead), and 108–109 (demons as monks); the description of the symptoms is from Evagrius, *History of the Church* 4.29 with P. Allen, *Evagrius Scholasticus the Church Historian* (Louvain, 1981): 190–194 on literary aspects of this and other plague narratives. For the economic impact, see H. Kennedy, "The Justinianic Plague in Syria and the Archaeological Evidence," in L.K. Little, ed., *The Plague and the End of Antiquity*, 87–95; P. Sarris, "Bubonic Plague in Byzantium," in L.K. Little, ed., *The Plague and the End of Antiquity* (Cambridge, 2008); 119–132.

53 **Economic relationship between the Balkans and Turkey:** D. Potter, "Cities in the Eastern Roman Empire from Constantine to Heraclius," in O. Dally and C. Ratté, eds., *Archaeology and the Cities of Asia Minor in Late Antiquity* (Ann Arbor, 2011): 247–260.

54 **Syria**: H. Kennedy, "From Polis to Madina: Urban Change in Late Antique and Early Islamic Syria," *Past and Present* 106 (1985): 3–27 remains the classic treatment. But, see qualifications in G. Avni, "'From Polis to Madina' Revisited—Urban Change in Late Antique and Early Islamic Palestine," *Journal of the Royal Asiatic Society Series* 3 21 (2011): 301–329, stressing the fact that there was no single cause for urban change.

55–6 M.G. Morony, *Iraq after the Muslim Conquest* (Piscataway, 2005): 27–124 for data on Sassanian finances.

56 N. al-Kaʿbi, *A Short Chronicle on the End of the Sasanian Empire and Early Islam: 590-660 A.D.* (Piscataway, 2016): 84 (Jews), 88 (Manicheans).

56 **Comment on Kusru**: see al-Kaʿbi, *Short Chronicle*, 32.

THE GREAT WAR

Crucial to any understanding of the historical record for this period is J. Howard-Johnston, *Witnesses to a World Crisis: Historians and Histories of the Middle East in the Seventh Century* (Oxford, 2010). W.E. Kaegi, *Heraclius, Emperor of Byzantium* (Cambridge, 2003).

57 **Capture of Jerusalem**: R.G. Hoyland, *Theophilus of Edessa's Chronicle and the Circulation of Historical Knowledge in Late Antiquity and Early Islam* (Liverpool, 2011): 64–65 and G.W. Bowersock, *Empires in Collision in Late Antiquity* (Waltham, 2012): 31–51.

58 **Siege of Constantinople**: Kaegi, *Heraclius*, 133–141.

58 **Battle of Nineveh**: R.W. Thomson (tr.), J. Howard-Johnston and T. Greenwood, *The Armenian History Attributed to Sebeos* (Liverpool, 1999): 83–84; C. Mango and R. Scott, *The Chronicle of Theophanes Confessor: Byzantine and Near Eastern History AD 284-813* (Oxford, 1997): 450–451 with Kaegi, *Heraclius*, 160–168 on location and what happened.

58–9 **Fall of Kusru and peace treaty**: see al-Ka'bi, *Short Chronicle*, 62–66; Thomson et al., *Sebeos*, 85; Mango and Scott, *The Chronicle of Theophanes*, 453–455 (end of Kusru); al-Ka'bi, *Short Chronicle* 66–68; Thomson et al., *Sebeos*, 85–87 (Kavad); al-Ka'bi, *Short Chronicle*, 70; Thomson et al., *Sebeos*, 88 (Ardashir); Mango and Scott, *The Chronicle of Theophanes*, 457; Thomson et al., *Sebeos*, 88 (peace treaty); and Kaegi, *Heraclius*, 187–190.

58–9 **The passage quoted comes from**: C.E. Bosworth (tr.), *History of Tabari* vol. 5 *The Sasanids, the Byzantines, the Lakmids, and Yemen* (Albany, 1999): 383; for the sources, see Howard-Johnston, *Witnesses to a World Crisis*, 347–348.

59–60 **Description of Heraclius at Nineveh:** Mango and Scott, *The Chronicle of Theophanes*, 449 (slightly adapted) with Howard-Johnston, *Witnesses to a World Crisis*, 278.

60 **Less dramatic version**: see al-Ka'bi, *Short Chronicle*, 60.

60 **For details of Heraclius' actions after the victory**: see Kaegi, *Heraclius*, 196–210 (more charitable than my take).

61 **Marriage of Heraclius and Martina**: Kaegi, *Heraclius*, 106–107.

MUHAMMAD AND MECCA

See, in general, S.A. Anthony, *Muhammad and the Empires of Faith: The Making of the Prophet of Islam* (Berkeley and Los Angeles, 2020); G.W. Bowersock, *The Crucible of Islam* (Cambridge, MA, 2017); J. Cole, *Muhammad: Prophet of Peace Amid the Clash of Empires* (New York, 2018); F. Donner, *Muhammad and the Believers at the Origins of Islam* (Cambridge, MA, 2010).

61 **Economic role of Mecca**: Bowersock, *The Crucible of Islam*, 48–57.

61–2 **Quotation** is from *Sura* 53.19–23; see, in general, A. al-Azmeh: *The Emergence of Islam in Late Antiquity: Allah and His People* (Cambridge, 2014): 164–275.

62 **Disintegration of Roman and Persian relations with the Jafnids and Nasrids**: R.G. Hoyland, *In God's Path: The Arab Conquest and the Creation of an Islamic Empire* (New York, 2015): 34–35.

62 **Relations between Ethiopia and Arabia**: G.W. Bowersock, *The Throne of Adulis* (Oxford, 2013): 92–133.

63 **Quotations with respect to Muhammad's critics** are from *Sura* 35.4; 7; *Sura* 36.48; 69–70.

63 **Muhammad tells his followers not to respond to critics with violence:** *Sura* 25.63.

63 **Range of believers:** *Sura* 2.62.

63 **Christians should stop fighting**: *Sura* 2.253.

64 **Death of Khadija and Abu Talib**: Cole, *Muhammad,* 87.

64 **Claim Muhammad lied about God**: *Sura* 34.8.

64 **Quotation from the Constitution of Medina** is taken from Donner, *Muhammad and the Believers,* 228.

65 **Muhammad on his followers:** *Sura* 8.72.

65–6 ***Sura* reflecting on an early conflict** is 8.15–16.

66 **"he is only a messenger":** *Sura* 3.144.

66 **Forgiving those who ran away:** *Sura* 3.153.

66 **Treaty of Hudaybiya**: Donner, *Muhammad and the Believers,* 48–49.

66 **"God has Truly fulfilled":** *Sura* 48.27.

66–7 **Muhammad on rabbis and monks**: *Sura* 9.31–3.

67 **Massacre at Najran**: see Bowersock, *Throne of Adulis,* 85–89; for reference in the Koran, see *Sura* 85.4–8.

67 **Harder line toward pagans:** *Sura* 9.3.

68 **Heaven and Hell**: *Sura* 13.38.

68 **Muhammad on the fall of Jerusalem**: see *Sura* 40.2–3, with G.W. Bowersock, *Empires in Collision in Late Antiquity (The Menakem Stern Jerusalem Lectures)* (Boston, 2012): 56 on the date and significance.

68 **Signs of trouble**: F. Donner, *The Early Islamic Conquests* (Princeton, 1981): 101–107 on the battle of Mu'ta in 629 (for which, see C. Mango and R. Scott, *The Chronicle of Theophanes Confessor: Byzantine and Near Eastern History AD 284-813* [Oxford, 1997]: 466).

68 **Noise outside the chamber**: *Sura* 49.2.

CONQUEST

This section draws heavily on F. Donner, *The Early Islamic Conquests* (Princeton, 1981); F. Donner, *Muhammad and the Believers and the Origins of Islam* (Cambridge, MA, 2010) R.G. Howland, *In God's Path: The Arab Conquest and the Creation of an Islamic Empire* (New York, 2015); H. Kennedy, *The Great Arab Conquests* (Philadelphia, 2007).

69 **Significance of Abu Bakhr's title:** Donner, *Muhammad and the Believers*, 98–99.

69 **Four *amirs*:** R.G. Hoyland, *Theophilus of Edessa's Chronicle and the Circulation of Historical Knowledge in Late Antiquity and Early Islam* (Liverpool, 2011): 92–93 with Hoyland's note on the chronology, which is followed here. **For another prophet**, see G.W. Bowersock, *The Crucible of Islam* (Cambridge, MA, 2017):59–63.

69 **Defeat of Khalid ibn al-Walid** is the battle at Mu'ta in 629, mentioned on p. 68 above.

69 **Heraclius refuses to pay Arab tribes**: see C. Mango and R. Scott, *The Chronicle of Theophanes Confessor: Byzantine and Near Eastern History AD 284-813* (Oxford, 1997): 466; for Christians in the Arab armies, see also Hoyland, *In God's Path*, 58. **For Heraclius and the Jews,** see *The Teaching of Jacob Newly Baptized* 1.1–4 (for which, see, conveniently, http://andrewjacobs.org/translations/doctrina.html). Maximus the Confessor, *Letter* 8 (http://andrewjacobs.org/translations/maximos.html) provides direct contemporary attestation; see otherwise M. Moosa (tr.), *The Syriac Chronicle of Michael Rabo (the Great): A Universal History from the Creation* (Piscataway, 2014): 455.

70 **Defeat of Theodore and capture of Damascus:** Mango and Scott, *The Chronicle of Theophanes Confessor*, 468; Hoyland, *Theophilus of Edessa*, 93–94 for other sources; see also W.E. Kaegi, *Heraclius, Emperor of Byzantium* (Cambridge, 2003): 230–231.

70 **Siege warfare**: see Kennedy, *The Great Arab Conquests*, 85–86 (siege of Homs); P. Sijpesteijn, *Shaping a Muslim State: The World of a Mid-Eighth Century Egyptian Official* (Oxford, 2013): 53 (in Egypt later).

70 **Succession of 'Umar**: Donner, *Muhammad and the Believers*, 146.

70 **Western understanding of the Arab community:** see R. Hoyland, *Seeing Islam as Others Saw It* (Princeton, 1997): 69; *The Teaching of Jacob Newly Baptized* 5.16.

71 **Battle of Yarmouk**: see especially N. al-Ka'bi, *A Short Chronicle on the End of the Sasanian Empire and Early Islam: 590-660 A.D.* (Piscataway, 2016): 80, 104–105; Mango and Scott, *The Chronicle of Theophanes Confessor*, 470; R.W. Thomson (tr.), J. Howard-Johnson and T. Greenwood, *The Armenian History Attributed to Sebeos* (Liverpool, 1999): 97; Hoyland, *Theophilus of Edessa*, 101–103 with Kennedy, *The Great Arab Conquests*, 83–85.

71 **Jerusalem**: see Kennedy, *The Great Arab Conquests*, 90–93; Hoyland, *In God's Path*, 48.

71–2 **The document quoted** is *P. Rain*. 30 n. 11.

72 **Conquest of Egypt:** see now Sijpesteijn, *Shaping a Muslim State*, 49–58.

72 **Rustam's worries:** Kennedy, *The Great Arab Conquests*, 111–115.

72 **Battle of Quadisiyya**: Donner, *Early Islamic Conquests*, 201–212 (important for sorting out issues with the sources) and Kennedy, *The Great Arab Conquests*, 115–117.

72 **Persian deserters**: Hoyland, *In God's Path*, 60.

73 al-Ka'bi, *A Short Chronicle*, 88 (Christian official).

73 **Bishop of Nineveh:** quoted from M.P. Penn, *When Christians First Met Muslims: A Sourcebook of the Earliest Syriac Writings on Islam* (Berkeley, 2015): 36.

THE RISE OF ISLAM

This discussion draws heavily on F. Donner, *The Early Islamic Conquests* (Princeton, 1981); F. Donner, *Muhammad and the Believers at the Origins of Islam* (Cambridge, MA, 2010); R.G. Howland, *In God's Path: The Arab Conquest and the Creation of an Islamic Empire* (New York, 2015); H. Kennedy, *The Prophet and the Age of the Caliphates: The Islamic Near East from the Sixth to Eleventh Century* (Harlow, 1986).

74 **Death of 'Uthman and 'Ali:** Donner, *Muhammed and the Believers,* 156–157; Kennedy, *The Prophet,* 73–78.

75 **Transition in qualifications for leadership:** see Crone and M. Hinds, *God's Caliph: Religious Authority in the First Centuries of Islam* (Cambridge, 2003): 24–42; Donner, *Muhammad and the Believers,* 170–193.

75 **Quotations from the inscription on the Dome of the Rock:** taken from Donner, *Muhammad and the Believers,* 234–235.

76 **For the title *Khalifa:*** see Crone and Hinds, *God's Caliph,* 1–23.

76–7 **Changes in coinage:** see Donner, *Muhammad and the Believers,* 210.

77–8 **Syriac accounts:** M.P. Penn, *Envisioning Islam: Syriac Christians and the Early Muslim World* (Philadelphia, 2015): 56–59; M.P. Penn, *When Christians First Met Muslims: A Sourcebook of the Earliest Syriac Writings on Islam* (Berkeley, 2015): 28 (Arabs of Mohammad), 33 (Hagarenes); N. al-Ka'bi, *A Short Chronicle on the End of the Sasanian Empire and Early Islam: 590-660 A.D.* (Piscataway, 2016): 78 (sons of Ishmael); Penn, *When Christians,* 81 (Hagarenes, who now rule, contrasted with pagans). **For Hagarism,** see especially Crone and M. Cook, *Hagarism: The Making of the Islamic World* (Cambridge, 1980): 12–15, 21–22; R. Hoyland, *Seeing Islam as Others Saw It* (Princeton, 1997): 89–90, 110–111, 218.

Chapter 3: The Protestant Reformation

CHURCH AND STATE

This discussion draws heavily on E. Cameron, *The European Reformation* 2nd edition (Oxford, 2012); D. MacCulloch, *The Reformation: A History* (New York, 2003); and P.H. Wilson, *The Holy Roman Empire: A Thousand Years of Europe's History* (London, 2016).

82 **Origin of the Ottomans**: see R.P. Lindner, *Explorations in Ottoman Prehistory* (Ann Arbor, 2007).

83 **Church and State**: Cameron, *The European Reformation*, 56–60.

84 **Sentence of Jan Hus**: the quotation is from Council of Constance; see http://www.legionofmarytidewater.com/faith/ECUM16.HTM. For the circumstances, see Wilson, *The Holy Roman Empire*, 99.

THE HOLY ROMAN EMPIRE

This section draws heavily from P.H. Wilson, *The Holy Roman Empire: A Thousand Years of Europe's History* (London, 2016).

86 Voltaire, *Essais sur les moeurs et l'esprit des nations et sur les principaux faits de l'histoire, depuis Charlemagne jusqu'à Louis XIII* 3 (Neuchâtel, 1773): 338–339. "Ce corps qui s'appelait, et qui s'appelle encore, le Saint-Empire Romain, n'etait en aucune manière, ni saint, ni romain, ni empire" (cited from https://archive.org/details/essaissurlesmoeu03volt/page/338).

86 **The Golden Bull**: see the text at https://avalon.law.yale.edu/medieval/golden.asp. The document took its title from the golden seal, or *bulla*, which was attached to copies that were circulated through the territory of the empire.

87–88 **Habsburg succession:** see Wilson, *The Holy Roman Empire*, 401–2.

88 D. Parrott, *The Business of War: Military Enterprise and Military Revolution in Early Modern Europe* (Cambridge, 2012) is crucial on economic aspects of warfare in the pre-modern period.

THE UNIVERSAL CHURCH

This section draws heavily on E. Cameron, *The European Reformation* 2nd edition (Oxford, 2012); J. le Goff, *The Birth of Purgatory* (tr. A. Goldhammer) (Chicago, 1981); and D. MacCulloch, *The Reformation: A History* (New York, 2003).

90 **Aquinas on sacraments:** see *Summa Theologica* part 3, question 60, for the summary in the text with discussion, in O-T. Venard, "Sacraments," in P. McCosker and D. Turner, eds., *The Cambridge Companion to the* Summa Theologicae (Cambridge, 2016): 269–287.

90 **Sacraments:** see H. Denzinger, *The Sources of Catholic Dogma* (tr. R.J. DeFerrari) (London, 1954): 220–225, from the Bull *Exultate Deo* issued on November 22, 1439.

92 **Augustine:** see J. le Goff, *The Birth of Purgatory* (tr. A. Goldhammer) (Chicago, 1981): 64–78.

92 **Lough Derg**: le Goff, *The Birth of Purgatory*, 193–201.

93 **Visions of Purgatory:** S. Greenblatt, *Hamlet in Purgatory* (Princeton, 2001): plate 1 (*Compendium of Theological Truth*); 54, Fig. 3 (mouth of a cat); 55, Fig. 4 (devils); 56, Fig. 5 (cauldron).

93 Dante, *Purgatorio, Canto* 25.96–7.

93 Denzinger, *The Sources of Catholic Dogma*, 201–202.

94 **Sixtus IV**: see Denzinger, *The Sources of Catholic Dogma*, 234–235 with D. MacCulloch, *The Reformation*, 118.

94 **Number of printed indulgences**: A. Pettegree, *The Book in the Renaissance* (New Haven, 2010): 94.

PUBLISHERS AND SCHOLARS

This discussion draws heavily on E.L. Eisenstein, *The Printing Revolution in Early Modern Europe* (Cambridge, 2005); M. Massing, *Fatal Discord: Erasmus, Luther and the Fight for the Western Mind* (New York, 2018); A. Pettegree, *The Book in the Renaissance* (New Haven, 2010).

95 See A. Pettegree, *The Book in the Renaissance* (New Haven, 2010): 23–33 for Gutenberg and his colleagues.

96 **Poggio's habits:** see C.B. Krebs, *A Most Dangerous Book: Tacitus'* Germania *from the Roman Empire to the Third Reich* (New York, 2012), and for **Valla,** see M. Massing, *Fatal Discord: Erasmus, Luther and the Fight for the Western Mind* (New York, 2018): 43–45; G.W. Bowersock, *Valla and the Donation of Constantine* (Cambridge, MA, 2007).

97–8 **This version of Erasmus' career** depends on Massing, *Fatal Discord*, 56–75, 109–116, 140–161, and 192–216.

MARTIN LUTHER

This section draws heavily upon S.H. Hendrix, *Martin Luther: Visionary Reformer* (New Haven, 2015); R. Marius, *Martin Luther: The Christian Between God and Death* (Cambridge, MA, 1999).

99 **Luther's birthdate** is controversial; for what is in the text, see: Hendrix, *Martin Luther* 17.

99 **Luther and his father**: see Marius, *Martin Luther* 18–23; Hendrix, *Martin Luther*, 18–20.

99 **For the storm**, see Hendrix, *Martin Luther*, 33; Marius, *Martin Luther*, 43.

99 **Trip to Rome**: Hendrix, *Martin Luther*, 81–84; M. Massing, *Fatal Discord: Erasmus, Luther and the Fight for the Western Mind* (New York, 2018): 162–165.

100 **Spalatin:** see Hendrix, *Martin Luther*, 31, 46; for **Staupitz**, see Hendrix, *Martin Luther*, 39, 43–47; Marius, *Martin Luther*, 134. For **Frederick's hostility to the new indulgence:** see B.S. Gregory, *Rebel in the Ranks: Martin Luther, the Reformation, and the Conflicts that Continue to Shape our World* (New York, 2017): 42; Hendrix, *Martin Luther*, 57; Marius, *Martin Luther*, 134.

100 **Complaints against the Church**: E. Cameron, *The European Reformation* 2nd edition (Oxford, 2012): 106.

101 See, for instance, *Inferno* Canto 10.120 (Cardinal Ottaviano degli Ubaldini); *Canto* 11. 8 (pope Anastasius); Canto 19.50 (pope Nicholas III); 82 (pope Clement V).

101 **Luther's training**: Hendrix, *Martin Luther,* 51–52; Marius, *Martin Luther,* 88–127.

102 There is debate as to whether Luther actually nailed the theses to the door. For the affirmative position, see Hendrix, *Martin Luther,* 61; less certain is Marius, *Martin Luther,* 137–138. What he certainly did was arrange for rapid publication; see A. Pettegree, *Brand Luther: 1517, Printing and the Making of the Reformation* (New York, 2015): 73–77.

102 Quoted here are (in this order): thesis 28; thesis 32; thesis 75; thesis 76; thesis 6; thesis 20; thesis 21.

103 **For the text of the indulgence:** see H.J. Hillerbrand, *The Reformation: A Narrative History Related by Contemporary Observers and Participants* (New York, 1964): 37–41.

104 **Tetzel's sermon:** see Hillerbrand, *The Reformation,* 44.

104 **Frederick and Albrecht:** see Hendrix, *Martin Luther,* 57–60.

THE LUTHERAN REFORMATION

This discussion draws heavily upon S.H. Hendrix, *Martin Luther: Visionary Reformer* (New Haven, 2015); R. Marius, *Martin Luther: The Christian Between God and Death* (Cambridge, MA, 1999); G. Parker, *Emperor: A New Life of Charles V* (New Haven, 2019).

105 **Publication of the Ninety-Five Theses**: A. Pettegree, *Brand Luther: 1517, Printing and the Making of the Reformation* (New York, 2015): 73–77.

106 **For the three major works:** see Hendrix, *Martin Luther* 85–98; Marius, *Martin Luther*: 237–274; Pettegree, *Brand Luther,* 124–131.

106 **Quotations from *To the Christian Nobility*** are taken from https://sourcebooks.fordham.edu/mod/luther-nobility.asp.

106 **Charles' initial response to Luther**: see Parker, *Emperor*: 117–118.

107 **Quotations from *The Freedom of the Christian Man*** are taken from https://sourcebooks.fordham.edu/mod/luther-freedomchristian.asp.

107 H.J. Hillerbrand, *The Reformation: A Narrative History Related by Contemporary Observers and Participants* (New York, 1964): 85 (incineration of the papal bull).

107 The quotation is given in various forms—for example, the language spoken to God being Spanish—but it is always German to the horse. To the point, see Parker, *Emperor,* 120. Charles did not speak a word of German in public before March 1521.

108–9 Luther is quoted from Hillerbrand, *The Reformation,* 91; for the question of "here I stand," see Marius, *Martin Luther,* 294.

109 See Parker, *Emperor,* 122–123 on the gesture.

109 **Charles' decree**: see Hillerbrand, *The Reformation*, 95–100.

109 **Wartburg**: see Hendrix, *Martin Luther*, 119–128.

109 See Parker, *Emperor*, 130–138 on the war in Italy.

109–10 **Luther's associates**: see Hendrix, *Martin Luther*, 128–148.

110 **Zwingli**: see B.S. Gregory, *Rebel in the Ranks: Martin Luther, the Reformation, and the Conflicts that Continue to Shape Our World* (New York, 2017): 97–133; D. MacCulloch, *The Reformation: A History* (New York, 2003): 166–174, and 245–261 for **Calvin**.

110 **Müntzer**: Hendrix, *Martin Luther*, 148–151; Hillerbrand, *The Reformation*, 221–227; P.H. Wilson, *The Holy Roman Empire: A Thousand Years of Europe's History* (London, 2016): 591–593 for the issues.

111 See Parker, *Emperor*, 165–173 on the sack of Rome.

PROTESTANT GERMANY

This discussion draws heavily upon S.H. Hendrix, *Martin Luther: Visionary Reformer* (New Haven, 2015); R. Marius, *Martin Luther: The Christian Between God and Death* (Cambridge, MA, 1999); D. MacCulloch, *The Reformation: A History* (New York, 2003); G. Parker, *Emperor: A New Life of Charles V* (New Haven, 2019).

111 **Speyer:** MacCulloch, *The Reformation*, 160 and Hendrix, *Martin Luther*, 177–180.

112 **Speyer 1529**: see http://www.gedaechtniskirche.de/fileadmin/user_upload/werke/bv-gedaechtniskirche/dateien/Text_Protestation.pdf with MacCulloch, *The Reformation*, 166–168.

112 **Turkish invasion:** Parker, *Emperor* 226–229.

113 **Augsburg Confession:** see https://www.stpls.com/uploads/4/4/8/0/44802893/augsburg-confession.pdf with M. Massing, *Fatal Discord: Erasmus, Luther and the Fight for the Western Mind* (New York, 2018), 731–733; MacCulloch, *The Reformation*, 169–170.

113 **Schmalkalden League**: see Parker, *Emperor*, 198.

113–14 **Zwingli and Calvin:** see MacCulloch, *The Reformation*, 170–174, 230–240.

THE ENGLISH REFORMATION

This section draws heavily on P. Marshall, *Heretics and Believers: A History of the English Reformation* (New Haven, 2017); D. MacCulloch, *Thomas Cranmer. A Life* (New Haven, 1996); D. MacCulloch, *Thomas Cromwell. A Revolutionary Life* (New York, 2018).

115 **Henry VII and Catherine:** MacCulloch, *Thomas Cromwell*, 13.

115 **Army costs**: S. Gunn, *The English People at War in the Age of Henry VIII* (Oxford, 2018): 73–95.

116–17 **Wolsey's early career:** MacCulloch, *Thomas Cromwell,* 14.

117 **The case of Richard Hunne:** Marshall, *Heretics and Believers* 88–95; the passage quoted is on p. 94.

117 **Henry VIII and Luther:** R. Marius, *Martin Luther: The Christian Between God and Death* (Cambridge, MA, 1999): 339–341.

117–8 **Cromwell's early career:** see MacCulloch, *Thomas Cromwell,* 22–74; for **Tyndale**, see M. Massing, *Fatal Discord: Erasmus, Luther and the Fight for the Western Mind* (New York, 2018): 688–691.

118 **Affair with Anne Boleyn**: MacCulloch, *Thomas Cromwell,* 77–79; for an **unflattering description of Anne Boleyn**, see H.J. Hillerbrand, *The Reformation: A Narrative History Related by Contemporary Observers and Participants* (New York, 1964), 317.

119 **Wolsey and the divorce:** MacCulloch, *Thomas Cromwell,* 75–85; G. Parker, *Emperor: A New Life of Charles V* (New Haven, 2019), 174, 184, 192 on Charles' role (essentially, Henry's request was going nowhere).

119 **Consultation of Luther:** Hillerbrand, *The Reformation,* 318 and H. Hendrix, *Martin Luther: Visionary Reformer* (New Haven, 2015), 239–240.

119–121 MacCulloch, *Thomas Cranmer* 25–37. For More's role, see Marshall, *Heretics and Believers,* 185–191; S. Greenblatt, *Hamlet in Purgatory* (Princeton, 2001), 134–150 for More and Purgatory.

121 **Separation from Rome and Cromwell's role**: MacCulloch, *Thomas Cromwell,* 156–230; for key documents, see Hillerbrand, *The Reformation,* 324–335.

122 **Ten Articles**: MacCulloch, *Thomas Cranmer,* 161–166.

122 **Cranmer on Purgatory:** Marshall, *Heretics and Believers,* 256.

122–3 **Pilgrimage of Grace:** MacCulloch, *Thomas Cromwell,* 372–397.

123 **Fall of Cromwell**, MacCulloch, *Thomas Cromwell,* 506–531.

THE BIRTH OF THE NETHERLANDS

This discussion draws heavily on J. Israel, *The Dutch Republic: Its Rise, Greatness, and Fall 1477–1806* (Oxford, 1995) and M. Van Gelderen, *The Political Thought of the Dutch Revolt* (Cambridge, 1992).

124 **Absence of feudal regimes**: Israel, *The Dutch Republic,* 106–107; Van Gelderen, *The Political Thought of the Dutch Revolt,* 22–23.

125 **Charles' response**: see p. 106 above.

125 **The Supplication of Beggars**: P. Marshall, *Heretics and Believers: A History of the English Reformation* (New Haven, 2017), 156–158.

126 **Economy**: Israel, *The Dutch Republic,* 116–122.

126 **Executions**: see Israel, *The Dutch Republic,* 93.

126 **Menno Simons and Dirk Philips**: Israel, *The Dutch Republic,* 91–93.

127 J. Calvin, *Institutes of the Christian Religion* (tr. H. Beveridge) vol. 2 (Edinburgh, 1863): 675 for when popular magistrates have been appointed to curb the

tyranny of kings (as the Ephori, who were opposed to kings among the Spartans, or Tribunes of the people to consuls among the Romans, or Demarchs to the senate among the Athenians. And perhaps there is something similar to this in the power exercised in each kingdom by the three orders, when they hold their primary Diets). "So far am I from forbidding these officially to check the undue license of kings, that if they connive at kings when they tyrannise and insult over the humbler of the people, I affirm that their dissimulation is not free from nefarious perfidy, because they fraudulently betray the liberty of the people, while knowing that, by the ordinance of God, they are its appointed guardians."

127 D. MacCulloch, *The Reformation: A History* (New York, 2003), 227–230, 294–296 (**Council of Trent**), 212–219 (**Loyola**); G. Parker, *Emperor: A New Life of Charles V* (New Haven, 2019), 326–336 (**Mühlberg and aftermath**).

128 **Mary Tudor**: see Marshall, *Heretics and Believers*, 356–416.

130 **Pragmatic sanction**: Parker, *Emperor*, 414–416.

130 **War with France**: Israel, *The Dutch Republic*, 131–136.

131–32 Israel, *The Dutch Republic*, 138–139 (**William and Granville**); Van Gelderen, *The Political Thought of the Dutch Revolt*, 73–74 (**Dathenus**).

132–33 Van Gelderen, *The Political Thought of the Dutch Revolt*, 77–81 (**de Bray and de Zuttere**).

133 Van Gelderen, *The Political Thought of the Dutch Revolt*, 91–93 (**Michaellam**).

133 **Council of Troubles**: Israel, *The Dutch Republic*, 158–160.

133 The quotation is from William of Orange, "Faithful exhortation to the inhabitants of the Netherlands against the vain and false hopes their oppressors hold out to them, 1568" in E.H. Kossman and A.F. Mellink, *Texts Concerning the Revolt of the Netherlands* (Cambridge, 2012) n. 12.

134–35 **The quotation of the Union of Utrecht** is from Kossman and Mellink, *Texts Concerning the Revolt of the Netherlands* n. 37.

135 **Declaration of independence:** Kossman and Mellink, *Texts Concerning the Revolt of the Netherlands* n. 49.

Chapter 4: Popular Sovereignty

PEACE

138 **Treaty ending the American Revolution:** see https://www.ourdocuments.gov/doc.php?flash=true&doc=6.

CIVIL SOCIETIES: BODIN AND HOBBES

This section depends (especially for the starting point with Bodin) on B. Straumann, *Crisis and Constitutionalism: Roman Political Thought from the Fall of the Republic to the Age of Revolution* (Oxford, 2016); R. Tuck, *The Sleeping Sovereign: The Invention of Modern Democracy* (Cambridge, 2015).

142–3 The quotations here are from J.H. Franklin (ed. and tr.), *Bodin: On Sovereignty* (Cambridge, 1992): 16, 6, 115.

143 **Bodin on magistrates:** see B. Straumann, *Crisis and Constitutionalism.* **Bodin on "enemies of the human race":** see D. Edelstein, *The Terror of Natural Right: Republicanism, the Cult of Nature & the French Revolution* (Chicago, 2009): 35.

145 **For this version of the origin of the English civil war:** B. Worden, *The English Civil Wars 1640-1660* (London, 2009): 1–39.

146 **Death Warrant of Charles I:** see https://www.parliament.uk/about/living-heritage/evolutionofparliament/parliamentaryauthority/civilwar/collections/deathwarrant/ transcribed at https://en.wikisource.org/wiki/Death_warrant_of_King_Charles_I.

146–7 **Hobbes' early life:** R. Tuck, *Hobbes* (Oxford, 1989): 1–27.

148–9 Quotations are from T. Hobbes, *Leviathan* (R. Tuck, ed.) (Cambridge, 1996): 88, 89, 120, 231, 237, 280, 402.

149 **Charge Hobbes was an atheist:** Tuck, *Hobbes,* 27–31.

150 The quotation is from Montesquieu, *The Spirit of the Laws* (tr. T. Nugent) (New York, 1949): 162.

LOCKE, MONTESQUIEU, AND THE ENLIGHTENMENT

For this section, see M. Jacob, *The Secular Enlightenment* (Princeton, 2019); S. Pincus, *1688 The First Modern Revolution* (New Haven, 2009); B. Straumann, *Crisis and Constitutionalism: Roman Political Thought from the Fall of the Republic to the Age of Revolution* (Oxford, 2016); R. Tuck, *The Sleeping Sovereign: The Invention of Modern Democracy* (Cambridge, 2015).

150–1 This discussion of Locke's career depends on J. Locke, *Two Treatises of Government* (P. Laslett, ed.) (Cambridge, 1970): 16–44.

152–4 **Quotations from Locke**, *Two Treatises* (Laslett, ed.) are from pp. 280 (rejection of Hobbes' state of nature), 269 (state of nature is state of perfect freedom), 283 (natural liberty), 293 (the rule of propriety), 296 (puts the difference of value), 301 (different degrees of industry), 306 (power of parents), 331 (one divests himself of his natural liberty), 326 (absolute monarchy is inconsistent with civil), 276 (judges in their own case), 351 (preservation of their property), 400 (tyranny begins), 398 (exercise of power), and 411 (people are at liberty).

155 **For the *Treatise of the Three Imposters* and the *Persian Letters:*** see Jacob, *The Secular Enlightenment* 92–96; quotations from Montesquieu, *The Spirit of the Laws* (tr. T. Nugent) (New York, 1949) are from pp. 3 (Man is reminded of God), 6 (Law, in general, is human reason), 17 (depositary of the laws),

151–152 (no liberty), 154 (chief inconveniences of a democracy), and 156 (there will be an end to liberty).

157 **Gibbon and Montesquieu**: R. Shackleton, "The Influence of French Literature on Gibbon," *Daedalus* 105.3 (1976): 37–48.

ROUSSEAU AND REVOLUTION: THE IMPACT OF LITERATURE

For this section, see in particular A.S. Curran, *Diderot and the Art of Thinking Freely* (New York, 2019); R. Darnton, *The Forbidden Bestsellers of Pre-Revolutionary France* (New York, 1995); D. Edelstein, *The Terror of Natural Right: Republicanism, the Cult of Nature & the French Revolution* (Chicago, 2009); J. Israel, *The Enlightenment that Failed: Ideas, Revolution and Democratic Defeat 1748-1830* (Oxford, 2019); M. Jacob, *The Secular Enlightenment* (Princeton, 2019).

159 **Rousseau's early life:** see J.-J. Rousseau, *The Basic Political Writings,* D.A. Cress tr. and ed., introduction and notes by D. Wooton, 2nd edition (Indianapolis, 2011): xii–xiii; Curran, *Diderot,* 38–41.

159 The discussion here tracks R. Darnton, *The Forbidden Bestsellers of Pre-Revolutionary France* (New York, 1995); for critics of the view, see H. Mason, *The Darnton Debate: Books and Revolution in the Eighteenth Century* (Oxford, 1999). My reasons for following Darnton's approach emerge in the text, but see also J.D. Popkin, *A New World Begins: The History of the French Revolution* (New York, 2019): 47–57.

159 For these entries in the *Encyclopédie,* see Curran, *Diderot,* 121–124.

160 **Rousseau and Diderot**: see Curran, *Diderot,* 37–41, 151–161.

161 **Rousseau on Hobbes**: see Rousseau, *The Basic Political Writings,* 61.

161 Rousseau, *The Basic Political Writings,* 24.

161 Rousseau, *The Basic Political Writings*; quotations are from pp. 128 (trample underfoot), 128 (securing the goods, life and liberty), and 131 (every prince).

162 **Tahiti:** see Edelstein, *The Terror of Natural Right,* 94–99; Curran, *Diderot,* 276–285.

162 **Diderot on natural law**: see http://www.ac-grenoble.fr/PhiloSophie/diderot-encyclopedie-article-droit-naturel/: "que celui qui refuse de la chercher renonce à la qualité d'homme, et doit être traité par le reste de son espèce comme une bête farouche, et que la vérité une fois découverte, quiconque refuse de s'y conformer, est insensé ou méchant d'une méchanceté morale," "Dans les principes du droit ecrit de tous les nations policées, dans les actions sociales des peuples sauvages et barbares; dans les conventions tacites des ennemis du genre humain entre eux et même dans l'indignation et le ressentiment" (my translation in the text).

163 Rousseau, *Basic Political Writings,* 156 (man in chains), 164 (defends and protects).

163–4 Rousseau, *Basic Political Writings,* 159 (natural authority), 247 (waste of time), 178 (all justice comes from God); for the significance, see Israel, *The Enlightenment that Failed* 467; Jacobs, *Secular Enlightenment,* 116–120.

164 Rousseau, *Basic Political Writings,* 174 (not even the social contract), 172 (general will always right), 170 (sovereignty product of the general will), 169 (private property), and 164 (each person then regains his first rights and resumes his natural liberty).

164–5 Voltaire quoted from I. Kramnick, *The Portable Enlightenment Reader* (New York, 1995): 194.

165 **For these alleged scandals:** see Darnton, *Forbidden Bestsellers,* 147–167.

165–6 T. Paine, *Common Sense and the American Crisis,* with an introduction by Richard Beeman (New York, 2012): 89; for **Paine's arrival on the scene**, see J. Ferling, *Apostles of Revolution: Jefferson, Paine, Monroe and the Struggle Against the Old Order in America and Europe* (New York, 2018): 30–55.

AMERICAN INDEPENDENCE

For the narrative, the text leans on R. Middlekauff, *The Glorious Cause: The American Revolution, 1763-1789* (Oxford, 2005); the view of Washington taken in what follows is essentially that of J.T. Flexner, *Washington: The Indispensable Man* (Boston, 1994). I am aware that it is quite possible to paint a less positive picture of Washington's role than I offer here, but I feel that the comparison between France and the United States reinforces Flexner's position that Washington was indispensable (and that indispensable does not need to mean perfect).

166–7 Middlekauff, *The Glorious Cause,* 214–279 for the outbreak of the war.

167 **Declaration of July 6, 1775:** quoted from J.K. Rakove, ed., *Founding America: Documents from the Revolution to the Bill of Rights* (New York, 2006): 53–59.

168 **Campaign of 1775 through July 4, 1776**: see Middlekauff, *The Glorious Cause,* 298–339.

168–9 **Quotations from *Common Sense***: T. Paine, *Common Sense and the American Crisis* with an introduction by Richard Beeman (New York, 2012): 14 (order of creation) and 21 (larger number of bad ones . . . armed banditti).

169 **For the connection between Paine, Adams, and Jefferson:** see J. Ferling, *Apostles of Revolution: Jefferson, Paine, Monroe and the Struggle Against the Old Order in America and Europe* (New York, 2018): 50–51.

170 ***Declaration of Independence:*** quoted from Rakove, ed., *Founding America,* 136–141.

TOWARD A MORE PERFECT UNION

This discussion draws heavily from B. Bailyn, *The Ideological Origins of the American Revolution* (Cambridge, MA, 1967); C. Berkin, *A Brilliant Solution: Inventing the American Constitution* (New York, 2003); J. Ellis, *The Quartet: Orchestrating the Second American Revolution 1783-1789* (New York, 2015); E.S. Morgan, *Inventing the People: The Rise of Popular Sovereignty in England and America* (New York, 1988). While I take Ellis' point, *The Quartet*, xiv, that things have moved on from the case made in C. Beard, *An Economic Interpretation of the Constitution of the United States* (New York, 1913), that the constitution was the product of a commercial faction, but we are still left with a model of a narrow group of individuals with similar backgrounds—former officers of the Continental Army—as the driving force behind the creation of the document.

171–2 **Articles of Confederation:** quoted from J.K. Rakove, ed., *Founding America: Documents from the Revolution to the Bill of Rights* (New York, 2006): 158.

172 **Newburgh mutiny:** (as the movement on March 1783 is also known); see R. Middlekauff, *The Glorious Cause: The American Revolution, 1763-1789* (Oxford, 2005): 603–605; for **Washington's speech**, see Rakove, ed., *Founding America*, 233–236.

173–4 **Rush**: see Rakove, ed., *Founding America*, 308–313.

174 **Western expansion**: see Ellis, *The Quartet*: 72–80.

174 **Shays' rebellion:** Ellis, *The Quartet*, 101–103; Middlekauff, *The Glorious Cause*, 621.

174–5 **Annapolis convention and decision to call the constitutional convention**: see Ellis, *The Quartet*, 97–120.

175 **Hamilton's letter**: see Rakove, ed., *Founding America*, 315.

175 **Resolution calling the Constitutional Convention**: see Rakove, ed., *Founding America*, 316.

175 **Critic's voice**: see Rakove, ed., *Founding America*, 435–475.

175 **For the continuing influence of Paine and views of government**: see Bailyn, *The Ideological Origins* 280–300.

176 **Awareness that radical change was the agenda of the core of the constitutional group**: see Berkin, *A Brilliant Solution*: 68–78.

176 **Distributions of food and alcohol and anti-government platforms**: Morgan, *Inventing the People*: 184–186 (also pointing out that the American style was imported from Great Britain where corruption was rampant).

176 **Madison in *The Federalist*, n. 10**: Rakove, ed., *Founding America*, 489.

177 **Madison in *The Federalist*, n. 48**: Rakove, ed., *Founding America*, 521.

177–8 Berkin, *A Brilliant Solution*, 169–190; Middlekauff, *The Glorious Cause*, 621.

FRANCE: 1787–1790

What follows owes a significant debt to the way issues are defined in P. Higonnet, *Sister Republics: Origins of French and American Republicanism* (Cambridge, MA, 1988); for the background, I have used J. Israel, *Revolutionary Ideas: An*

Intellectual History of the French Revolution from the Rights of Man to Robespierre (Princeton, 2014) (noting the critiques offered by D.A. Bell, *NYRB* July 10, 2014, and J.D Popkin, *H-France Review* 15 [May, 2015]); J.D. Popkin, *A New World Begins: The History of the French Revolution* (New York, 2019); S. Schama, *Citizens: A Chronicle of the French Revolution* (New York, 1989); and T. Tackett, *The Coming of the Terror in the French Revolution* (Cambridge, MA, 2015).

179–80 **Structure of the French tax system:** see Schama, *Citizens*, 61–79.

180–1 **The "pre-revolution,"** as the period before the summoning of the Estates General is known: see Tackett, *The Coming of the Terror*, 39–45.

181 Tackett, *The Coming of the Terror*, 51–53; Popkin, *A New World Begins*, 101 on climate problems.

181 **The discussion of the Estates General is based on**: Higonnet, *Sister Republics*, 273–280.

182 **Mirabeau**: see Popkin, *A New World Begins*, 82–84.

182 **Sieyès is quoted from**: L. Hunt, ed., *The French Revolution and Human Rights* (Boston, 1996): 66; see also Popkin, *A New World Begins*, 104–106.

183 **Oath of the Tennis Court**: see L. Mason and T. Rizzo, eds., *The French Revolution: A Document Collection* (New York, 1999): 60–61.

183 **Storming of the Bastille**: see Tackett, *The Coming of the Terror*, 51–59; Popkin, *A New World Begins*, 136–142.

183 **The Great Fear**: G. Lefebvre, *The Great Fear of 1789: Rural Panic in Revolutionary France* (tr. J.A. White) (Princeton, 1983).

183–4 **Marat and Brissot:** see Popkin, *A New World Begins*, 183–184.

184–5 ***The Declaration of the Rights of Man*** is quoted from Hunt, *The French Revolution*, 77–79; see also Popkin, *A New World Begins*, 161–167.

185 **The observer** is quoted from Tackett, *The Coming of the Terror*, 62.

THE END OF THE MONARCHY: 1790–1792

See here, too, P. Higonnet, *Sister Republics: Origins of French and American Republicanism* (Cambridge, MA, 1988); J. Israel, *Revolutionary Ideas: An Intellectual History of the French Revolution from the Rights of Man to Robespierre* (Princeton, 2014); J.D. Popkin, *A New World Begins: The History of the French Revolution* (New York, 2019); S. Schama, *Citizens: A Chronicle of the French Revolution* (New York, 1989); T. Tackett, *The Coming of the Terror in the French Revolution* (Cambridge, MA, 2015).

186 **For the election, see**: Tackett, *The Coming of the Terror*, 79–86.

187 **For the rise of the clubs, see**: Tackett, *The Coming of the Terror*, 86–90; Popkin, *A New World Begins*: 217–223.

187 **Mirabeau and Lafayette**: Schama, *Citizens*: 338–345, 532–543 (Mirabeau), 449–453 (Lafayette); Popkin, *A New World Begins*, 253–254.

187 **Flight of the king**: Schama, *Citizens*, 548–561; Tackett, *The Coming of the Terror*, 113–117; Popkin, *A New World Begins*, 237–244.

187–8 **"Field of Mars":** J. Hardman, *The French Revolution: Sourcebook* (1999): 136–137 (contemporary description); Popkin, *A New World Begins*, 248.

188 **Legislative Assembly**: Tackett, *The Coming of the Terror*, 148–165.

189–90 **Pilnitz and "vengeance":** see Hardman, *The French Revolution*, 141–142 (declaration of war); Tackett, *The Coming of the Terror*, 169; Popkin, *A New World Begins*, 279.

190 **Coup of August 9 and attack on the palace**: see Schama, *Citizens*, 613–618; Tackett, *The Coming of the Terror*, 186–191; Popkin, *A New World Begins*, 280–284.

191 **Electoral turnout and atmosphere**: M.L. Cook, *Elections in the French Revolution: An Apprenticeship in Democracy* (Cambridge, 1986): 79–101.

191 **Paine in France**: J. Ferling, *Apostles of Revolution: Jefferson, Paine, Monroe and the Struggle Against the Old Order in America and Europe* (New York, 2018): 248–272.

191 **Desertion of Lafayette**: see Tackett, *The Coming of the Terror*, 204; Schama, *Citizens*, 610.

191 **Valmy**: see Schama, *Citizens*, 639–642; Popkin, *A New World Begins*, 305–307.

THE TERROR: 1793–1794

See here, too, P. Higonnet, *Sister Republics: Origins of French and American Republicanism* (Cambridge, MA, 1988); J. Israel, *Revolutionary Ideas: An Intellectual History of the French Revolution from the Rights of Man to Robespierre* (Princeton, 2014); A.E. Mayer, *The Furies: Violence and Terror in the French and Russian Revolutions* (Princeton, 2000); J.D. Popkin, *A New World Begins: The History of the French Revolution* (New York, 2019); S. Schama, *Citizens: A Chronicle of the French Revolution* (New York, 1989); T. Tackett, *The Coming of the Terror in the French Revolution* (Cambridge, MA, 2015).

192 **Speech at the constituent assembly, June 22, 1791**: from https://www.marxists.org/history/france/revolution/robespierre/1791/death-penalty.htm.

193 **Robespierre on Terror**: see https://sourcebooks.fordham.edu/mod/robespierre-terror.asp.

193 **Robespierre's intellectual background**: see D. Edelstein, *The Terror of Natural Right: Republicanism, the Cult of Nature & the French Revolution* (Chicago, 2009): 170–256.

194 **For the law of June 10, 1794**: see http://chnm.gmu.edu/revolution/d/439/; see also J. Hardman, *The French Revolution: Sourcebook* (1999): 231–232 for extracts from the debate over the law (Robespierre's approach to "justice" had strong support).

194 **For the immediate death toll:** see Tackett, *The Coming of the Terror*, 329–330.
195 **Robespierre** quoted from Tackett, *The Coming of the Terror*, 231.
195 **Trial of Louis XVI**: see Schama, *Citizens* 649–663; Israel, *Revolutionary Ideas*: 305–311; for Saint-Just's statement, see Israel, *Revolutionary Ideas*, 307; for Robespierre's statement, see Hardman, *The French Revolution*, 161 (adapted).
196 **Description of Robespierre:** quoted from Israel, *Revolutionary Ideas*, 304. The description, dating to the autumn of 1792, is from Jérôme Pétion, the former mayor of Paris and former ally of Robespierre at this point.
196 **Trials of Marie Antoinette and Brissot**: see Schama, *Citizens*, 798–800, 803–804; Popkin, *A New World Begins*, 370–375.
196 **Fall of Robespierre**: see Tackett, *The Coming of the Terror*, 336–339.

THE SOVEREIGN PRINCIPLE

199–200 For the Gettysburg Address, see http://www.abrahamlincolnonline.org/lincoln/speeches/gettysburg.htm.

Chapter 5: Marx and Spencer

THE STUDY OF SOCIETY AS A SCIENCE

For the biography of Marx: see S-E Liedman, *A World to Win: The Life and Works of Karl Marx* (tr. J.N. Skinner) (New York, 2018); for **Darwin**, I've relied on P.J. Bowler, *Charles Darwin: The Man and His Influence* (Cambridge, 1990); J. Brown, *Charles Darwin: The Power of Place* (New York, 2002); for **Herbert Spencer**, M. Francis, *Herbert Spencer and the Invention of Modern Life* (Stocksfield, 2007); D. Wiltshire, *The Social and Political Thought of Herbert Spencer* (Oxford, 1978).
203 **Marx's family**: see Liedman, *A World to Win*, 39–45.
203–4 **University career**: Liedman, *A World to Win*, 68–74.
204–5 **"New Hegelians,"** see Liedman, *A World to Win*, 59–67. For **Marx's exclusion from an academic career:** see J. Israel, *The Enlightenment That Failed: Ideas, Revolution and Democratic Defeat 1748-1830* (Oxford, 2019): 906–915, esp. 907.
205 ***Rhenish Gazette*, marriage, and Engels**: see Liedman, *A World to Win*, 74–105, 126 (first meeting in 1842).
205 **Encounter with communists and socialists**: see Liedman, *A World to Win*, 112–115 with R.C. Tucker, ed., *The Marx-Engels Reader* 2nd edition (New York, 1978): 498 (existing society), 484 (abolition of private property).

206–7 **For the *Economic and Philosophic Manuscripts of 1844*** (so-called despite the actual dates of composition): see Liedman, *A World to Win*, 133–160; the quotations here are from Tucker, ed., *The Marx-Engels Reader*, pp. 150 "their political organization" and "conflict of their interests"), 151–152 ("war, pillage and murder"), 154 ("earth to heaven"), and 157 ("industry and exchange").

207–8 **For the circumstances under which the *Communist Manifesto* was written:** see Liedman, *A World to Win*, 219–240; the quotations here are from Tucker, ed., *The Marx-Engels Reader*, pp. 473 ("history of class struggles"), 475 ("most revolutionary part"), 481 ("the decisive hour"), and 500 ("order of things").

208–9 **Paris revolt in 1848**: see Liedman, *A World to Win*, 244–245; the quotations here are from Tucker, ed., *The Marx-Engels Reader* pp. 590 ("mark its doom"), 589 ("first great battle"), 590 ("monarchy against the people"), and 591 ("long live the revolution").

210 **Marx and the *New York Daily Tribune*:** Liedman, *A World to Win*, 312–316.

210–11 **Surplus value:** quoted from Tucker, ed., *The Marx-Engels Reader*, 700.

211 **Composition of *Capital*:** Liedman, *A World to Win*, 394–462.

211–12 **The English and revolution:** quotation from Liedman, *A World to Win*, 318.

212 Tucker, ed., *The Marx-Engels Reader*, 523 ("by peaceful means" and "moral authority"), 521 ("life's prime want").

212 **Paris Commune:** Liedman, *A World to Win*, 552–561.

212 **German Social Democrats**: Liedman, *A World to Win*, 563–572.

213 **Spencer's early years and employment as an engineer:** D. Wiltshire, *The Social and Political Thought of Herbert Spencer* (Oxford, 1978): 3–45.

214 T. Malthus, *An Essay on the Principle of Population*, Everyman's Library edition (New York, 1914): pp. 5 ("nourishment prepared for it"), 6 ("increase of their species"), 13 ("dignity of human nature"), 18 ("will be considerably greater").

215 C. Lyell, *Principles of Geology* 1 (London, 1830): 144.

215 C. Darwin, *The Origin of Species*, Barnes & Noble Classics edition (New York, 2004): 378.

216 C. Darwin, *The Origin of Species*, 370 (both quotations).

216 H. Spencer, *Data of Ethics* (London, 1879): iii ("a scientific basis").

216 H. Spencer, *Social Statics* (London, 1851): 37 ("adapting himself to them"), 65 ("whole organic creation"), 415 ("of favorable circumstances").

218 H. Spencer, *Essays Scientific, Political and Speculative* (London, 1858): 1, 30–31 ("some universal principle").

218 H. Spencer, *The Principles of Biology* (London, 1868): 462 ("one kind or other").

218 H. Spencer, *First Principles* (London, 1860): 216 ("differentiations and integrations").

218 **Darwin to Hooker**: quoted from https://www.darwinproject.ac.uk/letter/DCP-LETT-5135.xml. See also on P.J. Bowler, *Charles Darwin: The Man and His Influence* (Cambridge, 1990): 169–170.

218–19 H. Spencer, *The Principles of Biology* (London, 1868): 444 ("survival of the fittest"), 455 ("the savage races").

219 C. Darwin, *The Origin of Species* 5th edition (London, 1869): p. 72 ("sometimes equally convenient"), and pp. 92, 95, 103, 105, 125, 145, 149, 160, 168, 226, 239, 421, 566.

219 **Marx and Darwin**: see Liedman, *A World to Win*, 506 and Bowler, *Charles Darwin*, 206.

GALTON, SOCIAL DARWINISM, AND EUGENICS

For Galton, see: N.W. Gillham, *Sir Francis Galton: From African Explorer to the Birth of Eugenics* (Oxford, 2001); **for social Darwinism and eugenics, see**: R.C. Bannister, *Social Darwinism in Anglo-American Thought* (Philadelphia, 1979); A. Cohen, *Imbeciles: The Supreme Court, American Eugenics, and the Sterilization of Carrie Buck* (New York, 2016); P. Croon, *Darwinism, War and History: The Debate Over the Biology of War from the 'Origin of Species' to the First World War* (Cambridge, 1994); M. Hawkins, *Social Darwinism in European and American Thought 1860-1945: Nature as Model and Nature as Threat* (Cambridge, 1997); R. Hofstadter, *Social Darwinism in American Thought* revised edition (Boston, 1955).

220 H. Spencer, *Social Statics* (London, 1851): 84 ("arbitrary rule").

220 H. Spencer, *The Principles of Sociology* (London, 1864): 620 ("individual against the state").

221 H. Spencer in *Westminster Review* 57 (1853): 499–500 ("exemplified in Ireland").

221 T. Malthus, *An Essay on the Principle of Population*, Everyman's Library edition (New York, 1914) vol. 2: 55 ("a gross error").

221 H. Spencer, *A System of Synthetic Philosophy* (London, 1862) vol. 1: 156 ("lower human races"), 157 ("these few generations"). Spencer's later claim that he developed here the theory of "survival of the fittest" can generously be described as misleading.

222 F. Galton, *Hereditary Genius* (London, 1869): 35 "entire population" and "part in the gatherings"), 343 ("race would necessarily fail"), and 357 ("and the desponding"), with Gillham, *Sir Francis Galton*, 155–172.

224–5 F. Galton, *Inquiries into Human Faculty* (London, 1883): 24 n.1 ("express the idea"), 57 ("not tolerate among themselves"), 61 ("detests continuous labour"), 63 ("tends to be inherited"), 81 ("an intelligent society"), and 335–336 ("evolution of a higher humanity").

225 C. Darwin, *The Descent of Man* (London 1871): 157 ("slight corporeal strength"), 152 ("part of our nature"). See also P.J. Bowler, *Charles Darwin: The Man and his Influence* (Cambridge, 1990): 199–200.

226 **For Gautier**, see: Hawkins, *Social Darwinism*, 177. The Russian is Peter Kropotkin, on whom see Hawkins, *Social Darwinism*, 177–179. "British thought": Galton's work appears not to have influenced the Idiots Act of 1888; it did have some impact on the 1913 Mental Deficiency Act, which stopped short of mandatory sterilization, see H. Roberts, *Churchill: Walking with Destiny* (London, 2018): 143.

226 **James Hill**: see Hofstadter, *Social Darwinism*, 45.

226 **Quotations from the dinner at Delmonico's are taken from:** Bannister, *Social Darwinism*, 77.

227 M. Hawkins, *Social Darwinism*, 104–106 (early popularization of Spencer in the US).

227 R.C. Bannister, *Social Darwinism*, 97–113 on Sumner; J. Des Jardins, *Walter Camp: Football and the Modern Man* (New York, 2015): 29–30.

227–8 **Dugdale and Goddard:** see Cohen, *Imbeciles*: 49–53 and S. Kühl, *The Nazi Connection: Eugenics, American Racism, and German National Socialism* (Oxford, 1994): 40.

228 **Eugenics and restrictions on immigration**: Cohen, *Imbeciles*, 127–135.

228 **Carrie Buck**: see Cohen, *Imbeciles* passim. For numbers quoted in the last two sentences of this paragraph, see S. Jindia, "Belly of the Beast: California's Dark History of Forced Sterilizations," *The Guardian*, June 30, 2020.

229 **Hitler's interest in American eugenics legislation**: S. Kühl, *The Nazi Connection*, 37.

229–30 **Reception of social Darwinism in Germany:** see M. Hawkins, *Social Darwinism*, 132–148 (on Haeckl); Theodor Schiemann is the prominent thinker, see T.R.E. Paddock, *Creating the Russian Peril: Education, the Public Sphere, and National Identity in Imperial Germany 1890-1914* (Rochester, NY, 2010). See p. 63 for the quotation here.

230 **Meinecke:** see Paddock, *Creating the Russian Peril*, 147 ("Asiatic barbarism").

230 **"Pan-Slavism" and German thought:** Paddock, *Creating the Russian Peril*, 63 ("thoroughly hostile instinct") and 177.

230 **For von Benhardi's context, see:** J. Leonhard, *Pandora's Box: A History of the First World War* tr. Camiller (London, 2018): 62.

THE TSAR OF ALL THE RUSSIAS

For this section see J. Bergman, *The French Revolutionary Tradition in Russian and Soviet Politics, Political Thought and Culture* (Oxford, 2019); D. Lieven, *Towards the Flames: Empire, War and the End of Tsarist Russia* (London, 2015); R. Pipes, *The Russian Revolution* (New York, 1990); R. Service, *Lenin: A Biography*

(London, 2000); S.A. Smith, *Russia in Revolution: An Empire in Crisis 1890-1928* (Oxford, 2017).

231 C. Clark, *The Sleepwalkers: How Europe Went to War in 1914* (New York, 2012): 480–488; J. Leonhard, *Pandora's Box: A History of the First World War* tr. P. Camiller (Cambridge, MA, 2018): 89–90 on Russian responsibility; G. Wawro, *A Mad Catastrophe: The Outbreak of World War I and the Collapse of the Austro-Hungarian Empire* (New York, 2014): 197–198 (specifically on the absence of necessary artillery shells in the Russian arsenal).

232 **Nicholas and his coronation oath:** Pipes, *The Russian Revolution*, 227 .

232–233 **Structures of Russian society**: see Pipes, *Russian Revolution*, 61–90; Smith, *Russia in Revolution*, 32 (gentry landholdings).

233 **Enrollment in schools:** Smith, *Russia in Revolution*, 33.

233–234 **Universities as hotbeds of opposition**: see Pipes, *Russian Revolution*, 140–146; for **Lenin's early life**, see Service, *Lenin*, 40–41 (ability as a classicist), 56–58 (brother's revolutionary career), 67–71 (Kazan University), 116–125 (marriage and exile), and 129–137 (move to Switzerland). **For Russian terrorism, see**: C. Verhoeven, "'Une Révolution Vraiment Scientifique' Russian Terrorism, the Escape from the European Orbit, and the Invention of a New Revolutionary Paradigm," in K.M. Baker and D. Edelstein, *Scripting Revolution* (Stanford, 2015): 199–212.

235–236 **Quotations from *What is to be Done*** are from the translation in S.E. Bronner, *Twentieth Century Political Theory: A Reader* (London, 1997): 166 ("revolutionary socialist intelligentsia"), 167 ("only from without"), and 168 ("their profession").

236 **Party Congress in 1903**: see Service, *Lenin*, 152–156.

236 **Hostility of the intelligentsia**: Pipes, *Russian Revolution*, 122–135; the figure for plumbing in St. Petersburg is from Smith, *Russia in Revolution*, 36.

TEN YEARS OF TENSION AND TWO YEARS OF DISASTER

For this section see D. Lieven, *Towards the Flames: Empire, War and the End of Tsarist Russia* (London, 2015); R. Pipes, *The Russian Revolution* (New York, 1990); S.A. Smith, *Russia in Revolution: An Empire in Crisis 1890-1928* (Oxford, 2017).

236–237 **Revolution of 1904/5:** see Pipes, *The Russian Revolution*, 3–52; S.A. Smith, *Russia in Revolution*: 45–62. For **Trotsky**, see Smith, *Russia in Revolution*, 52.

237 **Quotation from *What is to be Done*** is from S.E. Bronner, *Twentieth Century Political Theory: A Reader* (London, 1997): 165.

238–239 **Nicholas and the Duma:** Pipes, *Russian Revolution*, 153–190.

239–240 **Divisions in Russian society**: see Lieven, *Towards the Flames*, 51–52 (alternative nationalisms); Pipes, *Russian Revolution*, 193–194; Smith, *Russia in Revolution*, 71–75 (labor unrest and expansion of participation in radical political groups).

240–241 **For the memorandum:** see Lieven, *Towards the Flames,* 303–307; the text of the Durnovo memorandum quoted in the text is from https://www2.stetson.edu/~psteeves/classes/durnovo.html.

241–242 **Discussions of the outbreak of World War I:** see works in the first note to p. 260.

242 **Russian losses in 1915**: see Pipes, *Russian Revolution,* 219; Smith, *Russia in Revolution,* 84–88.

243 **Nicholas and the Duma**: Pipes, *Russian Revolution,* 223–228.

243–244 **Polivanov**: see Pipes, *Russian Revolution,* 241–242. For **Rasputin's advice in 1914:** see D. Smith, "Gregory Rasputin and the Outbreak of the First World War," in T. Brenton, ed. *Was Revolution Inevitable* (Oxford, 2017): 48–65; for his **role in 1915,** see Pipes, *Russian Revolution,* 224–225.

244 **Economic issues**: see Pipes, *Russian Revolution,* 234–238, 272–275; Smith, *Russia in Revolution,* 93–98.

244 **Assassination of Rasputin**: Pipes, *Russian Revolution,* 262–266.

245 **Army in Petrograd**: Pipes, *Russian Revolution,* 278.

LENIN TRIUMPHANT

For this section see J. Bergman, *The French Revolutionary Tradition in Russian and Soviet Politics, Political Thought and Culture* (Oxford, 2019); S. Kotkin, *Stalin: Paradoxes of Power, 1878–1928* (New York, 2014); R. Pipes, *The Russian Revolution* (New York, 1990); R. Service, *Lenin: A Biography* (London, 2000); S.A. Smith, *Russia in Revolution: An Empire in Crisis 1890-1928* (Oxford, 2017).

245 **On the calendar, see:** A. Herman, *1917: Lenin, Wilson, and the Birth of the New World Disorder* (New York, 2017): 130.

245–247 **February 14–26, 1917:** see Pipes, *The Russian Revolution* 271, 274–279; Smith, *Russia in Revolution* 101–102.

246 **Formation of the provisional government**: Pipes, *Russian Revolution,* 289–304.

247 **Abdication of the tsar**: Pipes, *Russian Revolution,* 307–317.

247 **Zimmermann**: Herman, *1917,* 123–130, 141.

247 **Lenin's train ride**: Service, *Lenin*: 256–261.

247–248 **Kamenev and Stalin**: see Smith, *Russia in Revolution,* 113. On riots, see Pipes, *Russian Revolution,* 399–415. **Trotsky's agitation in the United States:** see Herman, *1917,* 225–226; for Miliukov's role in Trotsky's release see Krotkin, *Stalin,* 201.

248 **For the significance of not killing Lenin:** see O. Figes "The 'Harmless Drunk': Lenin and the October Insurrection," in T. Brenton, ed. *Was Revolution Inevitable*? (Oxford, 2017): 123–141.

248 **Increase in the number of soviets**: Smith, *Russia in Revolution,* 108; labor unrest, see Smith, *Russia in Revolution,* 117–124; for **General Order Number 1:**

see Pipes, *Russian Revolution,* 304–307; on the **spring offensive**, see Pipes, *Russian Revolution* 417–419.

249 **Kerensky and Napoleon:** Bergman, *The French Revolutionary Tradition* 149–50; 426.

249 **July riots:** see Pipes, *Russian Revolution,* 419–431; Service, *Lenin,* 281–285. **Charges that Lenin was a spy:** see Service, *Lenin,* 285; 293–294 contra Pipes, *Russian Revolution,* 410–412.

250 **Kornilov affair:** Smith, *Russia in Revolution,* 146–147; Pipes, *Russian Revolution,* 451–46; Kotkin, *Stalin,* 207–11.

250 **October revolution**: Pipes, *Russian Revolution,* 482–496.

251 **Lenin and Mommsen**: see Z. Yavetz, "Caesar, Caesarism and the Historians," *Journal of Contemporary History* 6 (1971): 190, noting that Lenin picked up the Mommsonian concept of "caesarism" (note esp. the vision of government at T. Mommsen, *History of Rome* (tr. Dickson) (Glencoe, Il., 1957) vol. 5: 412–413; **Lenin and Robespierre**: see Service, *Lenin,* 296–297; Bergman, *French Revolutionary Tradition,* 79–109; A.J Mayer, *The Furies, Violence and Terror in the French and Russian Revolutions* (Princeton, 2000): 255. I think it is fair to say that Pipes, *Russian Revolution,* 506–507 overstates the originality of Lenin's thought.

252 **Negotiations with Germany**: see Pipes, *Russian Revolution,* 567–605; Service, *Lenin,* 338–355; Smith, *Russia in Revolution,* 156–157.

252–253 **Murder of the tsar and his family**: see Pipes, *Russian Revolution,* 745–788; for **Dzerzhinsky as Fouquier-Tinville**, see Bergman, *French Revolutionary Tradition,* 172, and p. 496 on Lenin's moral compass.

254 **War Communism and the New Economic Policy:** see Smith, *Russia in Revolution,* 217–312.

FROM LENIN TO STALIN

For this section see S. Fitzpatrick, *The Russian Revolution, 1917–1932* (Oxford, 1982); G. Hosking, *The First Socialist Society: A History of the Soviet Union from Within* 2nd ed. (Cambridge, 1992); S. Kotkin, *Stalin: Paradoxes of Power, 1878–1928* (New York, 2014); S. Kotkin, *Stalin: Waiting for Hitler, 1929–1941* (New York, 2017).

254 Assassination attempt (possibly not carried out by Fanny Kaplan) see Kotkin, *Stalin, Paradoxes of Power,* 285.

254 Putin's grandfather, see Kotkin, *Stalin, Paradoxes of Power,* 413.

255 Trotsky misses Lenin's funeral see Kotkin, *Stalin, Paradoxes of Power,* 537–9.

257 Stalin as a teacher of terror, see Kotkin, *Stalin, Waiting for Hitler,* 435; for agricultural production in 1940, see Kotkin, *Stalin, Waiting for Hitler,* 816.

HITLER AND WEIMAR GERMANY

This discussion draws heavily upon R.J. Evans, *The Coming of the Third Reich: How the Nazis Destroyed Democracy and Seized Power in Germany* (London, 2003); B.C. Hett, *The Death of Democracy: Hitler's Rise to Power* (London, 2018); P. Longerich, *Hitler: A Biography* (tr. J. Noakes and L. Sharpe) (Oxford, 2019); V. Ullrich, *Hitler: Ascent 1889-1939* (tr. J. Chase) (New York, 2017).

257–258 **Hitler's years in Munich:** see Ullrich, *Hitler* 45–49 noting that Hitler did not exhibit violent anti-Semitism at this point; Longerich, *Hitler* 31–33 noting that Hitler later lied about his political views in this period.

258 **Hitler in the war**: see Longerich, *Hitler,* 33–45; Ullrich, *Hitler,* 50–72.

258 **Peace negotiations**: see J. Leonhard, *Pandora's Box: A History of the First World War* (tr. Camiller) (London, 2018): 467–468; Evans, *The Coming of the Third Reich* 57 (Social Democratic split); Leonhard, *Pandora's Box,* 782–790 for German negotiations.

258 Leonhard, *Pandora's Box,* 793–794, abdication of the kaiser; 799–817 on the end for Austro-Hungarian and the Ottoman Empires; 782–791.

259 Evans, *The Coming of the Third Reich,* 66–68 ("stab in the back"); Ullrich, *Hitler,* 77–78 (communist takeover in Bavaria); Longerich, *Hitler,* anti-Semitic propaganda.

260 **Weimar constitution**: see Evans, *The Coming of the Third Reich,* 78–88; B.C. Hett, *The Death of Democracy: Hitler's Rise to Power* (London, 2018): 24–27.

260 **Descriptions of Hitler's oratory:** quoted from Longerich, *Hitler,* 77.

260 **Hitler's move into politics**: see Longerich, *Hitler,* 57–72 (stressing the importance of anti-Semitism in contemporary conservative politics); Ullrich, *Hitler,* 73–91.

261 **Impact of the Versailles Treaty:** see Evans, *The Coming of the Third Reich,* 62–67 and 103–109 (hyperinflation).

261–262 **Hitler's speech** is taken from: http://www.worldfuturefund.org/wffmaster/Reading/Hitler%20Speeches/Trial/hitletrial.htm.

262 **Hitler's rise to influence in the NDSP**: see Longerich, *Hitler,* 98–108.

262 **Beer Hall Putsch and Hitler's imprisonment:** see Longerich, *Hitler,* 108–140; Ullrich, *Hitler,* 131–184.

263 **Hitler's team**: see Ullrich, *Hitler,* 104; 185–210. For violence in German politics more generally, see Evans, *The Coming of the Third Reich,* 70–76.

263–264 **New message**: see Longerich, *Hitler,* 173–190; Ullrich, *Hitler,* 200–212.

264 **Culture Wars**: see Evans, *The Coming of the Third Reich,* 118–138; for Thälmann, see Evans, *The Coming of the Third Reich,* 241–242.

THE NAZI SEIZURE OF POWER

This discussion draws heavily upon R.J. Evans, *The Coming of the Third Reich: How the Nazis Destroyed Democracy and Seized Power in Germany* (London, 2003); R. Gellately, *Backing Hitler: Consent and Coercion in Nazi Germany* (Oxford, 2001); B.C. Hett, *The Death of Democracy: Hitler's Rise to Power* (London, 2018); P. Longerich, *Hitler: A Biography* (tr. J. Noakes and L. Sharpe) (Oxford, 2019); V. Ullrich, *Hitler: Ascent 1889–1939* (tr. J. Chase) (New York, 2017); R.O. Paxton, *The Anatomy of Fascism* (New York, 2005).

265 **For the Young Plan changing reparations payments**: see T. Straumann, *1931: Debt, Crisis, and the Rise of Hitler* (Oxford, 2019): 3–38.

265 **Brüning's economic policy:** see Straumann, *1931*, 68–70, 91–92; R.J. Evans, *The Coming of the Third Reich*, 235–236.

265 **Campaign of 1930**: see Ullrich, *Hitler*, 228–240; Longerich, *Hitler*, 200–208.

266 **Hitler's campaign against Hindenburg**: see Ullrich, *Hitler*, 293–300; Longerich, *Hitler*, 235–242.

266 **Quotations from Hitler's stump speech** are from http://www.ihr.org/other/July1932Speech.

267 **Ban on SA**: see Evans, *The Coming of the Third Reich*, 274–275; Longerich, *Hitler*, 241; ban lifted, see Longerich, *Hitler*, 248.

267 **Results of the presidential election in 1932**: see Ullrich, *Hitler*, 331.

267 **Quotation from Goebbels** is taken from Evans, *The Coming of the Third Reich*, 288.

268 **July election results**: see Evans, *The Coming of the Third Reich*, 293–294.

268 **Quotations from Hindenburg and Hitler:** Evans, *The Coming of the Third Reich*, 297.

268 **November election results**: see Ullrich, *Hitler*, 331.

268 **Schleicher takes over**: see Ullrich, *Hitler*, 339; Hett, *The Death of Democracy*: 156–161.

268 **Schleicher offends Hindenburg**: see Ullrich, *Hitler*, 354–355, although see Hett, *The Death of Democracy*, 178–179 on Hindenburg's fears about his own legal liability.

268 **Papen** is quoted from Hett, *The Death of Democracy*, 182; see also Ullrich, *Hitler*, 365, for a similar statement.

269 **Reichstag fire**: favoring the possibility that Nazis set it, see Hett, *The Death of Democracy*, 189–193; against, see Ullrich, *Hitler*, 421; plausible but unproven, Longerich, *Hitler*, 289.

269 **Enabling Act**: see Ullrich, *Hitler*, 423–424.

270 **Violence**: see R. Gellately, *Backing Hitler: Consent and Coercion in Nazi Germany* (Oxford, 2001): 17–23.

270 **Cultural politics**: Evans, *The Coming of the Third Reich*, 405–431.

270 **Strike of April 1, 1933 and subsequent legislation**: Ullrich, *Hitler*, 442–445.

270 **Destruction of the SA**: see Ullrich, *Hitler*, 465–469; Longerich, *Hitler*, 380–394.
270 **"Toward the Führer":** see Ullrich, *Hitler*, 578; Evans, *The Coming of the Third Reich*, 337; for a dissenting view placing more agency with Hitler, see Longerich, *Hitler*, 368–394.
271 **Eugenics**: M. Burleigh, *Death and Deliverance: Euthanasia in Germany 1900-1945* 2nd edition (London, 2001).
271 **Nuremberg Laws**: see Gellately, *Backing Hitler*, 122–123; Longerich, *Hitler*, 435–437.
271 **Berlin Olympics**: D.C. Large, *Nazi Games: The Olympics of 1936* (New York, 2007).

Epilogue: January 6, 2021

For the alliance between evangelical Christians and white supremacists see E. Dias and R. Graham, "How White Evangelical Christians Fused with Trump Extremism," *New York Times* January 11, 2021. For the elements of an anti-democratic coup see S. Levitsky and D. Ziblatt, How Democracies Die: What History Reveals about our Future (New York, 2018): 23–24.

For the development of tech companies, see M. O'Mara, *The Code: Silicon Valley and the Remaking of America* (New York, 2019); for surveillance capitalism, see B. Schneir, *Data and Goliath: The Hidden Battles to Collect Your Data and Control Your World* (New York, 2015); S. Zuboff, *The Age of Surveillance Capitalism: The Fight for a Human Future at the New Frontier of Power* (New York, 2019); for the rise of populist nationalism, see E. Traverso, *The New Faces of Fascism: Populism and the Far Right* (tr. D. Broder) (New York, 2019); D. Renton, *The New Authoritarians: Convergence on the Right* (Chicago, 2019); J.B. Judis, *The Nationalist Revival: Trade Immigration and the Revolt against Globalization* (New York, 2018); for the issue with ventilators in particular, see N. Kulish, S. Kliff, and J. Silver-Greenberg, "The US Tried to Build a New Fleet of Ventilators. The Mission Failed" *New York Times* March 30, 2020; for Bill Gales and QAnon, see D. Wakabayashi, D. Alba, and M. Tracy, "Bill Gates, at Odds With Trump on Virus, Becomes a Right-Wing Target," *New York Times* April 17, 2020 with J. Bank, L. Stack, and D. Victor, "What is QAnon: Explaining the Internet Conspiracy Theory that Showed up at a Trump Rally," *New York Times* August 1, 2018 as background. Kate Ruane is quoted from K. Roose, "Who's Boss? 2 Tech Giants," *New York Times* January 10, 2021; Richard Blumenthal is quoted from K. Stacey and H. Murphy, "Now Republicans and Democrats Alike Want to Rein in Big Tech," *Financial Times* January 12, 2021.

INDEX